The Fourth World of the Hopis

The Fourth World of the Hopis

THE EPIC STORY OF THE HOPI INDIANS
AS PRESERVED IN THEIR LEGENDS AND TRADITIONS

Harold Courlander

Decorations by Enrico Arno

University of New Mexico Press
Albuquerque

Library of Congress Cataloging-in-Publication Data

Courlander, Harold, 1908–
  The fourth world of the Hopis.

  Reprint. Originally published: New York: Crown Publishers, 1971.
  1. Hopi Indians—Legends.   2. Indians of North
America—Arizona—Legends.   I. Title.
E99.H7C64   1987   398.2'08997   87-19197
ISBN 0-8263-1011-7 (pbk.)

University of New Mexico Press paperback edition reprinted 1987 by arrangement with
Harold Courlander.

Fifth printing,1992

Contents

"When a stranger comes to the village, feed him. Do not injure one another, because all beings deserve to live together without injury being done to them. When people are old and cannot work any more, do not turn them out to shift for themselves, but take care of them. Defend yourselves when an enemy comes to your village, but do not go out seeking war. The Hopis shall take this counselling and make it the Hopi Way."

—from the Palatkwapi story

Acknowledgments

I AM GRATEFUL AND MUCH INDEBTED to all those Hopis who made me feel welcome in their villages and homes, and who extended innumerable courtesies that helped to make this record of Hopi oral literature possible.

In particular I want to thank Albert Yava, of Hano (Tewa) Village, who contributed in many ways to this book, and who reviewed the finished manuscript before it went to press; Don C. Talayesva, of Oraibi; Emery Kinale, of Walpi; Bertha Kinale, of Walpi; Ned Zeena, of Walpi; Stewart Tubinaghtewa, of Polacca; Homer Cooyama, of New Oraibi; Louis Numkena, Sr., of Moencopi; Wallace Lomakema, Jr., of Sichomovi; Stanley Honahni, Sr., of Moencopi; Abbott Sekaquaptewa, of New Oraibi; Dewey Healing, of Hano; Juanita Healing, of Hano; Estelle Y. Fisher, of Parker, Arizona; and Mary Ruth Honie, of Walpi. Though my meetings with the late Peter Nuvamsa, Sr., of Shonogopovi were casual and infrequent, he helped me gain some valuable insights into the Hopi view of things, for which I am grateful. Nor have I forgotten the help of Bessie Condrey and Dallas Johnson, of Albuquerque, at the time when I was beginning the search for informants and narrators.

For reasons explained elsewhere in this book, I am not free to identify some of the persons who narrated the myths, legends and recollections. Even though their names do not appear here, they surely already know how much their contributions are valued.

Throughout our seemingly endless shuttle trips from one mesa or village to another, my wife, Emma, my daughter Susan and my son Michael showed much patience and understanding, for which I wish to express my deep appreciation.

The occasional music notations appearing in the story texts were made by John Benson Brooks from the original tape recordings of the narrations.

Some of the work on these materials was made possible by a grant from the Wenner-Gren Foundation for Anthropological Research.

Introduction:
The Coming of the Hopis

ACCORDING TO THEIR OWN MYTHOLOGY, the Hopis came into being when the people emerged from the Lower World through an opening in the earth. Yawpa, the mockingbird, addressed each person as he set foot in the Upper World, saying, "You shall be a Supai and speak the Supai language," or, "You shall be a Paiute," or, "You shall be a Hopi." In this way the tribes were set apart and made distinct from one another back in the days of the beginning. Putting aside the mythological explanation, we cannot know with any certainty when the Hopis became distinct from the other peoples of the Southwest. They speak a Uto-Aztecan language that suggests ancient ties to a great culture farther South. But anthropological evidence does not penetrate that far into the past. We know only that the Hopis, like their Eastern Pueblo cousins, somehow emerged out of an ancestral culture whose home was the San Juan Valley. Nearly two thousand years ago seminomadic seed-gathering peoples inhabited the valley and wide territories on each side of it. They clustered along the watercourses, hunting, harvesting wild food, and cultivating a primitive maize. They wandered back and forth across this extensive terrain, sometimes beyond it, and from time to time other small groups came in from other places.

It is generally assumed that what motivated these population movements was the endless search for surroundings that would provide for elemental human physical needs. But if surviving myths and legends are listened to with care they may tell us that these restless ancestors were also searching for places of spiritual harmony with nature. For throughout the myths and myth-legends are references to

9

flights from imperfection and evil, and to long journeys in fulfillment of moral prophecy.

By the fourth century A.D. there had come into being in this region of the Southwest a loosely knit culture of basketmaking peoples. Immigrating groups, probably from the south, brought the knowledge of pottery making. Stone houses and house clusters began to appear. By the eighth or ninth century the people were beginning to live in multiroomed apartments made of stone slabs or blocks. And where there were larger concentrations of population the room clusters became towns.

Having arrived at this stage of development, the San Juan people could have been expected to concentrate on their agriculture and give up their wandering ways. But as archeological records seem to show, there must have been a reluctance to remain fixed in one place. Though enormous energy was expended in the building of their villages and towns, the people—the late-arriving Navajos referred to them as Anasazis, meaning Ancient Ones—continued to be responsive to the wandering urge as though they were still seed gatherers. By the twelfth century they had developed technology associated with more sedentary life. They were growing cotton and a variety of maize comparable to what we know today. They were weaving cloth and making good pottery. And yet they abandoned their stone villages and the lands around them time and time again, escaping something or seeking something in a migration to still another place. The path of one migration crossed the trail of another. Stone villages, some of them almost monumental, came into being over a vast area of the Southwest, lived, and then died, sometimes after long occupancy, sometimes after only a few years.

While there may have been varied reasons for the migrations, it was probably a prolonged drouth toward the end of the thirteenth century that set into motion a southward movement from the San Juan region. In all probability the movement was piecemeal and spasmodic. New stone villages were built, lived in, and then left behind. It was a period of renewed migrations. Over a span of generations some people went far to the south and then returned to the north. Some departed from the scene altogether without leaving a trace. According to tradition there were parties of migrants that disappeared beyond the Grand Canyon country into what is now California, or southward into what is now Mexico.

One of the main courses of the migrations was east into the Rio Grande Valley. The settlements that came into being along that river were the ones to which the Spanish later gave the name Pueblos, meaning towns or town peoples. That these settlements reflected different migrations from different places of origin is attested to by the variety of languages spoken today in the Rio Grande villages. There was another movement, a series of migrations, southward from the San Juan region. Clans, family groups and perhaps fragments of tribes, building and then abandoning stone villages, went slowly toward the southern fringe of Black Mesa in what is now Arizona. The force that drew them to this place is not readily understood, for it was hard and arid country without a river and with sparse rainfall. It was a land of dramatic beauty, but it gave no promise of abundant crops or easy labor.

Some people rested for a while and then went on. But many stayed. One settlement after another grew up at the mesa's edge. New immigrants arrived, some speaking alien languages. Wandering clans continued to come out of the wilderness as though the Black Mesa country were a Promised Land. According to tradition some did indeed consider their arrival as the fulfillment of prophecy and the end of centuries of migrations. The people who remained in the Black Mesa country were the ancestors of the Hopis of today.

The Hopi villages now standing are grouped along three peninsula-like extensions of Black Mesa. Those extensions are known locally as First or Eastern Mesa, Second or Middle Mesa, and Third Mesa. The distance between the easternmost villages on First Mesa and the westernmost settlement, Moencopi (near Tuba City), is about seventy miles by the shortest route of travel. Within walking distance of every one of the existing villages are to be found the ruins of earlier settlements. Northward toward Kayenta and beyond, or toward Navajo Mountain whose Hopi name is Tokonave, southward far below Winslow and the San Francisco Mountains, westward to Grand Canyon, and east toward the Rio Grande— in every direction for many miles are the sites of old villages that the Hopis claim to have been inhabited by their ancestors. It was through this great stretch of country that the ancestral wanderings took place, and even though much of it is now occupied by Navajos and whites, the Hopis consider it, in a special way, their own.

Some of the Hopi traditions about the long journeys are shared with the Rio Grande Pueblo peoples. Through the centuries there have been continuing and frequent contacts between the Hopis and the Eastern Pueblos. They acted in concert in the 1680 revolt against the Spanish. Various Eastern Pueblo peoples came west from time to time to settle in Hopi country. The Hopi mesas were a sanctuary for Lagunas, Acomas and others seeking escape from Spanish authority virtually throughout the seventeenth century. At one time or another there were Eastern Pueblo settlements close to every one of the extant Hopi villages. For different reasons most of the Eastern Pueblos eventually departed from Black Mesa, some going farther west, or south, or back to the Rio Grande. Only one Eastern Pueblo group—the Tewas of First Mesa—remains among the Hopis today. Though it retains its own language and a certain sense of difference, it is in many respects as Hopi as any other village on the mesa.

In Hopi legends we have the only existing word records of the past. Most of them are not "history" as it is understood in literate cultures, but one cannot doubt that they contain within them dim recollections of the Hopi experience during the centuries of the migrations. The conservative Hopi regards them as authentic records of the clans and the crises that propelled them from one place to another, as elucidations of events long past, and, finally, as an explanation of the arrival and settlement at Black Mesa. These legends at heart are not for entertainment, but to keep alive a sense of human continuity. Though myth is often interwoven with legend, and legend with history, the stories must be reckoned as the repository not only of events, but of purposes and attitudes toward life and living things. Apart from the excavations and conclusions of anthropologists, the oral tradition is the only instrument we have for penetrating into the Hopi past. But it is a more revealing instrument in some ways than the archeologist's shovel. For out of the oral tradition we get insights about values and motivations that are not visible in potsherds.

It is regrettable that we do not have access to a more extensive body of this oral literature. One reason is that there has been no Hopi Homer to sing about the ancient trials, defeats and victories. But the Hopi past nevertheless appears truly Homeric. There is a great sweep of human conflicts and supernatural events. It begins at the time of the emergence from the Lower World and reaches into contemporary times. The people navigate back and forth across known and unknown lands, from mountain to river, from butte to mesa, and from lush canyon to desert, guided by sparks of fire and falling stars in the night. Prophecies, promises and omens set forth in the beginning become familiar landmarks in legend after legend. And toward the end there is no great surprise in discovering that a portion of the stone tablet made by the Fire Clan leader at the sipapuni still exists. The ancient beginning and the present are merely parts of a single long narrative in which, unnamed and unseen, Hopi Furies are ever-present.

There are different versions of the legends, and disagreements over which versions are the most true. Each clan and village has put the imprint of its own experiences on recollections of the past. So a Hopi Homer would have the impossible task of disentangling contradictions, and in working at it he would be certain to be accused by one clan or another, or one person or another, of heresies. The problems are exemplified by reference to the Reed Clan story, "The Lamehva People," in which it is stated that the original settlement on First Mesa was made by the Reed Clan. But Bear Clan tradition says that the Bear Clan was first. I have not attempted in any way to adjudicate the contradictions that are inherent in the oral literature. The material is "organized" only to the extent of being arranged as nearly as possible in a chronological sequence, conforming to recommendations made by Hopi informants. If the sections dealing with the Spanish period are not consistent with Spanish chronicles in a number of details, it is because this book is not concerned with a reconstruction of history but with Hopi recollections and, of course, the Hopi point of view.

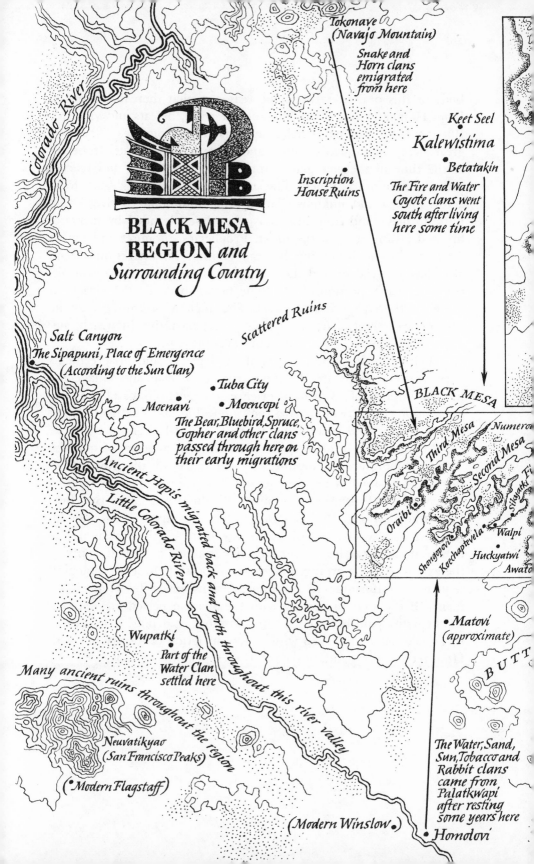

BLACK MESA REGION and Surrounding Country

Colorado River

Tokonave
(Navajo Mountain)

Snake and Horn clans emigrated from here

Keet Seel

Kalewistima

Betatakin

Inscription House Ruins

The Fire and Water Coyote clans went south after living here some time

Scattered Ruins

BLACK MESA

Salt Canyon
The Sipapuni, Place of Emergence
(According to the Sun Clan)

Tuba City

Moenavi

Moencopi

The Bear, Bluebird, Spruce, Gopher and other clans passed through here on their early migrations

Third Mesa

Numero

Second Mesa

Oraibi

Siswiki Fi

Shongopovi

Koechaptvela

Walpi

Huckyatwi

Awato

Ancient Hopis migrated back and forth throughout this river valley

Little Colorado River

Matovi
(approximate)

BUTT

Wupatki

Part of the Water Clan settled here

Many ancient ruins throughout the region

The Water, Sand, Sun, Tobacco and Rabbit clans came from Palatkwapi after resting some years here

Neuvatikyao
(San Francisco Peaks)

(Modern Flagstaff)

(Modern Winslow)

Honolovi

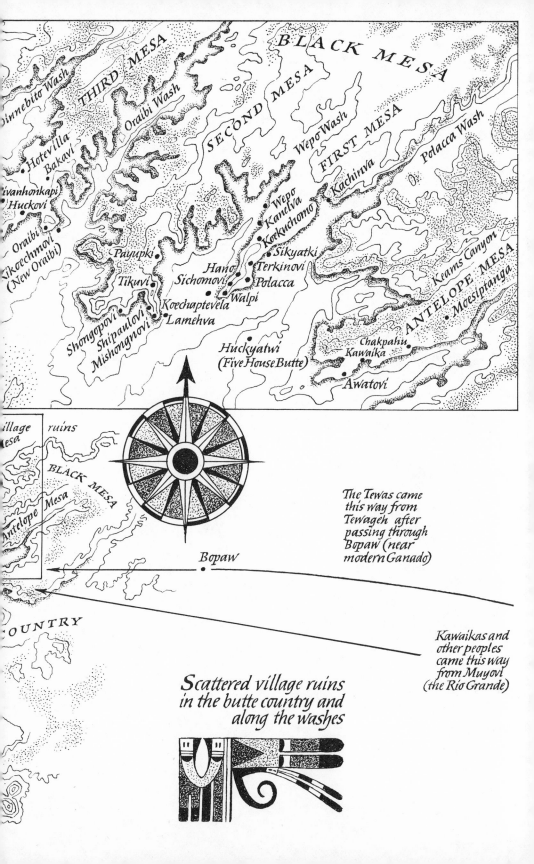

BLACK MESA

THIRD MESA

SECOND MESA

FIRST MESA

Dinnebito Wash

Oraibi Wash

Wepo Wash

Potacca Wash

Kachinva

ANTELOPE MESA

Keams Canyon

Hotevilla

Bakavi

Sivanhonkapi

Huckovi

Oraibi

(Nikoechmovi

(New Oraibi)

Payupki

Wepo

Kanelva

Korkuchomo

Sikyatki

Hano

Sichomovi

Terkinovi

Polacca

Tikuvi

Koechaptevela

Lamehva

Walpi

Shongopovi

Shipaulovi

Mishongnovi

Huckyatwi

(Five House Butte)

Chakpahu

Kawaika

Moesiptanga

Awatovi

village ruins

Mesa

BLACK MESA

Antelope Mesa

Bopaw

The Tewas came
this way from
Tewageh after
passing through
Bopaw (near
modern Ganado)

COUNTRY

Kawaikas and
other peoples
came this way
from Muyovi
(the Rio Grande)

Scattered village ruins
in the butte country and
along the washes

1 The Four Worlds

IN THE BEGINNING THERE WAS ONLY TOKPELLA, Endless Space. Nothing stirred because there were no winds, no shadows fell because there was no light, and all was still. Only Tawa, the Sun Spirit, existed, along with some lesser gods. Tawa contemplated on the universe of space without objects or life, and he regretted that it was so barren. He gathered the elements of Endless Space and put some of his own substance into them, and in this way he created the First World. There were no people then, merely insect-like creatures who lived in a dark cave deep in the earth. For a long while Tawa watched them. He was deeply disappointed. He thought, "What I created is imperfect. These creatures do not understand the meaning of life."

So Tawa called his messenger, Gogyeng Sowuhti, Spider Grandmother, and told her to go down and prepare the living creatures for a change. Spider Grandmother went down. She spoke to the insect creatures, saying, "Tawa, the Sun Spirit who made you, is unhappy because you do not understand the meaning of life. He says: 'The creatures are fighting among themselves. They see but they do not comprehend. Therefore I will change things. I will make a new world, and I will perfect all things that have life in them.' This is the message Tawa asked me to bring. Therefore, prepare to leave this place to enter the Second World." The creatures said, "If that is the way it must be, very well, let us depart from here."

Spider Grandmother led them on their journey, taking them to another great cave that lay far above the first one. The journey was long, and between the time they began and the time they finished, Tawa changed them into other forms of living things. When at last they emerged into the Second World they looked quite different. They were animals that somewhat resembled dogs, coyotes and bears. There was fur on their bodies, their fingers were webbed, and they had tails. They lived on in the Second World and were happy at first. But because they did not have any understanding they grew bitter and warred upon one another, even eating one another. Tawa saw how the creatures of his Second World were living. He saw that they did not grasp the meaning of life. And so again he sent Spider Grandmother to lead them on another journey.

While they travelled, Tawa created the Third World. He made the atmosphere a little lighter and gave them water to moisten their fields. When the creatures followed Spider Grandmother into the Third World they discovered that their bodies had changed again. Their fur, their webbed fingers and their tails had disappeared. Spider Grandmother said to them: "Now you are no longer merely creatures. You are people. Tawa has given you this place so that you may live in harmony and forget all evil. Do not injure one another. Remember that Tawa created you out of Endless Space, and try to understand the meaning of things." Then Spider Grandmother left them.

The people made their villages. They planted corn. They lived on. They were in harmony, and they were grateful to the Sun Spirit who had created them and given them a new world to live in. Yet things were not perfect. There was a chill in the air, and the light was only a grayness. Spider Grandmother came and taught people how to weave blankets and cloth to keep their bodies warm. She taught the women how to make pots out of clay so that they could store water and food. But the pots could not be baked and they broke easily. And the corn did not grow very well because warmth was lacking.

Then one day a hummingbird came to where some people were working in their fields. The people asked, "Why are you here?"

The hummingbird answered, "I have been sent by my master."

They said, "Who is your master?"

The bird replied, "He is Masauwu, Ruler of the Upper World, Caretaker of the Place of the Dead and the Owner of Fire. He has observed how you live here, and he says, 'The crops do not grow well because the people do not have warmth.'"

The people said, "Yes, it is true. Warmth is lacking."

The hummingbird said, "I have been sent to teach you the secret of warmth." And he gave them the secret, showing them how to create fire with a fire drill. After that he departed.

Now that the people had the knowledge of fire, they gathered grass and wood and made fires around their fields, and the warmth made their corn grow. But once they became careless and the fire spread to a nearby house and consumed it, including everything that was inside. When the ashes were cool the people found that their clay pots had become hard and did not break so easily. Thus they learned the secret of baking pottery. From this time on the people began to cook their meat instead of eating it raw. Those who had received the secret of fire from Masauwu's messenger became known as the Firewood or Fire People. They said, "Masauwu is our relative." Now things were better in the Third World.

It was the powakas, or sorcerers, who brought disruption and conflict among the people. They made medicine to injure those whom they envied or disliked. Worse yet, they turned the people's minds away from virtuous things. The younger people grew disrespectful of the older. Husbands sought other women, and wives sought other men. Instead of caring for their fields, men spent their time in the kivas gambling. And instead of grinding corn, women went into the kivas to join the men. Children wandered about unclean and uncared for, and babies cried for milk. What a man wanted he would take from another instead of fashioning it for himself. Dissension spread everywhere. Instead of seeking to understand the meaning of life, many began to believe that they had created themselves.

In the beginning, life in the Third World had been good. But because people succumbed to the evil unleashed by the powakas, things began to change. The cornstalks in the fields withered before the ears were formed. The flowing rivers moved more sluggishly and the springs dried up. Clouds drifted over the fields but did not release their rain. Squash and melon vines stopped growing, and sickness came into many houses.

Now, those who had not forgotten that Tawa was their father worried greatly about the way things were going. Night after night they met in the kivas to discuss the corruption that was spreading in the Third World. They encouraged the lazy to work, admonished women for their promiscuous ways, threatened the powakas with punishment and sought to create order, yet nothing changed. There was evil and chaos all around them.

Tawa saw what was happening to the world he had made. He called Gogyeng Sowuhti, Spider Grandmother, and sent her to the people with a message. Spider Grandmother went down. She entered a kiva where the people were gathered. She said: "Tawa, the Sun Spirit, is displeased with what he has created. The powakas have made you forget what you should have remembered. Therefore all people of good heart should go away from this place and leave the evil ones behind."

The people said to one another, "Where can we go? Is there another place?" But they did not know of another place anywhere, and they were troubled.

Then an old man said, "Have we not heard footsteps in the sky, as though someone is walking there?"

And other old men replied, "Yes, there has been someone walking above us up there. We have heard it many times when the air was still."

Other people said, "Let us discover what is there. Let us send a messenger to investigate things."

So the chiefs called for the medicine men to sit with them and consider things. They filled a pipe with tobacco and lighted it. They smoked, passing the pipe from one to another until their minds were tranquil. Then one of the chiefs said, "We must send someone to the place above the sky to see what it is like. If it is good, our messenger will request permission for us to come there. But who can make such a difficult journey?"

The medicine men pondered, and after a while one of them

said, "We shall create a messenger who can perform this task." The medicine men gathered some clay and shaped a bird out of it. They placed a kwatskiavu cloth, which is the robe made for brides, on the ground and placed the clay bird on it. They covered the clay bird with an ova cloth. They sat in a circle holding the edges of the upper cloth, singing and moving it gently up and down. They placed their hands underneath, doing what no one could see. When at last they removed the cloth there was a living swallow sitting there.

The swallow asked, "Why have you called me?"

The chiefs answered, "We have called you so that you may go up to discover whether there is another world above the sky. If you find someone living in that place, ask if we may come there and begin our lives again."

The swallow flew up. He circled higher and higher, until the people could no longer see him. His strength began to flow away, but still he went upward. At last he saw an opening in the sky. But he was too tired to go on, and he returned to the place where the chiefs and the medicine men were waiting. He fluttered weakly and settled on the ground. He said, "I went up. I found an opening in the sky. It was as though I were looking up through the entrance of a kiva. But my strength failed and so I had to return."

The medicine men decided to make a stronger bird. They began again, fashioning a figure out of clay and covering it with the cloth. They sang and made medicine, and this time when they removed the cloth a white dove sat there. The chiefs said, "How can the dove do what the swallow could not do?"

The medicine men answered, "It has great strength. Let it try."

The white dove spoke, saying, "Why am I here?"

The chiefs said, "We have called you to go above us to see what kind of a world is up there. Pass through the opening in the sky and tell us what lies beyond. If anyone inhabits that place, ask if we may come to find new homes for ourselves."

The dove went up and passed through the opening. He saw a vast land, but no living things, and he returned. He said, "It is true that there is an opening in the sky, and on the other side is a land that spreads in all directions, but I saw nothing that was alive."

The chiefs and the medicine men discussed the matter, recalling the sounds of footsteps in the sky. They said, "Surely someone lives in that place. We must know who he is."

Once more the medicine men fashioned a bird out of clay and brought it to life under the ova cloth. This time it was a hawk. The hawk also went up through the sky and explored the land above, but he returned without discovering what the people wanted to know.

The medicine men tried again, and this time they created a catbird. When the catbird asked, "Why am I here?" the chiefs replied, "You have been called because the swallow and the dove and the hawk have not been able to discover who it is that walks in the land above us. You, catbird, go up, discover who makes the sound of walking up there. Speak to him. Tell him the people of good heart wish to leave this place. Ask for his permission to enter his land. Go and return. Let us know how things are."

So the catbird flew up and passed through the opening in the sky. He passed the place where the hawk had turned back. He went on. He came to a place of sand and mesas. He saw large fires burning alongside gardens of squash, melons and corn. Beyond the gardens was a single house made of stone. A person was sitting there, his head down, sleeping. The catbird alighted nearby and waited. The person awoke and raised his head. His eyes were sunken in deeply, there was no hair on his head, and his face was seared by burns and encrusted with dried blood. Across the bridge of his nose and his cheekbones two black lines were painted. Around his neck were two heavy necklaces, one made of four strands of turquoise, the other of bones. The catbird recognized him. He was Masauwu, Spirit of Death, the Owner of Fire and Master of the Upper World, assigned to this place by Tawa because he had no other place for him.

Masauwu looked at the catbird, saying, "You, why are you here?"

The catbird said, "I was sent from down below to see whose footsteps are heard in the sky."

Masauwu said, "Yes, now you know that the footsteps are mine. Are you not afraid?"

"No," the catbird answered, "for I am only a bird fashioned out of clay just recently. I don't know enough yet to fear anything. I came because the Lower World is infested with evil, and there are many good people who would like to come here to live. Down below, the rain does not fall, the springs do not flow, the corn dries up in the fields, and there are numerous persons who do not respect the virtues of life. The people of good heart ask your permission to enter the Upper World and build their villages here."

Masauwu said, "You see how it is in this place. There is no light, only a grayness here. There is no warmth, and I must build fires to make my crops grow. But there is land and water. If the people wish to come, let them come."

The catbird left Masauwu and returned to the opening through which he had passed. He went down to where the chiefs and the medicine men were waiting. They asked him, "Did you arrive there and find the one who walks in the sky?"

The catbird answered, "Yes, I found the person who lives there. He is Masauwu, Spirit of Death, Owner of Fire and Master of the Upper World. His face is terrifying to see. But I spoke with him. He said: 'You see how it is. There is no light here and no warmth. But there is plenty of land and water, so if the people want to come, let them come.'"

Hearing this, the chief of the Fire People spoke. He said, "Masauwu is our spirit. We are the ones to whom he sent the secret of fire. He is our relative. Therefore we are willing to go." Others said, "Yes, let all of us who wish to escape from evil go there. The Fire People can lead us and speak for us to Masauwu. Let us prepare for the journey."

It was agreed, then, but the chiefs and medicine men looked upward, saying, "How shall we ever reach the sipapuni, the doorway in the sky?"

While they were thinking about this problem, Gogyeng Sowuhti, Spider Grandmother, appeared in the plaza with her young grandsons, the warrior gods Pokanghoya and Polongahoya. She said, "We are here. We will help you pass through the sipapuni." She sent the young warrior gods to find chipmunk, the planter. Soon they returned bringing the chipmunk with them. Spider Grandmother said to the chipmunk, "It is you who have been chosen to make a path for the people into the sky. For this you will always be remembered." And she explained what had to be done.

The chipmunk planted a sunflower seed in the center of the plaza. By the power of singing the people made it grow. If they stopped to catch their breath, the sunflower stopped growing, and Spider Grandmother called out, "Sing! Sing!" As soon as they started to sing again, the sunflower continued growing. In time the sunflower stalk reached toward the sky, but just as it was about to pass through the sipapuni it bent over from the weight of its blossom.

Spider Grandmother said, "Let us try again." This time the chipmunk planted a spruce seed and gave the people a song to sing. They sang the spruce tree into the sky, but when it had finished growing it was not tall enough. So now the chipmunk planted a pine seed, and by the power of singing they made it grow tall. But the pine, also, failed to reach the sipapuni. Once more the chipmunk planted. This time it was a bamboo. The people sang hard and made the bamboo grow straight and tall. Each time they stopped to catch their breath the growing stopped and a joint formed on the bamboo stalk. And when they resumed singing the bamboo grew again. Spider Grandmother went back and forth exhorting the people to sing the bamboo into the sky. Thus it went on. The people began to fear that they did not have breath enough to do what was required of them. But finally Spider Grandmother called out, "It is done! The bamboo has passed through the sipapuni!"

The road to the Upper World was finished, and the people rested. Spider Grandmother spoke, telling of things to come. She said: "The journey will be long and difficult. When we reach the Upper World, that will be only a beginning. Things there are not like things here. You will discover new ways of doing things. During the journey you must try to discover the meaning of life and learn to distinguish good from evil. Tawa did not intend for you to live in the midst of chaos and dissension. Only those of good heart may depart from the Third World. The powakas and all who perform wicked deeds must stay behind. As we go up the bamboo to the Upper World, see that no one carries evil medicine in his belt. See that no powakas go with us. Leave your pots and grinding stones behind. Up above you will make more of these things. Carry nothing that has to be held in your hands, for you will need your hands for climbing. When we have arrived in the Upper World I will tell you more about what is expected of you. Meanwhile, remember this: In the Upper World you must learn to be true humans." Then Spider Grandmother sent the people home to prepare for the journey, which would begin in four days.

The people prepared, and on the fourth day they gathered at the foot of the bamboo. The chiefs stood in front—the village chief, the crier chief, the singer chief and the war chief. Behind them the people stood waiting for the journey to begin. Spider Grandmother arrived with the boy warrior gods, Pokanghoya and Polongahoya. Pokanghoya, the elder, carried lightning arrows in his right hand and a thunderboard in his left. Polongahoya, the younger, carried a buckskin ball in his left hand, and in his right hand he held a nahoydadatsia playing stick. Spider Grandmother went up the bamboo first, followed by the boy warrior gods. The people moved toward the bamboo to begin their climb. But now the chief of the Fire People protested, saying, "Wait. We are the ones who are entitled to go first, for Masauwu is our special benefactor. We shall take the lead." The others deferred to the Fire People. After the Fire People began their ascent, whoever could get to the bamboo took his turn. The mockingbird fluttered around the bamboo, calling out, "Pashumayani! Pashumayani! Be careful! Be careful!" This is the way the people departed from the Lower World. They moved slowly upward, and in time the entire bamboo stalk was covered with human bodies.

As the first climbers emerged through the sipapuni and stepped into the Upper World, Yawpa the mockingbird stood at Spider Grandmother's side and sorted them out. "You shall be a Hopi and speak the Hopi language," he said to one. "You shall be a Navajo and speak the Navajo language," he said to another. "You shall be an Apache and speak the Apache language," he said to a third. He assigned every person to a tribe and a language, and to each tribe he gave a direction to go in its migrations. He named the Paiutes, the Zunis, the Supais, the Pimas, the Utes, the Comanches, the Sioux, and the White Men. The people began to make camp near the sipapuni. There were a great many of them. The chiefs discussed things and said, "Surely all the people of good heart have now arrived." But more were still coming up. The chiefs said, "All those who chose to depart from evil are here. Therefore, let no more come through the sipapuni." The village chief went to the opening and called down, "You who are still climbing, turn and go back. It is because of you that we chose to leave and come to the Upper World. Do not follow us. You are not wanted here."

But the climbers persisted, saying that they also wanted to be in the Upper World. So the warrior gods, Pokanghoya and Polongahoya, grasped the bamboo stalk and pulled its roots from the ground. They shook it and all those clinging to it fell back into the Lower World like seeds falling from ripe grass. The chiefs said, "Now we are secure from the evil ones. Let us make camp." The people camped near the sipapuni and rested.

Pokanghoya and Polongahoya looked around at the vast Upper World. Pokanghoya said, "Everything has a sameness. Something needs to be done." Polongahoya answered, "Yes, see how it is out there. The ground is soft. It is nothing but mud." So they took their buckskin ball and their playing sticks and began to play nahoydadatsia, following the ball wherever it went, running all the time. Wherever their feet touched the soft earth it became hard. They gathered the mud into great mounds and turned them into mountains. Wherever they passed, grass and trees came into being. They raced far to the north, and in an instant they created Tokonave, meaning Black Mountain, which in later times the White Men called Navajo Mountain. From there they ran far to the south, chasing their ball all the while, and created Neuvatikyao, which the White Men later named San Francisco Peaks. They went eastward then, making hills, mountains and mesas everywhere. They arrived at Muyovi, which the White Men came to call the Rio Grande, and near where the Zunis now live they created salt beds, and they also made salt beds at other places. When at last they had done enough things of this kind they returned to the sipapuni.

Spider Grandmother asked them, "Where have you boys been?"

They said, "We have been playing. We have made the Upper World good to look at. See what we have done."

But the light in the Upper World was a grayness and it was not possible to see very far, so what they had done was not clearly visible.

Pokanghoya said, "We need light in this place."

Polongahoya said, "Yes, and we need warmth also."

Spider Grandmother agreed, saying "It is true, light and warmth are needed."

She assembled the chiefs and the medicine men. She said, "Let us do something now to bring light and warmth to this place." She told the people what to do. They brought out many things that they had carried from the Lower World. They took a piece of buckskin and cut it in the shape of a disk, which they then fastened over a large wooden ring. They painted it with white clay and speckled it with black. When they were finished, they laid the buckskin disk on a kwatskiavu cloth and sang, as Spider Grandmother instructed them. Four chiefs took hold of the kwatskiavu cloth at the corners, and with a fast movement they lifted it and sent the disk soaring into the sky. By the power of singing they kept it moving upward until it disappeared from sight. But after a while they saw a light on the eastern horizon, and the buckskin disk rose from beyond the edge of things and moved slowly overhead.

Now the people could see a little better, but it was not yet light enough, and the earth still was not warm enough to grow corn. Spider Grandmother said, "Let us try again." They made another disk in the same way, but it was larger, and this time they painted it with egg yolks and sprinkled it with golden-colored pollen. They painted a face on the golden disk in black and red, and all around its edges they fastened corn silk. They attached an abalone shell to the forehead, and their work was finished. As before, the disk was placed on the kwatskiavu cloth. Four strong men grasped the corners, and with a quick lifting motion they sent the disk sailing into the sky. The people sang the disk upward until it disappeared. But after a while there was a bright glow on the horizon in the east, and a moment later the disk appeared there, shining brightly and making the whole land visible. Now the people could see the mountains and the other things created by the boy warrior gods. The disk also cast warmth on the earth. The people were glad, for now they had a moon and a sun.

The sun moved across the sky toward the west, rays of light and warmth spreading out from its corn silk edges. When the sun went down over the horizon the light faded, but the moon arose about this time and so there was not total darkness while the sun slept. The people were tired from their efforts and they rested now, but they forgot to put away all the things they had brought out to make their two sky disks. In the still of the night, Coyote came prowling among these things, examining them and turning them over out of curiosity. He discovered nothing that was edible or in any way useful to him, and in irritation he took a handful of small objects and hurled them into the air. These objects soon began to sparkle in the sky. And so the people now had many stars as well as their sun and moon. Coyote also picked up the paintpots, whose colors had been used to decorate the sun and moon, and threw them in all directions. The paint splattered against the rocks and buttes, marking them with the colors they have had ever since. These things Coyote did, and the people acknowledged that Coyote was responsible.

At the end of four days the people were ready to leave the place of the sipapuni and begin the next stage of their journey. Then, suddenly, the son of the kikmongwi, or village chief, fell sick and died. They buried him not far from the sipapuni and put stones over his grave. The kikmongwi grieved. He said, "There must be a sorcerer among us." And he instructed the people to find the one with the evil heart who had killed his son. The people looked about them. They examined each other's faces. They looked for the small black spot on the end of the nose that would identify a sorcerer, but found nothing. The kikmongwi said, "Look closely to see if anyone brought medicine from below in his belt." But they could not find anyone with medicine in his belt. The kikmongwi said, "Nevertheless, we shall discover the one with the evil heart." He made a ball of cornmeal and threw it into the air, saying, "May this ball of meal fall on the evil one." It fell on the head of a young woman, the very last person who had come through the sipapuni. The chief said, "Ah, then it is you."

She said, "Yes, I am the one."

The people said, "Why have you come? For all the powakas were instructed to stay below."

She answered, "That is so. But I did not wish to stay there any more. I want to be in the Upper World."

The kikmongwi took hold of her to throw her back through the opening into the Lower World, but the woman said, "Wait, do not throw me back. Your son is not dead. He lives on."

The kikmongwi replied, "No, the spirit has gone from his body, which is buried under the stones."

The woman said, "Yes, his body is under the stones, but even so he is not truly dead, for he lives on down below."

The kikmongwi answered, "How can such a thing be? For his body is cold."

The woman said, "Look through the sipapuni and see for yourself."

The kikmongwi looked down. He saw his son playing nahoydadatsia with other children in the village in the Lower World. He said, "Yes, I see that it is so. I see him there. My son lives on. Nevertheless there is no place in the Upper World for a powaka. You must return to the Lower World."

The woman pleaded, saying, "Let me stay here. Should things ever go badly I will use my powers to help the people."

There was a discussion. People argued about the matter. At last they decided. One of the old men said, "Let her stay in the Upper World. It is true that she is a powaka. But she has already contaminated the place by her presence. Good and evil are everywhere. From the beginning to the end of time good and evil must struggle against each other. So let the woman stay. But she may not go with us. After we have gone on she may go wherever she wishes."

So that was the way it was settled.

The time was drawing near for the people to leave the sipapuni behind. Yawpa the mockingbird said, "There is something still to be done—the selection of the corn." The people gathered around while the mockingbird placed many ears of corn on the ground. One ear was yellow, one was white, one was red, one was gray, some were speckled, one was a stubby ear with blue kernels, and one was not quite corn but merely kwakwi grass with seeds at the top. The mockingbird said, "Each of these ears brings with it a way of life. The one who chooses the yellow ear will have a life full of enjoyment and prosperity, but his span of life will be small. The short ear with the blue kernels will bring a life full of work and hardship, but the years will be many." The mockingbird described the life that went with each ear, and then he told the people to choose. Even while he was talking the people were deciding. The leader of the Navajos reached out quickly and took the yellow ear that would bring a short life but much enjoyment and prosperity. The Sioux took the white corn. The Supais chose the ear speckled with yellow, the Comanches took the red, and the Utes took the flint corn. The leader of the Apaches, seeing only two kinds of corn remaining, chose the longest. It was the kwakwi grass with the seeds on top. Only the Hopis had not chosen. The ear that was left was the stubby ear of blue corn. So the leader of the Hopis picked it up, saying, "We were slow in choosing. Therefore we must take the smallest ear of all. We shall have a life of hardship, but it will be a long-lasting life. Other tribes may perish, but we, the Hopis, will survive all adversities." Thus the Hopis became the people of the short blue corn.

Gogyeng Sowuhti, Spider Grandmother, said, "There is still one more thing to be done." She went to the sipapuni and covered it with water, so that it resembled an ordinary pond. To see it, one would not know it to be the place through which the people had emerged from the world below. Spider Grandmother said, "Here at the sipapuni the tribes will separate. We are ready to begin our journeys. When the sun rises tomorrow we shall leave."

The people slept, and when the next glow of the rising sun became visible the exodus began. Those who called themselves Paiutes, Apaches and Navajos departed, each taking the direction assigned to them by the mockingbird. Then the Zunis, the Supais, the Pimas, the Utes went out. There remained only the Bahanas, or White People, and the Hopis. As the Bahanas gathered their possessions and prepared to go, the leader of the Hopis saw that the sorceress was still there in the camp. He said to her, "Why do you remain here? Go somewhere, find your own way, for we intend to leave all evil behind."

The chief of the Bahanas said, "Let the powaka come with us. Even though she is evil she has great knowledge. We do not fear her. Her knowledge will be useful to the people." Then the Bahanas trailed out of the camping place and went toward the south, the powaka following them.

The leader of the Hopis said, "Because the powaka has gone with the Bahanas, they will grow strong. They will learn evil as well as good, and they will have secrets that are not known to us. Therefore, whenever we meet with the Bahanas let us listen with caution to what they say. Let us stand apart from their ways. However, it is said that in some distant time a certain Bahana whose name is not yet known will arrive among us from the direction of the rising sun, bringing friendship, harmony and good fortune to our people. When the time comes, he will appear. Let us watch for him. Let the dead be buried with their faces toward the east so that they will meet him when he approaches."

One of the elders of the Fire People said, "When such a person arrives, how shall we know for certain that he is the one we are expecting? What if a powaka comes, saying, 'I am the one you are waiting for'? He will take advantage of us and abuse us. He will destroy our way of life and give us cruelty instead of harmony."

Thereupon he took a small flat piece of stone and carved a picture of a man on it. Around the figure he made designs. And when he had finished carving this tablet he broke it into two parts. The part containing the head of the figure he handed to the chief of the Fire People, saying, "Let the Bahanas carry this piece. Let them hold it in trust for the White Brother who will come to us."

So the chief of the Fire People sent the fragment of the stone tablet to the Bahanas, who were still moving slowly southward. The messenger gave it to the leader of the Bahanas, saying, "On a certain day, at a certain place, a Bahana whose name is not yet known will come to us from the east, bringing harmony and good fortune to the Hopis. We must be certain of his identity. When the special Bahana comes, let him bring this fragment of stone with him. We will match it with the other portion. If the two parts fit together and the broken tablet becomes whole again, then we will recognize him as the person we are expecting."

The leader of the Bahanas accepted the fragment of the stone tablet, and the messenger returned to the sipapuni, saying, "It is done."

Now, when the Fire People claimed the right to leave the

Lower World first, the others had deferred to them. The migrations were about to begin, and the Hopis addressed themselves to the Fire People this way: "We are going to the place where our destiny awaits us. Because you are Masauwu's relatives, and because it is he who granted permission for us to come here, it is you who will take the lead and guide us. Direct us to do what is necessary and we shall follow."

But the Fire People did not accept. Their chief said, "No, we also are strangers here. If we take you to some place that is not good you will blame us. If the journey seems too long you will say, 'The Fire People don't know what they are doing.' If we are attacked by enemies you will say, 'The Fire People were careless. See what they have done to us.' If the corn dries up in the fields you will say that we are at fault. Therefore we don't care to lead. Choose whomever you wish for your leaders. We shall be responsible only for ourselves."

And so the Hopis selected other persons to lead them on the journey.

Gogyeng Sowuhti, Spider Grandmother, spoke. She said, "Remember the sipapuni, for you will not see it again. You will go on long migrations. You will build villages and abandon them for new migrations. Wherever you stop to rest, leave your marks on the rocks and cliffs so that others will know who was there before them. Tawa, the Sun Spirit, will watch over you. Do not forget him. There are other gods here as well. There is Masauwu, the Spirit of Death, who sent fire to the Lower World. This is his land, and so people must always be in the presence of death. If you see Masauwu's face you will recognize him though you have never seen him before. If you see a flame of fire moving in the night, that is Masauwu's breath. Speak well of him but avoid him. If he touches you the breath of life will depart from your body and go down to Maski, the Land of the Dead, from which it can never return. There is also Muyingwa, the spirit who germinates and makes things fertile. When you see him you will recognize him, for his body is made entirely of maize. There is Huruing Wuhti, the Hard-Substances Woman who owns all shells, corals and metals. Also living here is Balolokong, the Great Water Serpent who controls the springs and brings rain. All such things you have to know. You will learn about the forces of nature in your travels. The stars, the sun, the clouds and fires in the night will show you which directions to take. But the short blue corn that you chose at the sipapuni also will be your guide. If you reach a certain place and your corn does not grow, or if it grows and does not mature, you will know that you have gone too far. Return the way you came, build another village and begin again. In time you will find the land that is meant for you. But never forget that you came from the Lower World for a purpose. When you build your kivas, place a small sipapuni there in the floor to remind you where you come from and what you are looking for. Compose songs to sing in your ceremonies that will remind you how the sun and moon were made, and how the people parted from one another. Only those who forget why they came to this world will lose their way. They will disappear in the wilderness and be forgotten."

II The Migrations

AND NOW THE HOPIS BEGAN THEIR JOURNEY, travelling eastward. They camped at night and went on in the day, searching for signs to guide them. Some of the people saw a shooting star one night, and they turned southward to follow it. Others turned one evening to follow a red cloud, and when the sun rose again they were nowhere to be seen. Some saw the corn-silk rays of the setting sun point northward, and that is the way they went. Some saw birds flying in a formation that resembled an arrow, and they followed the arrow's flight. Others saw a glow at night on the peak of a distant mountain, and so they left the main party and travelled in that direction. A time came when the Hopis were scattered across the land, one group separated from another, but all looking for the place whose name they did not yet know. This is the way the great migrations began.

In those ancient days there were no clans, merely groups of relatives or friends travelling together. One of these groups arrived at a place where the carcass of a bear was lying. They paused to look at the dead bear, wondering if it was a sign that had to be understood. Their leader thought about the matter and finally he said, "Yes, there is a meaning to this. The meaning is that from this time on we shall be known as the Bear Clan. This name will distinguish us from all other Hopis." After the Bear Clan people rested there a while they went on.

Another group that was following them came to the same carcass. They cut strips from the bear's hide to make forehead straps for carrying heavy loads, and before they went on they took the name Strap Clan to distinguish themselves from others. More groups followed the same trail. Some people saw a bluebird pecking meat from the bear's carcass, and because of this they gave themselves the name of Bluebird Clan. Some came and found that although the bear's carcass was decayed there was still grease in the eye sockets of the skull, so they called themselves the Grease Cavity Clan. Others who arrived at that place saw a gopher digging a hole beneath the skeleton, and they became the Gopher Clan. Another party arrived and saw a spider spinning a web across one of the eye sockets, and these people took the name Spider Clan. And when the bear's bones were already bleached but still visible, yet another group came that way and saw a spruce tree growing through the skeleton, and for this reason took the name Spruce Clan. Because all of these clans acquired their names at the place of the dead bear, they considered themselves bound together. But after leaving the bear site they did not all go the same way, and some travelled faster than others, so that much time passed before they met again.

During these long migrations some children were lost in the canyons through which the people passed. The canyons were searched from end to end, but the children were never found, and at last the people had to go on. But a strange thing happened. The children were still alive, and they wandered from one place to another, eating wild berries and roots to satisfy their hunger. Eagles living on the high cliffs watched the children, soaring overhead to keep track of them. They felt sorry for the children and sought to comfort them. Sometimes they brought food and laid it on the ground nearby, and the children began to think of the eagles as their own people. They listened to the eagle calls and imitated them. One morning they awoke and discovered that they had turned into eagles. They flew into the air and perched on the high cliffs. In later days, if Hopis caught a small eagle they brought it home in a cradle board. They washed its head and gave it a small doll, just as though it were a human child.

As for the Bear Clan, it went northward, stopping whenever it had to plant corn and make a temporary village. When it had renewed its food supplies and rested it went on. How many villages the Bear Clan built and left behind in its northward migration is not known, but in time it reached a place where it had to turn back because the summers were too short for the blue corn to mature. The Bear Clan chief said: "Now, we cannot go in this same direction any more. This is what our corn tells us. We must seek what we are looking for somewhere in the south." Again the Bear Clan migrated, built temporary villages and abandoned them, arriving at last at a place called Moencopi, meaning Running Water, and there they rested again. How long the Bear Clan remained at this place is not known. But while they were still growing their corn there they were joined by the Spider Clan, the Strap Clan, the Bluebird Clan and the other related clans. All of these clans put their marks on the rocks and cliffsides as a record of their journeys.

After some years the Bear Clan chief said, "Yes, this is a good place and we shall remember it, but it is not the country where all the Hopis are supposed to gather again. Therefore we must go on." And so the Bear Clan left Moencopi behind, now going toward the east. They found a large mesa there, and somewhat below the rim of the mesa and not far from where the present village of Shongopovi stands they saw large fields of corn. Beyond the cornfields they saw a house. Standing before the house was Masauwu, the Giver of Fire, the Spirit of Death and the Owner of the Upper World. He was terrifying to see. He wore a rabbitskin robe. He had no hair at all, and no eyelashes, and his skin was marked with the scars of many burns. His eyes were sunken in and his face was splattered with blood.

Masauwu said, "Who are you and why have you come?"

The leader of the Bear Clan said, "We are Hopis. Our clan is the Bear Clan. We came through the sipapuni from the Lower World because our messenger, the catbird, said to us, 'Masauwu, the Owner of Fire, says that if the people want to come, let them come.' Now we are here. We have followed the clouds and the stars and they have brought us to this place, which is the center of things. We wish to settle and build our village. Assign us land to till so that we can plant the blue corn given to us at the sipapuni."

Masauwu replied, "Yes, you may remain here." He went to where the land was fertile, and there he stepped off the fields where the Bear Clan could plant. Then he returned, saying, "All the land around which I walked belongs to you and your clan children."

They asked, "Where may we build our village?"

Masauwu answered, "Over there, just at the foot of the mesa. Your village will be called Masipa."

They thanked Masauwu, and the Bear Clan chief said, "You, Masauwu, first you gave us fire in the world below, and now you give us land for our village and fields. Therefore, be our chief and govern us."

But Masauwu said, "No, I will not be your chief. You came from the Lower World of your own free will. I did not call you. I have no responsibility in the matter."

And after saying this, Masauwu turned and left them and disappeared from the place where he had been living. It is said by some that he went eastward to another part of the great mesa near where modern Walpi now stands, living on but remaining invisible unless he wanted to be seen. The people wished to bring pahos, or prayer sticks, to Masauwu, but they could not find him. So they built shrines for him at various places, and whenever they needed his help they carried pahos to these shrines.

This is how the Bear Clan people arrived, at last, in the country where they are living today.

The first night after they received their land from Masauwu the people camped in the valley. When they awoke in the morning they saw wisps of smoke rising from a plateau some distance to the east. They sent scouts to discover who was living in that place. The next day the scouts returned. They said, "Yes, on that mesa, there are people living there. The village is a large one. It belongs to the Bow Clan people, but other clans as well are among them. The smoke comes from the pottery fires. A pottery fire burns in front of every house. The village is called Awatovi, Bow Height. It has many houses and three plazas where the dances take place. How many kivas there are we do not know."

So the Bear Clan learned that it was not the first of the clans to arrive. But they built their houses at Masipa and settled there, growing their corn in the fields given to them by Masauwu. In the years that followed, some of the clans still migrating in the wilderness heard of the Bear Clan settlement, and they came to Masipa and were accepted there. The Bluebird Clan arrived, and after that there came the Strap Clan, the Spruce Clan, the Grease Cavity Clan and the Gopher Clan, each bringing with it some special ceremony or power to benefit the village.

The Fire People, who were the first to come through the sipapuni, wandered a longer time in the wilderness than some of the other groups. In the course of their migrations they became the Fire Clan, and later on they split into two separate parts. One part of the Fire Clan went eastward and arrived in time at Muyovi, the Rio Grande, where it remained for many years. The other part travelled northward to Kalewistima, near where the present town of Kayenta stands, and built a village there and settled. But the Fire Clan people were restless. They wanted to find the place that Masauwu had offered to the Hopis. And so, after putting their marks on the walls of the cliffs, they left Kalewistima and travelled southward. In time they arrived at Masipa, where the Bear Clan was living with its affiliated clans.

The chief of the Fire Clan asked for permission to settle his people in that place. But at the same time he contended that because Masauwu was particularly close to the Fire Clan, the Fire Clan should take the leadership in the village.

The Bear Clan chief, who was also the kikmongwi of Masipa, spoke to the Fire People in this manner: "Because you are related to Masauwu, and because it was you who first received fire from him in the Lower World, the people allowed you to be the first to come through the sipapuni. But once we were all in the Upper World you refused to lead us. You went your own way, just like the other clans. When we of the Bear Clan arrived in this place we spoke with Masauwu. He did not say, 'You are not the Fire Clan, therefore you are not my relatives.' He said, 'Settle here. I will give you land and a place to build your village.' Because Masauwu is the Owner of the Upper World we asked him to remain and be our leader. We said, 'Be our father and we will be your children.' But Masauwu said,

'No, it is not my responsibility. Make one of your own people chief.' Then he departed, going to the east so that he could be alone. Had he accepted the responsibility to lead us, you, his relatives, would have had a paramount position in Masipa. But he said, 'No, I cannot accept.' So the responsibility is ours."

The Fire Clan chief persisted. He said, "At the sipapuni before the tribes and clans parted from one another our leader gave half of a stone tablet to the Bahanas, retaining the other half. By these two fragments we will be able to identify the true Bahana who will come, some day, from the east, bringing harmony and well-being to the Hopis. Because we own half of the tablet, it is we who should be paramount in Masipa."

But the Bear Clan chief answered, "Yes, the tablet is an important thing. Nevertheless, Masipa was given to us by Masauwu. You may enter, you may stay, but the Bear Clan shall remain in authority."

At last the Fire Clan leader said, "Very well. We are here now. We shall stay. Apportion lands for us so that we can grow our corn." This is how one branch of the Fire Clan settled in Hopi country. The other branch arrived much later in a separate migration.

Following prophecies and signs in the sky, still other clans or parts of clans came together where the Bear Clan had settled. They could not all enter Masipa because there was not enough room for them, and so a number of other villages were built nearby. When the Squash Clan arrived after its journey from the Little Colorado River country it settled a few miles north of Masipa and called its village Tikuvi. When the Spider Clan arrived it remained for a while at a spring called Homikopu, where there are still ruins to be seen. Later on the Spider Clan asked for permission to move to Tikuvi, and the Squash Clan welcomed these people. Tikuvi grew large. After the Spider Clan people lived in Tikuvi for some years they moved again, to Masipa where their affiliated clans were living.

Now in Masipa, which in time came to be called Shongopovi, the kikmongwi had a brother named Masito. How it came about no one remembers for certain, but the kikmongwi and his brother fell out of harmony. Some say it was because Masito criticized the chief for the manner in which he carried out his leadership. Others say that Masito himself was criticized by the people for eating two ears of corn at once, one in each hand, during a year when food was scarce and some families had no corn at all. Still others recall hearing it said that Masito forced himself on the chief's wife and lay with her, causing bitterness to arise between the brothers. Whatever the reason for the estrangement, Masito disappeared from Masipa one day, taking his family with him. For a long time no one knew where he was. But later on, hunters found him at a place some distance to the west, where he was living in a house he had built near the foot of the mesa. They spoke, saying, "You are here, then. The people have been wondering about you. Your brother, the kikmongwi, wants you to come back to Masipa."

Masito answered, "Yes, here I live. This is my home. I cannot live in Masipa any longer. I do not want to have anything to do with it."

They asked him, "What is the name of this place?"

He answered, "It is called Ojaivi, Round Rock."

The hunters returned home. They told the chief where they had seen his brother. Then the chief sent special messengers to Masito to ask him to return. They found him in the fields where he was piling up stones to make a marker. They asked him what this marker meant.

Masito said, "These stones are our boundary. The land east of here, Masipa can keep it. On this side, toward the setting sun, everything belongs to Ojaivi."

The messengers replied, "Ojaivi? There is only one house there. What does one house need with so much land?"

Masito said, "Why are we counting houses? The marker separates us. Tell this to my brother."

The messengers returned to Masipa and told the chief what they had heard.

As time passed, people drifted away from Masipa, a few at a time, and went to join Masito. Whenever a family arrived, he assigned lands to it. Also, clans and portions of clans were still coming in from the migrations, and many of these people settled at Ojaivi. Fire Clan people arrived, Water Coyote Clan people and still others. A group of Badger Clan people from the south appeared near Ojaivi in the middle of winter. They camped in the valley and sent messengers to ask if they could enter the village and build houses there.

Three times they sent messengers without receiving an answer from Masito, for he wasn't sure the Badger people had anything good for the village. The fourth time the messengers came, Masito returned to their camp with them. Though everywhere else the ground was frozen and hard, flowers were growing all around the Badger Clan camp. Seeing this, Masito gave them permission to enter Ojaivi, and he gave them fields in the valley. The next day the Badger people went to Ojaivi in a procession, everyone carrying bean sprouts that they had grown with the aid of fire.

Ojaivi became large. In time its name changed to Oraibi and it moved to another place on higher ground that could take care of more people. And still later it went to the top of the mesa, near where it stands today. Because Masito belonged to the Bear Clan, all the chiefs of Oraibi have been members of that clan until recent times.

While Ojaivi was still young, other villages were springing up near Masipa, the first Bear Clan settlement. Mishongnovi appeared and began to grow. A small settlement named Waki, Place of Shelter, came into being. It grew larger and later on people changed its name to Shipaulovi.

The generations lived on, one after another, and still people kept coming in from the wilderness. Some had been on their migrations so long that they no longer spoke the Hopi language. They spoke the Shoshone language, or Paiute, or the languages of the Hamis people, the Zunis, and the Kawaikas, and they had to relearn Hopi, the language given to them at the sipapuni.

The Hopi villages stretched out from Awatovi and Kachinva in the east to Oraibi in the west, and from generation to generation still more villages were made. There were Payupki, Pivanhonkapi, Huckovi, Chimoenvasi, Sowituika, Matovi, Kateshum, Huckyatwi, Kawaika, Chakpahu, Akokavi, Moesiptanga and many others. And far to the north and south there were villages of other Hopis who had not yet finished their migrations. Some were along the Little Colorado River, some along the Rio Grande, some at Wupatki north of the San Francisco Peaks, some at the mountain of the north called Tokonave. Beyond the Colorado River to the west, and in the San Juan Valley in the north, and elsewhere in the wilderness there were Hopis who were moving imperceptibly toward the center of things, the land which had been given to the people by Masauwu, Owner of the Upper World.

But because the sorceress who had come with the people from the Lower World had taught her arts to others, the evil that people had sought to leave behind them had spread from place to place and was now to be found in one form or another almost everywhere.

III The Lamehva People

IT WAS DURING THE TIME THAT THE HOPI clans were still on their long migrations, before they arrived at the place where Masauwu lived. Gogyeng Sowuhti, Spider Grandmother, lived at that time in the wilderness with her grandsons, the warrior gods Pokanghoya and Polongahoya. The boys hunted game for Spider Grandmother and gathered firewood from the mesa, but mostly they spent their days playing nahoydadatsia and exploring the wide countryside that as yet was unmarked by human habitation. They went to one place and then to another, thinking, "Perhaps there are people out there somewhere." But they did not find any people, and they became lonesome.

They asked Spider Grandmother, "Are there no people in this country? Where can we find someone to talk to?"

Spider Grandmother answered, "No, in this country there are only the three of us."

Still, whenever Pokanghoya and Polongahoya went on their wanderings they would say to each other, "Let us go to the west, perhaps there is someone living there," or, "Let us try the valley below the mesa, maybe there is a village down there somewhere." But wherever they went they discovered nothing but endless land without people.

One day their wandering took them southward to the mesa's edge, and in the foothills they came to the spring called Lamehva. It was cool at the spring, and because the earth around it was moist, many reeds were growing there. Pokanghoya and Polongahoya played at the spring, shaping things out of mud. They made little mud houses. They made a little kiva. They made a complete village, and after that they made little mud people. They placed the mud people here and there, in front of the houses, in the kiva, and on the roofs. They had girls grinding corn, women making piki, and men weaving cloth. They felt as if they had discovered a living village.

When at last the sun was getting low in the sky the boys returned home. Spider Grandmother scolded them, saying, "Where have you been? It is late. You should have been here long ago."

"We went to the south," Pokanghoya said.

"We played at a spring," Polongahoya said.

"And did you find the people you were looking for?" Spider Grandmother asked.

They said, "No, there was no one there. But we made a village out of mud."

Spider Grandmother said, "You see, it is just as I told you. There are no people in this land."

When morning came the boys arose and said, "Now we are going back to the mud village."

But Spider Grandmother answered, "No do not return there today. Let the sun harden the mud for a while."

Pokanghoya and Polongahoya said, "Yes, really we should go to Lamehva. Our people are waiting for us."

But Spider Grandmother dissuaded them, saying, "No, it is better to let the village become dry. Do something else meanwhile. Go back to Lamehva on the fourth day."

So Pokanghoya and Polongahoya went in another direction with their buckskin ball and playing sticks, wondering why Spider Grandmother wanted them to stay away from the spring. On the morning of the fourth day they arose early, saying, "Now we are going back to see if our village has dried."

Spider Grandmother said, "Yes, go now. Your village has dried."

The boys went running to the south. They had almost arrived at the spring when Pokanghoya said, "I hear people talking."

Polongahoya said, "I also hear people talking."

Pokanghoya said, "Yes, it sounds as if they are at the spring."

His brother said, "Let us climb higher to see."

They climbed some high rocks. Now they were able to see the place where they had made their mud village. But what they saw was not a small village made of mud, but a large one with real houses made of stone, and with real people going here and there doing things. The houses, the kiva, everything was just where they had placed it.

"See the girl grinding corn!" Pokanghoya said. "She is one that I made!"

"And the man coming out of the kiva," Polongahoya said. "I am the one that made him!"

"Spider Grandmother has done this," they said. "This is what she meant by drying."

They approached a little closer, and as they did so a man sitting on a rooftop called out, "Kiavakovi! Someone is coming."

The people looked up and saw the boys. The chief of the village said, "Welcome them. They are our first visitors."

And from every house someone called out, "Come in, come in. Sit down and rest yourselves."

Pokanghoya and Polongahoya entered a house. The people gave them sweet corn and melons to eat. When the boys were finished there, they went into another house and were given more food. They entered every house in the village, and every family fed them. Then the chief took them into the kiva and they talked together. At last when the sun was sliding down in the west the boys returned home, taking with them much piki that the people had given them for Spider Grandmother.

Spider Grandmother was pleased with the piki. She said, "Did you find your village doing well?"

They said, "Grandmother, it was doing well."

She asked, "Was it dried?"

They said, "Grandmother, it was truly dried."

She asked, "And was there someone to talk to?"

They answered, "Yes, we talked to everyone. They treated us well."

Spider Grandmother said, "Well, now you know how it is. I

brought your village to life so that you would no longer be lonely. The village will take its name from the spring and be called Lamehva. And because of the reeds that grow there the people shall belong to the Reed Clan. You are the ones that shaped them out of mud and loneliness. Therefore you must always think of them as your children. They shall be dear to you, and you must treat them well forever."

Pokanghoya and Polongahoya said, "Yes, this is the way it will be."

So it was that the village of Lamehva and the Reed Clan people were shaped by the warrior gods and brought to life by Spider Grandmother.

Not far from Lamehva, a little higher up on the mesa, were two tall rocks that the people called Kaiotakwi, Corn Rocks, because they resembled ears of maize. The years went by, and in time some other people arrived and built a village at Kaiotakwi. So now there were two villages, one below and another above. Life was much the same in the two villages except for one thing. In Kaiotakwi they had a cat to help them with their hunting. For the people of Kaiotakwi the hunting was good because of the cat. But the hunters of Lamehva had nothing to help them, and sometimes it was difficult to get meat.

The kikmongwi of Lamehva had a son named Sikakokuh. The boy pondered on the hard times that the Lamehva hunters were having, and one night he went to the kiva to speak with his father.

He said, 'My father."

The chief replied, "My son."

The boy said, "There is a thing to discuss."

His father said, "Let us speak of it."

"Up above in the village of Kaiotakwi," the boy said, "they have a cat to help them catch rabbits and other game."

"Yet, it is so," his father said.

"We also should have something to help us hunt," Sikakokuh said.

"It would be good," his father answered.

The boy asked, "Where then can we find something better than a cat?"

The kikmongwi smoked his pipe. He thought a long while. At last he said, "I have heard that in a place far to the east, not far from the river called Muyovi, there are animals called dogs. They are larger than cats, and better hunters."

The boy said, "Good. Let us have a dog for our village."

His father answered, "It is not an easy thing to accomplish. The distance is far and there are many dangers. There are guards along the trail, and visitors to Suchaptakwi are turned away. Besides, who would make the journey?"

"I will go," the boy said. "I will get the dog, and he will help our village hunt."

"Very well," the chief said, "this is the way it will be. It is settled."

The boy's sisters prepared food for Sikakokuh to carry with him on the journey. The men of the village set to work making pahos, prayer sticks, for Sikakokuh to give to those who might help him along the way. Sikakokuh slept. When morning came he went out of Lamehva and followed a trail to the east. In time he came to a place of tall pine trees, and he found Spider Grandmother waiting for him there.

She said, "At last you are here. I have been expecting you, for it was I who breathed this journey into your mind. There are dangers on the way to Suchaptakwi. There is much to be understood. Therefore I am going with you."

The boy said, "I am grateful."

Then Spider Grandmother made herself small, and in the form of a spider she climbed up and sat on Sikakokuh's ear, saying, "Whenever there is something that needs to be done, I will tell you."

The boy continued his journey to the east. He slept in the pine forest that night, then went on. He came to a place where a rattlesnake guarded the trail. The snake sounded his rattles. When he spoke, it was with an angry voice. He said, "Turn back. No one may go beyond this point."

Spider Grandmother whispered in the boy's ear, "Give him a paho."

Sikakokuh selected a prayer stick and placed it on the ground before the rattlesnake, saying, "Accept this paho made by the people of my village."

The rattlesnake's anger melted away. He accepted the paho. He said, "For what you have given me I am glad. Therefore you may go on. Follow the trail to Suchaptakwi."

So the boy passed by. And some distance beyond he saw a large bear standing in his path. The bear spoke fiercely. He said, "Turn back. You cannot pass. It is not allowed."

"Give him a paho," Spider Grandmother whispered.

The boy offered a paho to the bear, saying, "I bring you a new paho made by my people."

The bear became gentle. He said, "I am grateful for this paho. You may pass."

Sikakokuh went on, and later he met a large buck deer. The deer menaced Sikakokuh with his antlers. He said, "Go back. This is a forbidden trail."

Again Spider Grandmother instructed the boy to offer a paho, and when the deer had received it he said, "Thank you. You may pass."

But Spider Grandmother whispered, "Wait. Do not go on yet. We must borrow his antlers."

Sikakokuh said, "Uncle, we have great need of your antlers."

The deer said, "Yes, you may have them for a while. Twist them gently and they will come off. Take them. When you return, leave them in this tree where I can find them."

The boy twisted the antlers and removed them. Then he resumed his journey. But once more an animal stood in his path. This time, however, it was only a small mole. He said, "You cannot pass this way. There are dangers ahead."

Sikakokuh was about to step over the small creature, but Spider Grandmother said, "Do not ignore him. Even though he is small, give him a paho, for you will need his help."

So the boy gave the mole a prayer stick. The mole said, "Thank you for this paho. I will remember you for it. Go on to Suchaptakwi."

Sikakokuh continued his journey. He came to a steep mountain whose sides were as smooth as glass. Whenever he tried to go up he slid back. Spider Grandmother said, "Use the antlers as walking sticks." And using the antlers this way, bracing the points against the slippery trail, Sikakokuh went slowly up the mountainside. At last he was near the top, and there he heard a strange barking sound.

He said to Spider Grandmother, "What is the sound I hear?"

She replied, "It is the voice of the thing for which you have made this journey. That is the sound of a dog."

He went on more quickly then, and when he reached the crest of the mountain he saw the dog. It ran back and forth, barking. It turned and trotted ahead of Sikakokuh, leading him to what appeared to be a water hole. Protruding from the water was the top of a ladder. The dog began to descend the ladder, and as he did so the water disappeared.

"Follow him," Spider Grandmother said. "This is the kiva of the dog people."

Sikakokuh followed. He went down the ladder and found himself in a large kiva, just as Spider Grandmother had said. Above his head water again covered the entrance. A man was sitting in the kiva. He said, "Well, you have arrived at last. We have been expecting you. Our messengers told us you were coming. Sit down with me and smoke."

Now, the tobacco that the man placed in the pipe was very powerful. Only the dog people could smoke it without being overcome. Sikakokuh did not know this, and almost at once when he began to smoke, his body felt strange and numb. He felt as though he were being enveloped in a dark cloud. He heard the man say, "Smoke, do not hesitate. Smoking brings harmony to the heart." Sikakokuh went on smoking. It seemed to him that his spirit was about to depart from his body. But Spider Grandmother saw what was happening. She went out of the kiva unseen and found the mole to whom Sikakokuh had given the paho. She gave him instructions. The mole began burrowing. He burrowed a hole below the kiva and came up underneath where Sikakokuh was sitting. Then Spider Grandmother went down below Sikakokuh and drew out the smoke from his anus. She blew the smoke through the tunnel made by the mole, and it came out of the ground some distance from the kiva. Sikakokuh felt better. His head cleared. He finished smoking the tobacco.

The man was watching him. He said, "Yes, you are a good smoker. Let us refill the pipe and go on with the smoking." He put fresh tobacco in the pipe and lighted it. After puffing on it a little, he returned the pipe to Sikakokuh. The boy smoked again, and Spider Grandmother continued to draw out the smoke from below and expel it through the mole burrow. At last the man said, "Well, I see that you are not an ordinary person. You have remarkable powers. Let us talk now. Why are you here?"

Sikakokuh answered, "I have travelled far. In my village we hunt rabbits and other game for meat, but the hunting is hard. We do not have enough to eat. In another village nearby the people have what they call a cat. It helps them catch game. But we have heard that dogs are the best of hunters. We need a dog in our village. That is why I have come to Suchaptakwi."

The man considered what he had heard. He put his pipe aside, saying, "Rest and refresh yourself now. I will think about it." He called for food for the boy. Girls came from another room in the kiva bringing corn, melon and fruit. The boy ate, and when he was finished he sat waiting for the man to speak.

The man said, "I am the first uncle and advisor to the dogs. But there is another uncle who must be consulted. I have sent for him."

Spider Grandmother whispered, "The uncle who is coming is a hard man. He speaks roughly. He will not agree easily to what you want. You must persuade him."

The second uncle arrived. He said, "Why is this stranger in our kiva?"

The first uncle replied, "He comes from the village of Lamehva far to the west. He wants a dog to take home with him."

The second uncle said, "It is here in Suchaptakwi that dogs are meant to live. They will remain here forever."

Sikakokuh spoke then. He said, "Uncle, the people of my village made these pahos for you." He handed three pahos to the man. Then he went on: "In Lamehva the people are suffering because they don't have enough meat. We go hunting for rabbits. Sometimes we find them in their burrows, so we have a little meat. When we see them running in the fields we use our throwing sticks. But it is not easy to get enough meat, and often we have no meat at all. In the upper village of Kaiotakwi the people are more fortunate because they have a cat that helps them hunt. My father, the kikmongwi, told me that the dog people live here. He said that dogs are the best of hunters. If we have a dog in Lamehva our life will be better. This is the reason I have come on this long journey."

The second uncle said, "You are courageous to have made such a dangerous trip. And I am glad for the pahos that you gave me. Because of these things, and because of what you have told me about your village, you may take one dog back to Lamehva." After saying this he left the kiva.

The first uncle of the dogs said, "Well, now it is arranged. It will be done this way. We shall have a dance. You will see all the dogs, and you will select one of them." He sent a message to an inner room of the kiva telling the dog people to prepare for the dance. The dancers made themselves ready. They went to where their dog pelts were hanging on the wall and took them. As each person put on his pelt, he became transformed into a dog. All the people became dogs. They came to the center of the kiva, formed a line, and began to dance. As they danced, they sang:

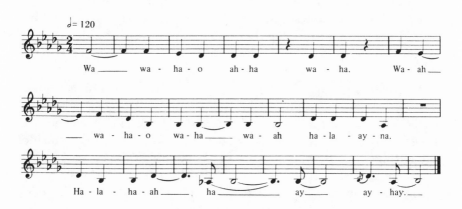

They danced all night until the rising of the sun. Sikakokuh watched them, wondering, "Shall I take this one? Or shall I take that one?" Some were large, some were small. Some had long fur, some had short. Some were black, some were brown, some were spotted. Sikakokuh could not decide. When the dancing came to an end, the first uncle of the dogs said, "You have seen them all. Now make your choice."

Sikakokuh looked at the largest dog, but Spider Grandmother

whispered, "Not that one. Take the small one at the end." The boy looked at the small one. It was only a puppy. Spider Grandmother said again, "Take the small one."

So the boy said, "Yes, I have decided. I want the little one with the spots in back."

The man nodded his head, saying, "You must have great understanding of these things. The one you have chosen will be the fastest and best hunter among us. Very well, he is yours. Take him back with you to your village."

The boy took the puppy and held it. He fed it, and they became friends. The other dogs went back to the inner room and took off their dog pelts and became people again. Everyone slept. When morning came Sikakokuh prepared to leave.

The first uncle said to him, "You have chosen one of our people to go with you. He will grow into a good watchdog and a great hunter. Treat him well. Speak to him gently. Never strike him or abuse him. If you treat him well he will bring good luck to your village. Whoever abuses him will suffer in return. If something should happen and the dog dies, bury him as you would bury one of your own people. After four days he will return to us here in Suchaptakwi to live again with us in our kiva."

Sikakokuh said, "Uncle, I will remember what you have told me." Carrying the puppy in his arms, he ascended the ladder. As he neared the top, the cover of water dissolved, and when he had passed through the opening the water reappeared. From the outside, the entrance to the kiva again looked like an ordinary water hole.

The boy began his return journey. He came to the place where he had met the deer, and he left the antlers there in a tree. He went on past where he had met the bear and the rattlesnake guards of the trail. And when he arrived at the spot where he had met Gogyeng Sowuhti, Spider Grandmother, she left him there and he went on with his dog. As he approached his village he saw his two sisters standing on a high rock waiting for him. Every day since his departure they had come there to watch for his return.

Sikakokuh put the puppy on the ground, saying, "Here is our dog."

The girls were glad, but they asked, "Can such a one as this truly hunt?"

They arrived at their house. The girls called out, "Mother," and their mother came out. They called, "Father," and their father came out. Other people came. They looked in wonder at the dog.

The chief said, "My son, I see that you have brought something with you."

The boy answered, "My father, I have brought him. Now we have a dog to help us."

The people of Lamehva crowded around. They touched the dog and rubbed his fur, saying, "So this is what a dog looks like." They spoke to him gently, as though he were a child. The next day there was a ceremony. The dog's hair was washed, and they gave him a name, Tintopakokoshi, meaning Spotted-in-Back.

A day came when Spotted-in-Back was old enough to go hunting. The men and boys went out to look for meat, and they took the dog with them. What they saw greatly surprised them, for Spotted-in-Back could pick up the scent of a rabbit and follow him swiftly. He caught many rabbits and brought them back to the hunters. That day no hunter went home without meat. And afterwards when they went hunting again, things were the same. Good fortune had come at last to the village of Lamehva.

But in the upper village, Kaiotakwi, the people heard what had happened and they were jealous, for they had only a cat to help them. They became angry with the people of Lamehva. As for the dog, they said to one another, "He is an evil creature, he steals all the game."

Things went on this way. When he was not hunting, Spotted-in-Back went here and there exploring the countryside. He went up on the buttes, he followed the washes, and he wandered on the mesa. And one night when everyone was asleep he found his way into the upper village and prowled among the houses. He found some meat hanging there, and he ate it. When day came, people discovered that their meat had been stolen. The next night more meat disappeared, and the next night also. The men of Kaiotakwi examined the ground and found the tracks left by the dog. They were very angry. They said, "It was the evil creature from Lamehva. Let us put bait out for him tonight and wait for him. We will catch him and kill him."

They prepared the bait. They put a piece out in the village

plaza. And when night came the men hid on the rooftops with sticks and clubs in their hands. They waited. There was a bright moon, and late in the night they saw the dark shadow of the dog moving across the plaza. Spotted-in-Back came to the meat and began eating. The men jumped down from their hiding places and surrounded him. They beat him. Spotted-in-Back could not escape. They killed him. Then they took his body to the edge of the village and threw it into a ravine.

Morning came. In Lamehva the people were looking for Spotted-in-Back, but they could not find him. "Perhaps he will return soon," someone said. They waited until the sun was high, and then they began to search for him. Following his tracks here and there, they discovered that Spotted-in-Back had been in Kaiotakwi, and at last they found his body in the ravine.

Sikakokuh went to his father. He said, "A terrible thing has happened. We have lost Spotted-in-Back, our friend and helper. The people of Kaiotakwi killed him and threw his body into a ravine. Now, once again, our hunting will be hard."

The chief said, "That is an evil deed. Who can live with people who do such things?"

Sikakokuh said, "Yes, it is true, one cannot live with people like that. But the uncle of the dogs in Suchaptakwi warned that anyone who treated Spotted-in-Back badly would suffer for it. I think something will happen to the cruel men in Kaiotakwi."

They took the body of the dog to the foot of a great rock, and there they buried Spotted-in-Back as though he were a person. They put stones on the grave and left prayer sticks just as they would have for anyone in the village, and after that they returned to their homes.

For the next four days the people of Lamehva did nothing. They did not work in their fields, they did not weave, they made no pottery, they ground no corn. They merely sat in their houses or their kiva mourning the death of their friend. On the fourth day they returned to the place where they had buried the dog. But he was no longer there. His grave was empty. They saw the marks of his feet on the ground, and the tracks led toward the east.

Sikakokuh said, "Yes, it is just as they said it would be. Spotted-in-Back has gone to live with his own people in Suchaptakwi."

From that time on there were bitter feelings between the villages of Lamehva and Kaiotakwi. If people from the two villages met on the trail or in the fields, neither would speak to the other, but merely passed in silence. And soon a strange thing happened in Kaiotakwi. All the men who had a part in the killing of the dog became lame. Their knee joints swelled and they felt great pain. They could move from one place to another only with the help of walking sticks, and later on some of them could not walk at all. For this misfortune they blamed the village of Lamehva. They said that the people of Lamehva were powakas.

In Lamehva the people discussed the situation in the kiva. "We cannot live in this place any more," one person said. "It is like a sickness to be so close to Kaiotakwi."

Another said, "Yes, that is the way it is. The name Kaiotakwi leaves a bitter taste in the mouth."

Still another said, "We must find another home. The tracks that Spotted-in-Back left are a sign telling us to go in that direction. There, somewhere in the east, we will make a new village." All night long the discussion went on.

They agreed that something must be done, and when morning came the people prepared to abandon Lamehva. They took what they could carry and left everything else behind. The people of Kaiotakwi saw them depart, going eastward. But then a heavy mist descended from the sky and enveloped the people of Lamehva so that they were no longer visible. In the heart of the mist they journeyed until they came to a broad shelf of land below the heights of the great mesa. There the mist lifted, and they saw that they were in a good land. They built their houses at that place and called their new village Koechaptevela, meaning Ash Hill, and down below in the valley they planted their corn. Once more things were in harmony, and the people shaped out of mud by the warrior gods and given the breath of life by Gogyeng Sowuhti lived on.

Now, the Bear Clan people who had received land from Masauwu at Masipa also made settlements near where the great mesa sheltered Koechaptevela, and as time passed there came to be controversy over who had arrived first. Some said one thing, some another, but as they were all Hopis they accepted life together and their village became strong.

IV The Destruction of Palatkwapi

SINCE THE BEGINNING OF THINGS much time had passed. People had journeyed from one place to another, built villages, abandoned them and gone on, following the instructions of their wise men and the signs that appeared in the sky. Somewhere far, far to the south of where the Hopis now live, a band calling itself Patkiwoema, the Patki People, moved through the wilderness. They had taken the name Patki, meaning a dwelling-on-water, or houseboat, because in ancient times they had escaped from a place of wickedness by floating in houseboats across a great sea. After a long voyage they came to land and continued their migrations on foot. How long they journeyed by land is not known, but at last they came to the place they called Palatkwapi, and there they settled and built their village. Other related bands, such as the Cloud People and the Frog People, joined them at Palatkwapi, and in days to come they all became clans. Later on, because they were so closely bound together by their experiences, they were all known as the Water Clan. Other clans came also. There were the Sand Clan, the affiliated Tobacco and Rabbit Brush clans, the affiliated Eagle and Hawk clans, the Sun Clan, and some clans whose names have now been forgotten. But the Water Clan was the first in Palatkwapi, and it held the paramount authority there.

The people who gathered in this village in ancient days did not assume it to be their final settlement, but as the years passed they began to forget about the migrations. Life was good to them. Their corn matured, there was always water in the nearby river, the rain fell and there was plenty of game. The older people, however, did not forget the sipapuni and the meaning of life. In their songs they asked, "Who are we? Where do we come from? Why are we here?" They recalled that they were made by Tawa, that they had been admonished to leave evil behind, and how they must search for the place where all the migrating Hopis would meet again. Already they had heard from the old ones about a certain place called Sichtilkwi, Flower Mound, and they understood that a time would come when they would journey there. Yet while some people recalled these things, there were many who did not think of them any more.

Palatkwapi was small at first, then it grew large, and by the time it was old there were numerous persons in the village who rejected virtue. As one generation followed another there were more and more people who could not answer the question, "Why are we here?" Evil and corruption entered the village. Instead of gathering in the kivas to examine the meaning of life, men and women used the kivas for playing totolospi, kokotukwi and other gambling games. They neglected their fields and forgot to make pahos for the gods. Young people abandoned respect for older people and old ways, harassing the aged even when they went out to relieve themselves at the edge of the village. Married women accepted the companionship of men who were not their husbands, lying with them wherever it was convenient. A shadow seemed to be falling over Palatkwapi.

The kikmongwi and the leaders of the clans met frequently to discuss what was happening. At last they decided that they must do something to warn the people about the consequences of their bad behavior. So in the dark of night they summoned a young man of the Water Clan and dressed him in the costume of a Tsaveyo monster. Over his head he wore a large black mask with horns at the sides and huge protruding eyes. It had long black jaws with sharp white teeth, a bird foot painted on the forehead, a collar of fur, and five radiating eagle feathers in the back. The Tsaveyo monster wore a buckskin cape and a quiver full of arrows. In one hand he carried a bow and in the other a large stone ax.

The young man went out of the village and hid until the sun appeared in the east. Then, impersonating the terrifying monster, he came to the edge of Palatkwapi and called out in a great voice, "I am entering!" The kikmongwi went to where the monster was waiting and offered him pahos, saying, "Why are you here?" The Tsaveyo replied, "I have come to talk to the people."

So the kikmongwi led him to the plaza. There the Tsaveyo moved back and forth brandishing his stone ax. The people gathered. The Tsaveyo said: "You people of Palatkwapi, you have forgotten why human beings exist. It was Tawa who brought you here so you could lead virtuous lives. But you are profaning the kivas with careless and evil ways. You are neglecting your duties. The corn is suffering because the young men do not work in the fields with their fathers. The young women should be in their houses grinding corn, but instead they run about looking for pleasure. You men, why have you stopped making pahos to place at the shrines? You women who lie down in the fields with anyone who smiles at you, have you no husbands? You young people, why do you harass the old ones who cannot protect themselves? Palatkwapi is sick. I am here to warn you. Unless Palatkwapi returns to a good way of life it will cease to be a living village."

There were many who listened to what the Tsaveyo said. But others were impatient to leave because they wanted to go back to the kivas to gamble. When the Tsaveyo moved about brandishing his stone ax they laughed. And when at last in the evening he left the plaza and departed from the village, they hurried away to do the things they had been deprived of. Still, for a while after that things were a little better in Palatkwapi.

But when another year had passed everything was in great disorder again. Women seeking diversions in the kivas even forgot to feed their children, and sometimes the men had to bring babies to the kivas so that they could be suckled. The kikmongwi and the clan chiefs were distressed, not knowing what to do next. Now, the kikmongwi was considered the father of the village, and his wife was considered the mother of the people. They were expected to demonstrate by example the virtuous way of life. But the kikmongwi's wife succumbed to the evil all around her. And when the kikmongwi discovered her lying with other men he was aroused to great anger.

He said, "Palatkwapi has returned to the chaos of the Third World. Now we are back where we began." And he descended then into the kiva that was reserved for him alone and remained there four days without coming out.

On the fourth day he sent for his nephew. The chief said, "My nephew."

His nephew said, "My uncle."

The chief said, "My nephew, there is an important thing that must be done."

His nephew replied, "My uncle, tell me what I must do."

The kikmongwi said, "You are an excellent runner. But you must surpass what you are now capable of doing. Build your strength. Go out of the village when the sun shows itself in the east. Run toward the south where the dark mountain is, circle it, and return to the village."

In the morning the young man went running toward the dark mountain in the south. But long before he reached the mountain he tired and had to return. The kikmongwi said, "Yes, that is the way I expected it to be. Try again tomorrow." The next day the young man reached the foot of the mountain before he had to stop. Again he returned and reported to the chief. The kikmongwi said, "Tomorrow try again." On the third day the young man circled the mountain and was halfway home before he had to stop. On the fourth day he did not stop running until he had circled the mountain and returned to Palatkwapi. The kikmongwi said, "My nephew, now you are ready for your task. Come to me in the kiva tomorrow morning and I will tell you about the thing that must be done."

When morning came, the young man descended into the kiva. The kikmongwi handed him two prayer sticks that he had made during the night. He said, "Today you will need all your running skill. Go out to the valley in the west. Hunt for a buck deer. When you see him, pursue him and capture him. Give him these prayer feathers to take with him to the next world. Kill him and remove one of the small spike horns from his head. Then return to the village."

The young man went to the west. He saw some deer there and began to pursue one of them. The deer was fleet, but the young man followed him without faltering. They ran for a long time, and gradually the deer veered around until he came back to the place where the chase started. The deer could not run any more. The young man caught him and threw him down.

The deer said, "Are you going to be severe with me?"

The young man answered, "Yes, but it is not because I want to. I must do as I have been instructed by my uncle. You have to die, and for this I am sorry. I have brought you two prayer sticks. When you are dead, perhaps these pahos will do something good for you in the other life to which you are going."

The deer said, "Thank you for the pahos. Do now what you have to do."

So the young man killed the deer and took one of the spike horns from his head, after which he returned to his uncle in the kiva. The kikmongwi received the spike horn. He attached it to his nephew's head, saying, "This horn, no matter what happens to you, do not remove it." Then he instructed the young man this way: "What you must do now is full of dangers. It may cost you your life. Are you willing to accept it?" The young man said, "Yes, I accept it," and the kikmongwi continued: "Here are four masks that I have prepared for you. Here also is a medicine to put on your tongue so that fire will come from your mouth. Take these things. Return to the dark mountain tomorrow and stay there until night comes. Put these masks on, one over the other. Run back to Palat-kwapi in the darkness and circle through the village. Pass through the plaza and climb to the highest roof. Corn-grinding stones will be there. Kneel there, grind corn, and sing the song that I will give you. After that, leave the village and return to your hiding place at the dark mountain."

He gave the masks to his nephew one at a time. The first one was a Kiwan mask, like those now worn by kachina dancers; the second was an Owhalani mask, like the masks now used by dancers in the Soyal ceremonies; the third was a Talavai mask, like the ones now worn by the Dawn Kachinas; and the fourth was the mask of Masauwu, the Owner of Fire and the Spirit of Death. Attached to the Masauwu mask was a necklace made of human bones. The kikmongwi instructed his nephew again in all the details, and the next morning the young man went to the dark mountain in the south.

Night came. The young man put on the Kiwan mask. Over that he put on the Owhalani mask. Over that he put on the Talavai mask. And the fourth mask that covered the other three was that of Masauwu, the Spirit of Death. Then the young man put the fire medicine in his mouth, and the flame that came out resembled Masauwu's breath. After that he began running. He came to Palatkwapi and ran around it at the outer edge. He entered the village and ran through the streets, passing through the plaza and mounting to the highest roof. The grinding stones were there, and he went through the motions of grinding corn. He sang:

Tu-ta - heh!   Tu-ta - heh!   Tu-ta voe-na heh!   Tu- ta voe-na heh!   Heh heh heh!

Most of the people who were still awake were in the kivas playing games. But there was a man lying on top of one of the kivas. He called down to the others, "Come quickly. There is a fire going around the village. It goes from one place to another."

But the people down below only laughed, saying, "Why do you tell us such stories? Who has ever heard of a fire going from one place to another?"

The man called down again, saying, "Yes, it is true. Now the fire is grinding corn upon the roof and singing a song."

Again the people in the kiva called back, "Go home, old man, and sleep."

When the kikmongwi's nephew finished his grinding and singing he left the village. The man on top of the kiva called out, "Come quickly, the fire is going away now."

But no one paid any attention.

The next night at the same time the young man came again, running through the village, passing through the plaza, and mounting to the roof of the highest house. Again he ground corn and sang:

> *"Tu-tah-heh! Tu-tah-heh!*
> *Tu-ta voe-na heh! Tu-ta voe-na heh!*
> *Heh-heh-heh!"*

The same man as before was there on top of the kiva, and this time when he called to those below a friend came up. He also saw the fire and heard the song. He saw the fire come down from the roof, pass through the plaza, and depart from the village. He said to those in the kiva, "Yes, it is true. A fire went through the plaza. It is departing now." So some other men came out of the kiva and they saw the fire moving toward the south.

On the third night the kikmongwi's nephew came again. This time there were many people outside the kiva. They said to one another, "Yes, it is so. There is a man running there. Fire comes out of his mouth. He grinds corn on the highest roof and sings. What is the meaning of it? It is a serious matter." They went below, telling the people in all the kivas what they had seen. There was no more laughing. They decided that if the runner with fire in his mouth came again they would catch him and get an explanation of the affair.

The next night they hid inside houses near the plaza and on the rooftops. After a while someone said, "See, it approaches." They saw the fire coming. It encircled the village, passed through the streets and entered the plaza. They saw then that it was a man. He climbed to the highest roof, and there he ground corn again, singing:

> *"Tu-tah-heh! Tu-tah-heh!*
> *Tu-ta voe-na heh! Tu-ta voe-na heh!*
> *Heh-heh-heh!"*

While he was singing, the people came from their hiding places and blocked all the passageways leading from the plaza. When the kikmongwi's nephew descended from the roof they seized him and took him down into a kiva. In the light of the kiva fire they saw the Masauwu mask he was wearing and became fearful. They removed the Masauwu mask, revealing the Talavai mask. They removed that mask also, expecting to see a man's face, and discovered the Owhalani mask. Removing that mask they saw the Kiwan mask. When they removed the fourth mask they saw the face of the kikmongwi's nephew. In surprise they asked, "Ah, is it you?"

He answered, "Yes, it is I."

They said, "What are you doing? What is the meaning of this

thing?" But he did not answer them. They became fearful. "Who instructed you in this matter?"

He replied, "My uncle, the kikmongwi, who is the leader of the Water Clan."

"Why should the kikmongwi give you such a task?"

The young man said, "I do not know. Perhaps it is because of what you have done to his wife."

The people were silent for a while, perceiving the seriousness of the affair. They remembered that the outer mask was the face of the Death Spirit, Masauwu, and that fire is Masauwu's breath. They said, "It is a bad thing the kikmongwi and his nephew have done. There is an evil purpose in it. Let us kill the nephew and be done with it."

Hearing this, the young man said, "I hope you will not be severe with me, for I did only what I was instructed to do. But if you do put me to death, you must leave the spike horn on my head and leave one of my hands unburied."

They said, "What is the meaning of that? Why does he tell us what we must do and what not to do?"

Someone replied, "We do not know the meaning of it. Let us kill him. But let us leave the horn on his head and one hand protruding from the ground. Perhaps it is best that way."

It was morning now. They took him out of the kiva. They killed him. They dug a grave in the center of the plaza and put his body in it. As they began to cover the grave someone said, "Yes, leave his hand on the outside. Who knows what the consequences will be if we do not follow the instructions?"

After considering the matter again they took the young man's arm and raised it, leaving his hand protruding from the earth. The thumb was folded over, so that four fingers pointed upward. They left the grave and went away.

Early the next morning when the people came from their houses they looked at the hand, and they saw that the index finger was folded downward, leaving three fingers pointing toward the sky. They wondered about the meaning of this, and felt a foreboding. Nevertheless, the ones who valued pleasure above a good life went to do the things to which they had become accustomed.

The next morning they saw that the second finger of the hand was folded down, leaving only two upright. On the third morning the third finger was folded down, leaving only the little finger pointing upward. Seeing this, the people of Palatkwapi understood that there were forces at work that could not be turned back, and they became afraid.

On the fourth morning when they came to the plaza the sun was red, and though there were no clouds in the sky the light was subdued. They looked at the place where the body was buried and saw that the last finger was turned down, marking the end of the cycle of four. There was a rumbling in the distance. The sound grew louder as it came closer. The earth began to shake. Large stones slid from their foundations and the walls of the houses cracked. The buildings began to crumble and fall. Out of the gray cloudless sky rain poured down, and a cold wind swept through the plaza. The people of Palatkwapi fled to their houses seeking refuge, but even as they did this, water began to flood out of their fireplaces, washing through the rooms and the doorways. In the plaza the floodwaters rose. The violent shaking of the earth caused more walls to collapse. Where once the people had danced in the plaza there was now a deep pond. From the earth underneath this spot, where the kikmongwi's nephew had been buried, the head of the great water serpent Balolokong appeared. Balolokong's head reared higher and higher as his body emerged out of the earth. On the back of his head was a single horn like the one worn by the young man who had been interred there. Balolokong's eyes turned this way and that, surveying the crumbling walls of Palatkwapi. The people fled in terror, but there was no more sanctuary in the village, which by now was submerged in the surging water. In the flight to the safety of high ground outside the village some children were lost or swept away, and some of the old and the crippled were left behind.

Outside Palatkwapi the survivors found refuge among the rocks and caves. The kikmongwi and the clan chiefs discussed what might be done to quiet Balolokong. They agreed that a prayer offering must be made. They set to work making pahos, and when the pahos were finished there was the question of who would take the offerings back to Palatkwapi. They chose a boy and a girl to carry out this mission. The boy's name was Choong'o, meaning Smoke Pipe.

They dressed him. They combed his hair and put feathers in it. They put turquoise beads around his neck and gave him a kilt to wear. They painted his legs, and they painted a black line across his cheeks and the bridge of his nose. The girl was called Kachinmana, meaning Kachina Girl. They fixed her hair in the ancient style and placed eagle down in it. They painted her legs black with moss from a water hole, and her chin was painted black also. After that they put an atu'i robe with blue, white and red stripes over her shoulders. Then the old men gave the children the pahos they had made, instructing them to return to the ruined village and offer the pahos to Balolokong.

The children did as they were told. As the people saw them go they were silent, for the children were not likely to come back again from Palatkwapi.

And now the clan leaders called all the survivors together, and the chief of the Water Clan, who was also the kikmongwi, addressed them in this way: "We are here among the rocks and caves. Our village, Palatkwapi, we may not go back to it any more, for it is a ruin and a cursed place that will be haunted until the end of time by the evil deeds that were committed there. The chiefs said over and over again, 'Do not forget who you are and why we are here.' But the people did not want to remember. Therefore we must now begin again at the beginning as we did when we came out of the Third World. Palatkwapi is dead to us. It will be covered with wind-blown sand, and the writings we have put on the rocks will be weathered away and become invisible. As it was at the sipapuni, so it is now. Again we will journey, each clan on its own migration following the signs that are known to it. Our fathers have said that somewhere there is a place called Sichtilkwi, Flower Mound. There our people will find one another again. Let us begin."

The people picked up the few things they had saved from the destruction and began their journeys. The Rabbit Brush Clan, or Rabbit Clan as it came to be known, and the Tobacco Clan were the first to go. After them the Hawk and Eagle clans departed. Then the Sun Clan left, followed by others. The Water Clan and its subclans waited with the Sand Clan until the others had gone. The Water Clan chief, using a flint knife, inscribed on a large rock nearby the message that the Water People had come, lived for a while, then moved on, and he signed his message with the picture of a frog. When that was done, the Water Clan people and the Sand Clan people left this place, gathering a few ears of corn from the fields as they went, and began walking toward the north.

Meanwhile the two children, Choong'o and Kachinmana had entered the plaza of Palatkwapi. The great water serpent Balolokong, rearing out of the floodwaters there, turned his fearsome eyes on them. They held out the pahos for Balolokong to see, whereupon he stopped thrashing his body about and the shaking in the earth subsided. He spoke to the children, saying, "Do not be afraid of me. I am your uncle. Come closer." They waded into the water, but after a few steps they stopped. Again Balolokong said, "Do not be afraid of me." Once more they went forward, holding out the pahos, and when they were close enough Balolokong took them and, holding them against his breast, slowly sank beneath the water. As he did so the rain stopped falling, the sky became light, and the rays of the sun stretched out and touched the ruins that had been Palatkwapi.

Balolokong descended into the earth with Choong'o and Kachinmana, and they found themselves in a large kiva. Balolokong removed his serpent skin and hung it on the wall, appearing now in the form of a man. He said, "You see, there is nothing to be afraid of here. I am your uncle." They gave him the pahos, which he received with gratitude. He said, "Rest now. Do not feel sad. Later on you will return to your families." He gave them food to eat. He said, "Because the people forgot the meaning of things, the village lives no more, and they must go on and begin life again. You will tell them the things I want them to know. They must remember forever why Palatkwapi perished. I will give you songs to take to the people. In these songs they will find the history of the Hopis, back to the beginning of things."

Balolokong taught the children many songs. He said: "These songs shall be sacred to the Water Clan, and they shall be sung in the kivas. Once every year at the time of the winter solstice the people must hold a ceremony commemorating what happened here in Palatkwapi. They must build a special shrine and deposit pahos there for me. I will show you how the pahos must be prepared. Only a person of the Water Clan may make this offering. And only a single person at a time is to know my sacred name. He may not divulge it to another until he feels death approaching. He who knows the sacred name will speak to me in a low voice at the shrine where he places the pahos, saying, 'You, Palatkwavehe (at the place of Palatkwa), I offer these pahos to you. Take care of us. We need rain.'

"If these things are done properly I will send rain when the people are in need. But they must also live good lives. When a stranger comes to the village, feed him. Do not injure one another, because all beings deserve to live together without injury being done to them. When people are old and cannot work any more, do not turn them out to shift for themselves, but take care of them. Defend yourselves when an enemy comes to your village, but do not go out seeking war. The Hopis shall take this counselling and make it the Hopi Way."

Balolokong went on, "There is one thing more. The single horn that you saw on my head is my symbol. Therefore, let the priests of the Kwan Society wear a horn in this fashion to symbolize the knowledge of things that I give to the Hopis."

Balolokong continued giving instructions to the children. And on the morning of the fourth day he put on his serpent skin again and took the children to the plaza overhead, which by this time was covered with mud, the water having drained away. He set them down. He handed Choong'o a knife, saying, "Now you must cut a piece of skin from my neck."

Choong'o hesitated. He said, "How can I do such a thing? For you have been gentle with us."

Balolokong said, "Take the skin. It will not injure me." He put his head forward and Choong'o cut a piece of skin from the back of the great water serpent's neck. Balolokong said, "Carry this skin back to your people. When they offer pahos to me in the winter ceremonies they must first rub the pahos on the skin. It will help their prayers to be heard, and it will remind them that I am truly at Palatkwapi."

Then the great water serpent disappeared below the ground, and there was a silence over the dead ruins of the village. The children followed the tracks leading northward. They came in time to where some of the clans were camping while the men made bows

and arrows so that they could hunt game. They were greeted by
their families as though they had returned from the land of the
dead. And while the people were still at the camping grounds,
Choong'o and Kachinmana told of their descent into the kiva of
Balolokong, and about what had happened there. They reported to
the Water Clan chief everything that Balolokong wanted the Water
People to know, and gave him the sacred songs that had been en-
trusted to them.

Now back in Palatkwapi while the earth was still shaking and
the people were fleeing, some old men were left behind. These old
men made their way to a small house that was still standing on the
eastern edge of the village, thinking that they would be safe there.
But the floodwaters entered the house, and in fear that they would
be drowned the old men climbed up to a high storage shelf and
squatted there facing the wall. The water rose and lapped at them
from behind, marking them with white foam. A good spirit saw the
old men clinging there, and out of compassion it turned them into
turkeys. It is because of this that turkeys have white marks on their
tails where the water touched them.

There were still two other men alive in Palatkwapi at this time.
One was blind, and the second man was crippled and could not
walk. Neither one knew that the other was there. When the floodwaters receded they began to call out, hoping to locate other survivors.

The crippled man said, "I hear you, but wherever you are I
cannot walk there because I cannot stand on my legs."

The blind man answered, "I hear you also, but I cannot see
you because I am blind."

The crippled man pulled himself forward a little at a time with
his hands, and the blind man groped from place to place, and at last
they came together.

The crippled one said, "So it is you, my cousin. Are we the only
persons left in Palatkwapi?"

The blind one answered, "Yes, I believe it is that way. I heard
the others leaving, and since the earth stopped shaking and the rain
stopped falling there have been no other voices, only yours and
mine. We have been abandoned here."

The crippled man said, "This village is dead. Somehow we must go away."

The blind man said, "Perhaps with your eyes and my legs we can follow the clans."

They agreed. They found some bows and arrows in the village and prepared to leave. The crippled one got on the blind one's back, and the blind man carried him with the aid of a carrying strap which he braced against his forehead. Travelling this way, they went out of Palatkwapi following the northern trail taken by the clans. They journeyed slowly, the crippled man saying, "Go this way," or "Go that way," and the blind man going wherever he was directed. They became weak with hunger, and because of this they had to travel very slowly.

But one morning they came upon a grazing deer. The crippled man said, "I see a deer nearby. Stop here." He placed an arrow in his bow. He said, "Go forward a little, gently. Stop. Turn a little to the right. Turn back a little." When the moment was right he let his arrow fly and killed the deer. Working together this way, the two men skinned the deer, cut up the meat, and hung it in a tree to dry. They made a fire and placed the deer head in the coals to roast. It was still roasting when the sun went down. But things were still visible, and at this moment the crippled man saw a movement in the distance. He said, "There is something out there lurking in the shadows."

The blind man took an arrow from his quiver and offered it to the crippled man, asking, "What do you see?"

The crippled man said, "I see it now. It goes from one place to another. It is moving around us in a wide circle. It is very large and fierce. It walks on two feet like a man, but it has a black face and white eyes the size of gourds. Its jaws are filled with sharp teeth. It carries a bow and many arrows."

The blind man said, "Yes, it is clear. It is a Soyoko monster. Can you kill it with an arrow?"

The crippled man said, "Yes, it is certainly a Soyoko. But he moves too fast. He goes behind one rock and then another. He is looking at us now."

The blind man said, "Prepare your arrow."

The crippled man replied, "It is no use, he moves too quickly."

The Soyoko went up on a high rock, put an arrow in his bow, and aimed at the men.

The crippled man called out, "The Soyoko is sending an arrow now." And as he spoke, the Soyoko's arrow came flying at their campfire. It struck the roasting deer head, which exploded with a loud noise, sending smoke, hot coals and bits of meat flying everywhere.

Overcome with fright, the two men scrambled away from the fire. Suddenly the crippled man was running and the blind man could see. The Soyoko went away.

The man who had been blind said, "Something has happened. My eyes have been opened."

And the man who had been crippled said, "Yes, something has happened, for now I can walk on my legs."

They rebuilt their fire and put another piece of meat on it. They ate. All night long they sat by the fire discussing what had happened to them.

And later, after the meat was dry enough to carry, they resumed their journey, following the trail left by the clans, both of them seeing and both of them walking equally. They arrived at the place where the people were camping. Everyone was surprised to see the blind man with sight and the crippled one walking. They said, "Look, a strange thing has happened."

The two men said, "Yes, everything is different for us now." They told of their meeting with the Soyoko, and everything that happened at that place.

People said, "A good spirit must have seen how you struggled and sent the Soyoko as a messenger to help you."

The two men made a shrine nearby and offered pahos to the spirit that had sent the Soyoko. Then they distributed the meat that they had brought. When at last the people left their camping grounds and continued their journey, the two men led them, walking in front and searching for the signs in the sky.

This is how the people departed from Palatkwapi. Not everyone left the village, for many perished there. Those who escaped did not all travel in the same direction. Some went southward, some to the west and some to the north. Of those who went to the south nothing more was heard again. Some clans travelled alone, others in groups. Sometimes they encountered people who had not yet formed clans, or people of other tribes, and many young men among the Hopis chose wives from these groups. It is said that there were battles with other nomadic peoples in which Hopi men were killed and Hopi women and children captured by the enemy. Because of this, certain clans or parts of clans disappeared before they finished their journeys. Also because of this some enemy tribes identified themselves with the clans of their Hopi captives, and in this way became related to the Hopis.

V Homolovi and the Journey Northward

THE CLANS THAT WENT NORTH FROM PALATKWAPI stopped at one place and another, building winter villages, and then moving on. It is said that they settled at a place called Kunchalpi for some years. There they rested and grew their blue corn. Old people died and children were born, and thus in time there were many for whom Palatkwapi was only a word in the mouths of the grandfathers. But one night there was a bright shooting star in the northeastern sky, and it was taken as a sign that the migration should be resumed. So the people abandoned Kunchalpi and travelled again, drifting a little to the east, until they came to a site they named Hohokyam. There they settled again, planting their fields and resting from the journey. After many years they departed from Hohokyam and moved on to another place, Neuvakwiotaka, which is now known as Chaves Pass, and there they remained for a long time. And later on, after many harvests at Neuvakwiotaka, they went on until they came to the Little Colorado River near where the present town of Winslow stands. There they made a settlement that they called Homolovi, Small Mound, consisting of two villages, a larger one and a smaller one. The people of the Water and Sand clans occupied the smaller village. Sharing the larger village were the Tobacco and Rabbit clans, the Sun Clan, and various others, including the Eagle, Hawk, Turkey and Moon clans. After a time they were joined by the

Badger Clan and a group that called itself the Reed Clan, though it was not the same Reed Clan that originated at Lamehva. Then some other groups began to arrive from the direction of Muyovi, the Rio Grande, in the east. Among them were the Fox Clan; certain people who as yet had no clan name but who would later become the Coyote Clan; and a branch of the Fire Clan. And, from time to time, still more groups drifted in from different directions. Thus Homolovi grew large and populous.

But while the people were living at this place they came to be threatened by wandering earth-giant monsters called Cooyokos. The chiefs of the clans in Homolovi sent messengers to the warrior gods, Pokanghoya and Polongahoya, to ask for help. The young brothers arrived. The village fed them and made them welcome. The chiefs explained about the Cooyokos, and the brothers said, "Yes, do not worry about it. We will take care of the matter." Polongahoya, the younger, and Pokanghoya, the elder, fastened their bows and their lightning arrows on their backs and went out from the village playing stickball. At a certain place they saw one of the Cooyokos. They put their playing sticks aside, took their bows from their backs, and killed the Cooyoko with lightning arrows. Then they went on playing stickball until they found another monster, and they killed him also. They searched out all the Cooyokos and one by one they killed them all. After that they returned to Homolovi. In gratitude the people made for the warrior gods not pahos but a new buckskin ball, because Pokanghoya and Polongahoya had worn out their old ball during the expedition.

For a while after that Homolovi was at peace. But then bands of Apaches began drifting into this part of the land, and Homolovi was threatened again. The Apaches attacked the people in the fields and took away their crops. Succeeding in this, the Apaches raided the village itself and took away not only corn but sometimes women and children. The marauders did not go away after the raids but remained encamped at spots from which they could return to Homolovi whenever they wanted new stocks of food. Seeing the way things were, the Homolovi clan chiefs again sent messengers to the warrior gods to ask for help.

"We are besieged by the enemy," the messengers told Pokanghoya and Polongahoya. "They are camped all around us. They come to steal our corn, our women and our children. We fight, we drive them away, but each time they come we lose something more. We are suffering from their raids and we need your help."

The young warrior gods said, "Very well. We will come." They took their bows and their lightning arrows and went to Homolovi. Some days passed. Then one morning just at dawn the village scouts came running, saying that the Apaches were approaching. Pokanghoya and Polongahoya went out to meet the enemy. They saw the Apaches moving in great numbers toward Homolovi, their faces painted, their lances and bows in their hands. There were as yet no horses in the land, and therefore all the warriors were on foot. Pokanghoya and Polongahoya stood in the path of the Apaches, their lightning arrows hidden in their clothing. At first the Apaches laughed at the sight of the two boys, saying, "Are there no men left in Homolovi?" Then the warrior brothers slung heavy stones and killed some of the enemy, whereupon the laughing stopped. The Apaches shot some arrows, but Pokanghoya and Polongahoya moved quickly this way and that and escaped the arrows. After that the Apaches rushed forward, and now each of the brothers took out a lightning arrow and shot it. The arrows struck with a great flash and a thunderous noise. Many of the enemy lay dead or dying on the ground. Again the Apaches attacked, again the warrior gods loosed their lightning arrows, and the ground was now covered with corpses. Those Apaches who were still alive fled from the field, but Pokanghoya and Polongahoya pursued them, shooting lightning arrows until no more of the enemy stirred. The warrior gods found the body of the chief and removed his scalp, after which they returned to Homolovi, where they were warmly greeted by the people.

Pokanghoya said, "The Apaches will not come again. We have destroyed them all. Here is the scalp of their chief."

There was a celebration in Homolovi. The people danced in the plaza in honor of the victory of their warrior gods. When the dance came to an end, the clan chiefs came to Pokanghoya and Polongahoya, saying, "You have done everything for us. You have killed all our enemies, the Cooyokos and the Apaches. Therefore we want you to be our kalatakmongwis, our war chiefs. When danger threatens us you will lead our men into battle."

But Pokanghoya answered, "No, we cannot be your war chiefs.

We cannot remain in Homolovi forever. Select a war chief from among your people." The clan chiefs persisted, saying that the warrior brothers should be their leaders in war. Pokanghoya said again, "No we cannot accept. However, I will select a kalatak-mongwi for you." Therepon he flung his scalp trophy into the air so that it fell among a group of men standing behind the clan chiefs. It landed on a certain man, and Pokanghoya said, "There, it is decided. The man on whom the scalp fell, he is your war chief now." And in this way the question was resolved.

The warrior brothers went back to their home, where they were living with Gogyeng Sowuhti, Spider Grandmother. She asked them, "Well, have you done what you went out to do?"

They said, "Yes, it is done. The people over there in Homolovi are now living in peace."

The village remained at peace for a long while, until a large and fierce bear began to prey on the people. He killed many persons, men in the fields, women at the springs, and old ones who could not move fast enough to escape. The hunters went looking for him. Sometimes they saw him and tried to kill him with arrows. But the bear's skin was tough and the arrows did not penetrate. So once more the people decided to ask for help from the warrior gods. They made a new buckskin ball, and messengers carried it to the house where the brothers were living with Spider Grandmother. They gave the ball to the boys. They said, "A great bear is harassing us. He has killed many persons. Our hunters pursue him, but they cannot kill him or drive him away. We want you to help us."

The boys were lighthearted about the matter. They said, "Yes, we will do it for you." They took their bows and arrows. They also took their new ball and their nahoydadatsia sticks. Playing stickball, they travelled rapidly, looking for bear tracks all the while. They found the bear tracks and followed them to a cave. The bear came out of the cave and confronted them. The boys placed arrows in their bows. Both shot at the same time. Both arrows struck the bear in the neck and he fell dead.

Polongahoya, the younger, said, "Let us cut off his head."

But Pokanghoya said, "No, let us skin him."

So they skinned the bear in a special way, making a long cut along each of the legs and pulling the entire hide off the carcass as though it were a shirt. Then they stuffed the skin with grass and sewed up the legs, after which they set it on its feet. It resembled a live bear. Pokanghoya tied one end of a long cord to the bear's neck, and the other end he fastened around his own waist. When he walked he pulled the bear behind him. They returned to Homolovi, and as they approached the village Polongahoya ran ahead, shouting, "The great bear is pursuing Pokanghoya!" People came out to see what was happening. They saw Pokanghoya running and a great bear pursuing him. Everyone fled. Women and children went up the ladders onto the roofs. Men went to get their weapons. Pokanghoya went here and there through the village. Men shot arrows at the bear, but the bear did not seem to notice. Pokanghoya ran through the plaza, scattering the people in all directions. He left the village, a few of the hunters still chasing the bear. He came to Spider Grandmother's kiva. Polongahoya shouted down through the opening, "A great bear is pursuing Pokanghoya!" Then Pokanghoya untied himself and pushed the stuffed skin into the kiva. Spider Grandmother saw it coming. She cried out. She fell down. She lay as though the spirit had left her body. The boys laughed. They shook her. They said, "See, it is only a skin stuffed with grass."

Spider Grandmother arose. She whipped the young warrior gods, saying, "Oh, you boys. Is this a decent way to treat your grandmother?"

Now that the predatory bear was dead, the village was at peace again, and Homolovi lived on.

One night in the northern sky there was a brilliant display of moving lights, and the clan leaders came together in the kiva to discuss the meaning of the event. They agreed that it was a signal for the people to go on with the migration that had stopped at Homolovi many years before. They announced to the people that they should prepare for a resumption of their journey.

People asked, "Where are we going?"

Their leaders said, "Long ago it was foretold that at the end of our travels we would come together again with our Hopi brothers. It is time now for us to continue our search."

So the clans prepared to leave. While they did so their leaders made their marks on the rocks, signifying that such and such a clan had rested there and then moved on. On the evening before the departure, Pokanghoya and Polongahoya came into the kiva where the old men were making plans. They said: "There is something to be done, now that Homolovi is being abandoned. The piece of skin from Balolokong's neck, it was meant for all who once lived in Palatkwapi. Therefore it should be divided now so that each clan has a portion. In this way all of the Palatkwapi clans will have powerful medicine for bringing rain."

The Water Clan chief brought out the Balolokong skin from its hiding place and divided it among all those clans that had come from Palatkwapi. Each clan chief who received a portion placed it in a section of bamboo for protection. Likewise they gathered together all the other sacred paraphernalia from their altars and wrapped them in buckskin. And now they were all ready to go.

As the sun came up the next morning the people went out of Homolovi. Most of the people went northward, where the lights in the sky had been seen. But there was an argument among the Water Clan elders. While some wanted to go north, there were others who insisted that they should go westward along the river to a place which, they said, was waiting for them to arrive. They could not resolve the dispute, and so there was a split. A group of Water Clan families went toward the west and a little to the north, following the river. In time they passed through Neuvatikyao, now called the San Francisco Mountains, and there turned north. A little beyond the tall peaks they came to the place called Wupatki, where already there was a settlement of Hopis, and there they remained.

The largest part of the Water Clan and all the other clans from Homolovi took the northern trail. They travelled across a barren land of sand, rocks and buttes. They stopped and camped a while at a place known as Bird Spring. After that they continued travelling until they came to Little Ruin Mound, not far from where Walpi is today. They camped at that point and sent scouts out to see who might be living on the great mesa that was plainly visible.

At this time the Tobacco and Rabbit clans were in the lead. Their scouts went to a high place and a little to the east, where smoke was rising as though there were a village there. When they returned they said, "Yes, there is a large village up on top. It is owned by the Bow Clan and it is called Awatovi." So a delegation went to Awatovi to inquire if the Tobacco and Rabbit clans might come and live there.

The Awatovi chief asked, "What can you people do that will be good for our village?"

The messengers replied: "The Tobacco and Rabbit clans are affiliated, and the powers we have are shared between us. The Tobacco Clan is the one to whom tobacco was given in the beginning by Tawa. Tobacco is an important thing. The smoking of tobacco in the kivas brings harmony between men. This is what we have to offer Awatovi."

The Awatovi chief considered everything, and at last he agreed that the Tobacco and Rabbit clans could enter the village and settle there.

The Water and Sand Clan people reached Little Ruin Mound a little later. They also sent messengers to ask if they might come to Awatovi. But the Awatovi chief answered, "No, we have already taken in the Tobacco and Rabbit clans, and we have no more room to spare." So the Water and Sand People went a little farther and arrived at the point of the mesa on which Koechaptevela was situated, and not far from there they made a small village which they called Pakatkomo. Here they lived on for a while. From Pakatkomo they could see the smoke rising from Koechaptevela's fires. They established contact with Koechaptevela, where several other clans were already living, including, it is said, the Bear Clan. The chiefs of the two villages exchanged visits and became friends. The Koechaptevela chief learned that the Water and Sand clans had a special claim to Balolokong, and that they possessed a piece of the great water serpent's skin, which they used in the making of pahos. Some of the people in Koechaptevela said, "Let us invite these new clans to live in our village." But the ones on whom the decision depended were not yet certain. So the kikmongwi, or village chief, and the war chief went down to Pakatkomo one day and said, "Let us see something you can do."

The Sand Clan people went out and gathered sand from some nearby dunes. They spread it on the ground and planted corn seeds in it. Then the Water Clan people gathered there and sang ceremonial songs. The power of their singing was great. Clouds formed overhead. There was thunder and lightning, and rain fell. Even as the Koechaptevela chiefs watched, corn shoots sprouted out of the sand and cornstalks formed. Seeing that, the kikmongwi of Koechaptevela said, "Yes, it is just as you told me. You possess great powers. Come and join us in our village. We will give you land. You will assist us in our ceremonies."

The Water and Sand clans went to Koechaptevela, and their special knowledge was used for the benefit of all. Water Clan members were brought into all the important secret fraternities, and it was they who were given the main responsibility for initiating young men and teaching them, mouth to ear, the things that had to be known—where the Hopis had come from and what their moral duties were. It was always a Water Clan uncle who passed on the teachings of Balolokong.

As the Water and Sand clans were settling in their new home, other groups were still moving northward. Among them were a large segment of the Fire Clan and some of its relatives such as the Masauwu Clan, the Fox Clan and the Wolf Clan, and also the Coyote group which as yet had not taken its clan name. How the Coyote Clan acquired its name is this. On the long march from Homolovi there was a certain child who was continually crying and who could not be comforted. Its mother tried everything. She sang, offered food, and did whatever she could think of. The father carved dolls out of cottonwood for the child. Nothing made any difference. People said a bad spirit was tormenting the child. Then one morning a man searching for firewood discovered a litter of young coyotes in a den. He brought one of the coyote puppies to the ch?' who instantly stopped crying and became happy. People "Surely this young coyote was given to us by a good spirit. The. is a meaning in it." And so they decided to call themselves the Coyote Clan.

The Coyote, Fox and Fire people and their kindred clans came in time within sight of Awatovi. Just as the Water and Sand clans had done, they sent emissaries to Awatovi to ask if they might enter the village and build houses there. But they were refused, so they went on, turning toward the west, and came to a place lying somewhat east of Koechaptevela. At the foot of the mesa they found a good spring, and they decided to settle at that spot.

They built a village on the foothills below the mesa, almost in the shadow of the cliff. They terraced some of the slopes and made gardens, and on still lower ground they laid out many rectangular fields and marked them off with stone walls. The people called their village Sikyatki.

Later the people who called themselves the Reed Clan arrived. They went past Sikyatki and Koechaptevela, past Shongopovi and several other villages, and stopped at last in the valley near Oraibi. Their chief went to Oraibi to ask for permission to settle there. But the kikmongwi and clan chiefs in Oraibi hesitated. They said they would have to think about it. It was late summer when the Reed Clan made its first contact with Oraibi, but when winter came they were still encamped in the valley because Oraibi had not made up its mind. The cold weather began to flow across the land, and the Reed People built stone shelters to protect themselves from the elements. Snow fell and covered the earth. Again the Reed Clan chief sent a message to Oraibi, asking, "When can we come?" Still there was no answer. But one morning the kikmongwi of Oraibi stood on a high place and looked down on the Reed Clan encampment. He noticed that while there was snow everywhere else, there was none around where the Reed People were staying. It puzzled him. So he went down into the valley to visit the encampment, and arriving at that place he saw that summer flowers were growing on all sides. He spoke to the Reed Clan chief, saying, "Never before have we seen flowers growing at this place in the middle of winter. Your people truly have a special power. Therefore, you are welcome in Oraibi." So the Reed Clan people left their camp and went up to Oraibi, where they lived on.

After a while the Badger Clan also arrived in the valley. It was still winter, and they rested not far from where the Reed People had been staying. From Oraibi it could be seen that there were large fires burning in their camp, and some people went down to see what was happening. They discovered that the Badger People were growing bean sprouts in the sand, using the fires for heat. The Oraibi People reported this to their kikmongwi and their clan chiefs. The chiefs said, "The Badger Clan people have a good power. Let us invite them into the village." So the Badger Clan also was admitted. When the Badger People entered Oraibi they came in a procession carrying bean sprouts in their hands.

Of all the clans that had begun their journeys at Palatkwapi, the Sun Clan, along with some other people travelling in the same party, was the last to arrive. The Sun Clan passed a settlement where the Cistern and Corn clans were living. They went on until they reached Kwalaipka, Eagle Mesa Point, where they stopped and rested. They saw smoke rising from Awatovi and sent messengers to ask if they might enter that village, but Awatovi said it had no room for them. So the people continued on their journey until they neared Masipa, or, as it was coming to be known, Shongopovi. They sent messengers to that village also. The kikmongwi of Shongopovi, who was of the Bear Clan, asked them, "What powers do you have? What can you bring us?"

The messengers said, "The warrior gods, Pokanghoya and Polongahoya, are related to us. They help us when we need them. They are fierce in battle. As everybody knows, it was they who destroyed the giant monsters. The spirit Tawa is the father of all living things. As Tawa is our father, so the Sun Clan is the father of all the creatures of the earth and treats them with kindness." Thereupon the messengers displayed small stone figures of all kinds of animals—deer, wildcats, wolves, bears, coyotes and many others. They said, "As these figures show, we have special concern for all life, and for this reason we have a close bond with all creatures who share this world with us. That is what we can bring to Shongopovi."

The kikmongwi and the clan chiefs discussed the matter, and at last they gave permission to the Sun Clan and the others in their party to enter Shongopovi. The messengers returned to their camp. They said, "Yes, it is arranged. Tomorrow morning we are to go there."

So the people slept their last night in the camp and arose early in the morning to go on to the village. But at this moment a Sun Clan woman began to give birth to a baby, and all those of the Sun Clan decided to wait with her until the baby was born. They told the others who were travelling with them to go on. So the advance party left and entered Shongopovi just as the sun was rising and showing its forehead over the horizon. For this reason, these people took the name Sun Glow or Forehead Clan. The real Sun Clan did not arrive until the sun was high overhead. It was the last of the Palatkwapi clans to come to the great mesa where the other Hopis were living.

VI Tokonave: The Snake and Horn People

AT THE TIME OF THE MOST ANCIENT MIGRATIONS some of the people left the sipapuni and travelled an erratic course, finally going westward and settling in what is now known as California. Their village was called Taotoykya, and they came to speak a language akin to Paiute. They lived on there for many generations, after which they abandoned Taotoykya and journeyed to the east, coming at last to Tokonave, Black Mountain, which the Whites later named Navajo Mountain. At Tokonave they built another village, Wuhkokiekeu, where they remained a long while. As yet they had no clans, and were known merely as the people of Wuhkokiekeu, or the Tokonave people.

It is said that the kikmongwi of the village had a son who was always sitting at the river's edge watching the water flow by. He sometimes threw bits of bark into the river and watched them float away to the south, asking himself questions as he did this. Why does the water always go in that direction? Where does the river empty itself? What is it like in such a place? What people are living there? These questions were continually in the mind of the kikmongwi's son.

His father saw him sitting by the river one day. He said, "My son, your spirit may flow away with the water if you watch the river too long."

The boy answered, "My father, if the water always moves in one direction it must arrive somewhere. Does anyone know what is at the end?"

His father said, "No, we do not know. But in the end it must join somewhere with Patowahkacheh, the Great Water. Some of our grandfathers were there in ancient times, but no one now living is familiar with all of the land through which the river passes. It is said that for a while the water runs between great cliffs, and beyond that there is desert on all sides with no living thing growing there except cactus. This much we have heard about, but the rest has been buried with our ancestors."

Time passed. The boy became a young man. He worked in the fields with his father and did other things that young men do, but still he often wandered to the river's edge and pondered on where the moving water went. And one day he went to his father and said, "My father, I am going on a journey to find out where the river ends. Surely there must be something there worth knowing."

His father said, "Sit down, let us smoke." The young man sat with his father. They smoked in silence for a while. Then the kikmongwi said, "Many years ago it was foretold that one of us would undertake the journey you speak of. Ever since you were small I knew it would be you. Now you say you are going. So here is the rest of the prophecy. The old ones said that whoever makes this journey will travel in a tree hollowed like a drum. Therefore let us consider what has to be done."

And after some days had passed the kikmongwi and his son went out and found a large pine tree, of which a great many were growing at Tokonave. They cut it down and hollowed it out so that a person could lie inside, and made a tight cover to seal the opening. When that was done they dragged the hollowed tree to the river.

"Tonight," the kikmongwi said, "we shall make pahos for you to take on the journey, and tomorrow you will begin."

That night the kikmongwi sat near the fireplace in his kiva making prayer sticks, and in the house his mother and sister prepared tushi, a meal made of baked corn, and piki for the young man to carry with him.

The mother said, "Why do you feel compelled to go on this

trip? It is dangerous. Have we not lived well without knowing where the water goes at the end?"

The young man said, "Do not fear for me. I will return when I have found out what I have to know."

His father said, "Yes, he must go. For it was always known that one of our people would do this. A good spirit has put it in his mind. He will go, he will return. The prophecy says that the one that makes this journey will bring a great good to the village when he returns."

Then the kikmongwi addressed his son, saying, "The good thing that you will bring back, we do not know what it is. But there is something else at the place where you are going. It is said that Huruing Wuhti, the Sea Woman, lives near where the river meets the sea. The Sea Woman is the owner of all shells, turquoise and coral. We are greatly in want of these things. Therefore, when you reach that place entreat her to give us some, whatever she can spare."

The young man said, "Yes, I will do it."

In the morning he entered his drumlike boat and lay there on his back. His father gave him the pahos he had made, and his mother and sister gave him baskets of food. Then the kikmongwi placed the cover over the hollow log, fitting it tightly, and pushed the craft into the water. The river took it and carried it away. This was the beginning of the journey.

The young man lay in darkness. The log moved smoothly at first, turning slowly this way and that in the current. But in time it came to turbulent rapids where it was tossed violently up and down and from one side to another. The young man thought, "Ah, now I see how it is. Will I survive this journey?" But the craft was strong, and it came safely to smooth water once more. The young man could feel the movement of his craft and knew that he was still going forward, but he did not know if it was night or day. He slept, awakened, slept, awakened many times. And then he felt the log grating on the sand. He removed the cover and stepped out. Around him in all directions there was nothing but desert, and no living thing was growing there except cactus. He thought, "Surely this is not my destination. I do not see Patowahkacheh, the Great Water." So he pushed his log from the sandy shore, entered, and replaced the cover. He went on. Much time passed, and at last, once again, he felt his craft ground itself against the shore. He came out. Lying before him was the Great Water. He stood there, saying, "This indeed is a marvelous thing."

And now, removing his pahos and the remains of his food from the hollow tree, he began to walk. At first he saw nothing and heard nothing but the surf washing in toward the land. But soon he came to a small house built on the coastal rocks, and there he found Gogyeng Sowuhti, Spider Grandmother, living.

She said, "Well, you have arrived. I was expecting you."

He answered, "How did you know that I was coming?"

She said, "My bird messengers brought me the news."

The young man said, "Yes, I have come. I have seen Patowahka-cheh. But where am I?"

Spider Grandmother said, "Why, you have just told me where you are. You are here at the edge of things. This is the land of the Snake People. And out there on that island lives Huruing Wuhti, the Sea Woman who owns all shells, turquoise and coral."

The kikmongwi's son said, "Yes, Huruing Wuhti, I must visit her. But how shall I get there?"

Spider Grandmother answered, "I will give you a path when the time comes. But as for now, come in, be welcome, and rest yourself from your journey."

The young man entered Spider Grandmother's house. She fed him. After that he slept. When he awoke the sun was just rising. He ate some of his piki. Then he said, "Grandmother, I must cross to the place where Huruing Wuhti lives."

Spider Grandmother said, "Yes, I will arrange it. Come with me."

They went to the edge of the water, and Spider Grandmother pointed her finger toward the island. Instantly an arched path like a rainbow appeared, bridging the water to the island where Huruing Wuhti lived. She said, "Cross over now. When you are ready to return I will give you the path to walk on."

The young man said, "Thank you, Grandmother, for you are truly my grandmother."

He entered the rainbow path and walked on it. He went on. It was a long way to the island. He arrived there, and when he did so the path from the mainland disappeared. He went searching for Huruing Wuhti. He saw a house standing on a butte and approached it. He saw that the butte itself was made of coral. The ground around him was covered with beautiful shells of all kinds. And when he came close to Huruing Wuhti's house he saw that it was made entirely of turquoise. At the door an ugly, toothless old woman was waiting. There were sores on her skin, her flesh was wasted away, and moisture dangled from her nose.

She said, "Why are you here?"

He replied, "I am looking for Huruing Wuhti, the Sea Woman."

She said, "Yes, I am the Sea Woman. What do you want with me?"

The kikmongwi's son was greatly surprised, having heard it said that the Sea Woman was beautiful. He was disturbed by her unpleasant appearance. But he handed her four of the pahos made by his father, saying, "These prayer sticks, I have brought them from Tokonave for you. That place is far from here. Things are good in my village, which is called Wuhkokiekeu, but the old people say that they greatly want shells, coral and turquoise. Therefore I have come to you to get some of these things."

Huruing Wuhti said, "Do you think I hand out such precious articles to anyone who comes saying, 'I need some of this,' or 'I need some of that'? No, that is not the way it is. Anyway, come in and rest yourself from your journey."

The young man entered the house. He sat on a rug on the floor. Huruing Wuhti brought him food, but seeing the ugly old woman handling it he had no appetite. Nevertheless, he ate. She asked him for many details of his journey. And after a while she said, "Yes, it is possible that I can help you. You must remain here tonight. If all goes well, perhaps I can let you have the turquoise and other things your village needs."

When night came Huruing Wuhti said, "Now let us sleep." She motioned to the place where the young man was to lie down. He lay down. She went into another room, and when she returned she lay down with him and embraced him. The kikmongwi's son grew faint in his heart, for she was truly repulsive to him. But there was a flickering light from the fireplace, and he saw that Huruing

Wuhti was no longer a toothless old woman but a young and lovely girl. He became happy. He embraced her, and they were both content the way things were. After that they slept.

In the morning when he awoke he was alone in the house, but on the blanket next to him was a buckskin bag. He opened it, discovering that it was full of turquoise, coral and many rare and beautiful shells. He took the bag, knowing that it was meant for him, and went down from the butte to the edge of the sea. When he came to the shore he stood there wondering how he would cross again to the mainland. At that very instant Spider Grandmother's rainbow bridge appeared, and walking upon it he returned to the other side of the water. When he arrived there the rainbow bridge disappeared. He came to Gogyeng Sowuhti's house. She greeted him. She fed him.

He said, "Now I have the coral, the shells and the turquoise. What there is to do now, I do not know, though my father says a great good will come of it."

Spider Grandmother said, "The happenings of which he spoke will find you."

The young man said, "You say that this is the country of the Snake People. But I have seen no people."

Spider Grandmother said, "Their village is a little way to the east. I will go with you to advise you." And making herself small, she went up and sat on the young man's ear. He walked toward the east, Spider Grandmother directing him, "Go this way, go that way." She said, "There are many snakes around us. Do not step on them." As he approached the village the kikmongwi's son saw rattlesnakes, bull snakes, water snakes, and many other kinds of snakes moving here and there on the ground. These snakes did not flee to cover, but paused to watch the young man as he passed.

When he entered the village an old man approached him, asking, "Where do you come from?"

"From the mountains in the north called Tokonave. I have floated down the great river. I ended my journey here. I wanted to see what it was like where the river flowed into the Great Water."

The old man said, "You are welcome. Enter our kiva." He started down the ladder.

Spider Grandmother whispered, "Follow him. Give him four

prayer sticks. Do not be afraid of what you see down there."

The young man went down the ladder. The kiva was a large one and there were many people inside.

The old man said, "I am the kikmongwi of this village. Let us sit and talk."

"Yes," the young man said, "that will be good. First, accept these pahos which were made by my father for you. He is the kikmongwi of our village, which is called Wuhkokiekeu."

The old man said, "Thank you for these pahos. Let us smoke."

They smoked a while. The tobacco was very strong, and the young man began to feel faint. So Spider Grandmother went down to his anus and drew the smoke out so that it would not overcome him. Everyone in the kiva was watching him. At last the old kikmongwi said, "You are a strong one. Surely you have a good spirit helping you. Now let us put the tobacco aside. Tell me about your journey."

The young man described his journey. After that the kikmongwi said, "Well, you have discovered what lies at the place where the river meets the Great Water. We are Snake People. We are different from other people you know. Now we will show you something."

The people who had been sitting quietly in the kiva all arose and took snakeskins down from the wall. They went into an adjoining room, and in a few minutes they returned in the form of snakes, crawling on the floor of the kiva. The young man was surrounded by bull snakes, rattlesnakes, king snakes, and many others. They approached him menacingly, but Spider Grandmother whispered, "Do not be afraid of them. They do not intend to harm you." So the young man sat without flinching even when the snakes brushed against him or put their heads in his lap. When the kikmongwi gave a signal the snakes returned to the other room and removed their skins.

"Now you have seen who we are," the kikmongwi said.

"Yes," the young man said, "now I understand."

The old man said: "You are a person of good heart. We accept you as one of us. I take you as my nephew. Remain with us for a while. We will teach you many things. In this way you may take something worthwhile with you when you go back to your village."

The young man said, "My uncle, I am grateful."

And so he remained with the Snake People for four days. They taught him their ceremonies. They taught him prayers. They taught him songs to bring rain. They taught him how to talk to snakes, how to handle them, and how to dress for the snake rituals. They told him all the things that must be done to bring a good life.

On the fourth day the old man said, "There is nothing more to tell you now. You are one of us forever. Only one thing is left to be done. Select one of our girls to take home with you as your wife. She will help you in carrying out the ceremonies and remembering the songs."

The young man had seen many beautiful girls in the kiva. He said, "Yes, I will gladly choose a wife."

So the old man sent out word for all the unmarried girls to come to the kiva. When they arrived they took their snakeskins from the wall and became snakes, and the floor was covered with snakes of every kind. Again they went from one place to another and looked menacing. The young man was not afraid. But he was confused, not knowing which of the snakes to choose. Spider Grandmother whispered in his ear, "Choose the gray rattler over there. Pick it up. Stroke it with a feather to calm it. Tell the kikmongwi, 'This is the one I choose to be my wife.'"

The young man stood up and walked among the snakes. He picked up the gray rattler and stroked it with a feather, speaking to it in the way he had been taught. He said, "Yes, this is the one. I can see that she is beautiful and that she has knowledge. I will take her with me to my village."

The old kikmongwi said, "You are truly our son. You have chosen wisely."

The girls removed their snakeskins and appeared in human form again. The young man was happy when he saw the one he had chosen. The two of them left the kiva and began the journey northward. When they had gone some distance from the village Spider Grandmother took her larger form and returned to her own house. The young man and his wife followed the river. The way was often difficult, and sometimes they had to leave the river's edge and go inland. In time they came to the cactus desert where the hollowed tree had drifted ashore. They stopped there and built a shrine, and after that they went on. The journey was a long one. At last they came to Tokonave and entered the village of Wuhko-kiekeu. The young man, with his wife, went to his house. His family was waiting for him.

His father said, "You have come again."

He answered, "Yes, I have returned. I have brought someone. She is my wife. I have also brought shells, coral and turquoise from Huruing Wuhti."

The kikmongwi said, "My son, you have done well."

They entered the house. Everyone was glad.

Later the kikmongwi said, "My son, let us go below, in the kiva, and smoke."

They went into the kiva and the young man sat with his father. They smoked for a while.

The kikmongwi said, "Tell me about the journey."

His son told everything, and spoke about the knowledge given to him by the Snake People. "They are now my Snake Fathers," he said. "They gave me the secrets to bring back, and the chants to call rain. Is this what was in the prophecy?"

"The details were never told to us," the kikmongwi said, "but surely this is what the prophecy meant. What is more important than the knowledge of how to summon rain?"

The village of Wuhkokiekeu lived on. The young man and his wife made a house of their own. They also lived on. There came a summer without rain, and the corn in the fields dried up. Then the kikmongwi's son said to his father, "Surely now is the time to apply the knowledge brought from the Snake People."

The kikmongwi answered, "Yes, let us get on with it."

They called the men of the village together, saying, "Let us prepare to perform the snake ceremonies." But some of the men said, "No, this has nothing to do with us," and they went away. Those who stayed said, "Yes, we will do what is necessary. Teach us." So the kikmongwi's son instructed them in everything. They learned the songs that had to be sung and the rituals that had to be carried out, and in all this they were assisted by the young man's wife. After that they began the eight-day ceremony. For four days the men went about the countryside searching for snakes, which they brought back and placed in large earthen vessels in the kiva.

The next four days were spent at making moccasins and costumes for the dance. And at night the men prayed and sang in the kiva and rehearsed what was yet to come. On the eighth day the dancers went into the plaza. The snakes were brought out and the dancers carried them around, holding them gently between their teeth. More sacred songs were sung. In all these things the young woman who had come from the village of the Snake People helped them. She was the one who sprinkled the sacred meal. When the dancing was finished, the men carried their snake brothers back to open country and released them, asking them to remember how gently they had been treated. They gave the snakes pahos and entreated them to carry the prayers of the village into the sky so that it might rain. Clouds formed and approached from the south. They reached Tokonave. The rain fell, and the parched fields became moist. The dying corn revived and began to grow again. So the village of Wuhkokiekeu was spared from famine.

In time the young man and his wife had a number of children. As they grew, the children played with other children in the village. But sometimes they bit the children with whom they played, causing them to become sick or even to die. The people of Wuhkokiekeu were angered. They said, "This cannot go on. Our children are dying from the bites of the Snake People. The Snake People must leave."

And so the kikmongwi's son and all who assisted him in the ceremonies gathered their possessions and left the village, camping for a while near a good spring. Then they travelled east of Tokonave. And when the summer was almost gone they came to a canyon where other people were already living, not far from the present town of Kayenta. There were several villages in the canyon, but all were small. Numerous clans were there, including the Water Coyotes and a branch of the Fire Clan. The place was called Kalewistima, where still to be seen are the ruins now known as Betatakin, Keet Seel and Inscription House. The people from Tokonave built their own village in Kalewistima and remained there a long time, one generation after another, and came to be known as the Snake Clan.

It is said that the people of Kalewistima eventually left that place because of a drought, but that was at a much later time. When the Snake Clan lived there life was good. There was plenty of water and plenty of corn. Because life was so good to them the people did not work as hard as they had in earlier times. They also began to forget the ceremonies and all the things they were supposed to remember. The old men began to worry. They said: "We chose the blue corn at the sipapuni, and with it a hardworking life. Here at Kalewistima things are too easy. It will end in our destruction. Let us move on before it is too late."

And so a day came when the Snake Clan people abandoned their village at Kalewistima and journeyed south to find the other clans that were there, first making their marks on the rocks to show that they had lived in that place and then moved on. They stopped at one place and another to build temporary villages and to renew their stocks of corn. Sometimes the people asked, "Where are we going?" And the old men answered, "To the south some-where is the place that was prophesied in ancient times. It is called Sichtilkwi, Flower Mound. That is what we are looking for."

It was a long journey, but at last the Snake Clan came to Wepo Valley, and there they camped by a spring. They could see a large mesa in the east, and the old men said, "Perhaps on that mesa some-where is Flower Mound. They saw smoke rising from a shelf of the mesa, and they sent a scout to find out who was living there. When he returned he said, "I met some people working their fields. They told me that the place where the village stands is called Sichtilkwi, Flower Mound. The village itself is known as Koechaptevela. Living there are several clans, and the Bear Clan holds the chieftainship."

The Snake Clan leader said, "Let us rest here a while and think about what is to be done."

Now, from the top of the mesa above the village Masauwu, the god of fire and death, saw the Snake Clan people down below in Wepo Valley. He went to the kikmongwi of Koechaptevela, saying, "In the valley down there, new people are coming. Go down and see who they are."

But the kikmongwi declined. He said, "No, all this land around here belongs to you. It is more fitting that you find out who they are."

So Masauwu changed his appearance to make himself look hu-man, and he went to where the Snake Clan was camping near the spring. He spoke to the clan chief, asking, "Who are you people and why are you here?"

The clan chief said, "We are the Snake Clan. Though our language is somewhat different from yours, we are Hopis. We come from Kalewistima. Before that we lived at Tokonave. Our ancients told us that some day we would meet with other Hopis at Flower Mound. Now we have almost concluded our journey. We want to join those other Hopis living up there on the mesa. We have something to contribute. We have the Antelope Society. We have the Snake Ceremony and the secret of calling the clouds."

But Masauwu was not certain that he wanted the Snake People to come, and he decided to frighten them away. He said, "Wait for me. I will return." He went behind some rocks and changed himself to his true and terrifying form. He gave a wild wolf cry and emerged into view. His skin was white and raw, marked by burns and splattered with blood. There was no hair on his head and he appeared as though he had just come out of the heart of a fire. When he breathed, flames came from his mouth.

The Snake People were overcome with fright. Some turned and ran, and others fell unconscious on the ground. But the Snake Clan chief, who was also the chief of the Snake Society, stood without flinching. Even when Masauwu approached him and breathed fire into his face, still the chief of the Snake Clan did not fall back.

Masauwu said, "Do you know me?"

The chief answered, "Yes. Who does not know you? You are Masauwu, the Spirit of Death, the Giver of Fire and the Owner of the Upper World. But why should we fear you? Are you not the one who sent fire to us in the Lower World? Are you not the one who invited us to come and live here in the Upper World? Therefore I do not fear you." Then he gave Masauwu a paho, saying, "Help us. We want to go up above and join the Hopis already living on the mesa."

Masauwu said, "I don't know. Perhaps there is something special about you, since you did not turn in fear at the sight of me. I will think more about this matter." He went behind the rocks and changed back into human form. When he returned he said, "Well, now, you have boasted about your powers, so show me what you can do."

The Snake Clan chief instructed his people and they prepared things. They put on their dancing kilts. They put on necklaces made of seashells and coral. They put on parrot, bluebird and eagle feathers and painted their arms and bodies. Each man held an eagle feather in his hand. Facing Masauwu, they began to dance, and as they moved, their necklaces gave off the sound of rattlesnake rattles. They sang one of the sacred songs brought back to Tokonave by the kikmongwi's son.

Snakes began to appear from all directions. They came out of the rocks and washes. Soon there were hundreds of them. They crawled without fear around the feet of the dancers. The men picked the snakes up and carried them in their hands, sometimes in their mouths, talking to them, brushing them with feathers to soothe them. As the singing and dancing continued, clouds formed in the sky and covered the sun. Rain began to fall.

When Masauwu saw this he said, "Very well, you have showed me something. The Snake People have strong powers. I will give you fields in which to plant your corn, and the people of Koechaptevela will receive you." Saying this, Masauwu departed and went back to the place where he lived on the highest part of the mesa.

The people stayed by the spring in the valley for four days. On the fourth day a messenger came from the village. He said, "Come and build your houses near ours. When we need rain you will perform your ceremonies for us." So the people of the Snake Clan at last moved into the village of Koechaptevela. There they remained.

Now, many years after the kikmongwi's son and the other Snake People left their ancient home at Tokonave, trouble came to the village of Wuhkokiekeu. The rain stopped falling and the corn did not mature. The old men said, "Our ancients told us that our corn would guide us. Now we must go somewhere where our corn will grow properly." Others said, "If we could find the Snake People who departed from here long ago we could be assured of rain, for it is they who own the ceremony for calling the clouds." And soon afterwards the people abandoned their village and their fields. By this time the people had organized into clans. Among them were the Horn Clan, the Divided Spring Clan and a number of others. Each clan went in a different direction. The Horn Clan travelled east. Here and there it discovered signs made on the rocks by the Snake Clan, and left its own marks to be read by others who might pass that way.

It went on to Kalewistima, where it learned that the Snake Clan had long ago departed from that place. It reached a village called Lenyanovi, Place of the Flute, where the Flute Clan people were living. There the Horn Clan remained for some time, during which it combined with the Flute Clan. When the combined Horn-Flute Clan abandoned Lenyanovi it went on, reading the signs on the rocks, until it arrived at the site of a spring called Kwaktapavi. There it camped while scouts went out in search of the Snake Clan. In a few days the scouts returned with the news that the Snake Clan was living at Flower Mound in the village of Koechaptevela, less than a day's journey away. So the Horn-Flute People continued their journey, passing by Wepo Spring, Kanelva and Gogyengva, meaning Spider Spring, which was just at the base of that part of the mesa on which Koechaptevela was situated. At Spider Spring they rested long enough to cleanse themselves of the dust of their travels, and from there they went directly up to Koechaptevela. At the village edge they were met by the kikmongwi and the chiefs of the clans.

They were asked, "You people, who are you, where do you come from, and why are you here?"

The Horn-Flute leader said, "Do you not recognize us? We come from Tokonave. We are searching for our cousins, the Snake People, who left us many years ago. We wish to be reunited with them."

The Snake Clan chief came forward. He said, "Is it you?"

The Horn-Flute chief said, "Yes. We are the ones who lived with you at that place, in the village of Wuhkokiekeu. Surely you can tell by the language we speak, which also was your language. Permit us to enter and make our lives here. We come in a spirit of harmony, and we bring with us our Flute Ceremony."

The Snake Clan chief said, "Yes, we recognize you as our cousins. Enter the village. We will show you where to build your houses. We will assign fields where you can plant. You are welcome to Koechaptevela."

Then the kikmongwi and the chiefs of the various clans moved aside, opening the way, and the Horn-Flute People entered the village.

VII Pakabva and the Kachinas

THE PEOPLE WHO CAME TO THE HOPI villages in the great mesa country brought ceremonies of many kinds. The Snake and Horn-Flute clans brought the Snake, Antelope and Flute rites. The Water Clan brought the Kwakwan and Lalakon ceremonies. The Squash Clan brought the Aal and Wuwuchim ceremonies. And there were many more such ceremonies in the villages. Nevertheless, there were still some villages that did not yet know about the spirits called kachinas, who lived at Tokonave, Black Mountain, far to the north.

Among the villages that did not know the power of the kachinas was Pakabva, and there were also villages to the east of Pakabva that did not have this knowledge. At Tokonave the kachinas sometimes discussed going to these places to offer their help. But for a long while they did not do so, waiting to see if the people would come to them to ask for assistance. Not knowing that kachinas existed, these villages did not send any messengers to Tokonave.

It happened one time that a group of Nuva or Snow Kachinas was travelling across the mesa a little north of where the present Hopi villages stand. The uncle, or counselor, of the Snow Kachinas was an Eototo Kachina. He said to the others, "A few hours' walk to the south of us is Oraibi. A little east of that place are Shongopovi

96

and Mishongnovi. East of those villages is Koechaptevela. And just beyond that is Pakabva, Reed Spring. In Pakabva, the people living there do not yet know about us. At that place the people are having a hard time with their corn. We can help them by bringing rain. Let us go there and do something to make life better for them."

The Snow Kachinas replied, "Yes, certainly we should do something to help them. Let us go there and dance. We shall bring rain to their fields."

So the kachinas went toward Pakabva, but before they reached that place the sun went down and darkness came. Nevertheless they continued their journey, arriving in Pakabva in the middle of the night. The people were sleeping and the village was silent. The kachinas entered the village and went to the central plaza. There they began to dance, invoking the rain to come and water the fields. Not wanting to awaken the people from their sleep, they did not sing. But the tortoiseshell rattles they wore on their legs made a sound that was heard in all the houses. People came to the edge of the plaza. They saw strange beings there, dancing without singing, and they were afraid. They said to one another, "Who are those ghostly persons from whose mouths no song comes? What do they want here? They are surely making evil against us. Let us get rid of them."

The men of Pakabva went to their houses for their weapons. Seeing what was happening, the Eototo said to the other kachinas, "The people do not understand who we are. They intend to attack us. Let us leave."

So they departed from the village, going out in a procession, the Eototo in the lead and the Snow Kachinas following. Before they had gone far, however, the men of Pakabva came after them giving war cries and shooting arrows. The kachinas fled across the mesa with the Pakabva war party in pursuit.

They came to the edge of the mesa, but they could not descend there because the cliff was too steep. So they turned and went in another direction, the war party still following. They reached a place where there was a deep crack in the mesa floor. The Eototo Kachina climbed into it and the Snow Kachinas did the same thing. They were lying wedged in a pile at the bottom. They remained silent in the hope that the Pakabva warriors would not find them.

The Pakabva men came to the crack in the earth and one of them held a torch over the edge. They saw the kachinas down below. They shot arrows at them and threw down flaming wood so that the fire would burn them up. After that they returned to Pakabva.

All the kachinas were killed except the Eototo. He survived because he was at the bottom of the pile and was not touched by the arrows or the fire. He lay there until daylight came. He crawled out from under the dead bodies. He looked back at Pakabva, then he started walking toward Tokonave. He chanted a mourning song as he went. He arrived at Tokonave. The kachinas living there heard him coming. They heard the sound of his tortoiseshell rattle. They heard him singing:

> *"The ungrateful people of Pakabva*
> *Poured arrows and fire on us.*
> *We offered them rain,*
> *They offered us death.*
> *The Snow Kachinas are dead,*
> *Only Eototo survives."*

The kachinas went out to meet him. They asked him the meaning of his song. He did not reply, but went on singing. They saw that his body was splattered with the dried blood of the Snow Kachinas. They saw that fire had scorched his kilt and his moccasins. They arrived at their kiva and went down. They smoked. After that the Eototo spoke.

He said: "Yes, what my song said is true. We went to the village called Pakabva because we saw that their corn was thirsty. Even though it was night we went to the plaza to dance for the people and bring rain. We sang our prayers silently within us so as not to awaken the village. But the people heard the sound of our rattles. They came to the plaza and threatened us, so we went away. But they pursued us, crying out and shooting arrows. We returned to the top of the mesa. Still they pursued. We came to an opening in the earth where the rock had split apart and we went down into it. At the bottom it was very narrow and we were all wedged together. We remained there without making any sounds. But even in the darkness the Pakabva war party found us. The men poured arrows on us and threw fire on us. All the Snow Kachinas perished.

I, Eototo, survived because their bodies lay upon mine like a shield. This is the terrible thing that happened at Pakabva."

The kachinas listened. They reflected on things. They sang a mourning song. After that they sent out messages to all the kachinas living at Tokonave, asking them to assemble. The kachinas came from all directions. Every kind of kachina was there, each dressed in his own way. They began a Soyohim or Mixed Kachina Dance, urging the clouds to gather at a certain place. They danced on and on without stopping to rest.

At Pakabva the people were doing ordinary things, weaving and making pottery in the village, weeding corn in the fields. Someone noticed a cloud moving in the sky. He called out, "A cloud is coming. Perhaps there will be a little rain." The cloud moved to a place in the sky just above the village, and there it rested. Other clouds appeared. They moved across the sky from different directions and gathered over Pakabva. People said to one another, "Yes, we surely shall receive some rain today." The clouds continued to gather over Pakabva, mounting one over another. The sky became dark, but as yet no rain fell. It seemed as though night were falling. People could see the rays of the sun breaking through some distance to the west near Koechaptevela. And there was light in the east in the direction of Muyovi. But over Pakabva and its fields there was only blackness. The people became afraid. They asked one another, "What is happening? Why do the clouds remain there without dropping rain?"

At Tokonave the Soyohim Kachina dance was still going on. And now the kachinas took up their lightning frames and their thunderboards and put them into motion.

At Pakabva there was a great bolt of lightning in the sky, followed by a roll of thunder. The houses in the village shook. Again there was lightning, again there was thunder. Four times the lightning and thunder came. Then the rain began to fall. At first it came down only a little, then the clouds spilled out all their water on Pakabva. Great hailstones fell from the sky with the water. People sought refuge wherever they could find it, but some were killed by the hailstones before they could reach their houses. Water covered the fields and washed through the village. The kiva was flooded and some who had sought safety there were drowned. Water surged through the houses, and along the edge of the hill on which the village was built walls collapsed and roofs fell in. Then, suddenly, the rain and hail stopped falling. The clouds drifted away in the directions from which they had come. The sun was visible again and people emerged from their hiding places. They looked at their fields and gardens and saw that everything was destroyed. The corn was lying flat, almost covered by sand that had washed down from the mesa top. The melon vines were twisted and broken. The squash vines were tangled and dying. Everything that grew in the fields was lifeless.

It was only then that the people of Pakabva understood that they had given great offense to the spirits. The old men discussed what had happened. They journeyed to Koechaptevela and talked to the learned ones there. When they returned they said to the people of Pakabva: "It is clear now that those dancers we drove from our village were not ordinary people. They were kachinas, sacred beings who have the power to bring rain. When we saw them in the plaza they were calling the clouds to water our fields, but we treated them as enemies. We pursued them and killed them where they took sanctuary among the rocks. We did not understand about things. The storm that fell upon our village has shown us the power of the kachinas. Never again shall a kachina be treated badly. Any kachina who comes among us must be welcomed and respected. They meant to bring good to us. We brought evil to them. Now we have been repaid."

The village of Pakabva was blighted with the memory of what had been done there, and its leaders ordered that it be abandoned. The people took what they could carry and dispersed. Some went eastward toward Muyovi. Some went south and found new homes at Huckyatwi. Some, who were of the Bear Clan, were received into Koechaptevela. Others went elsewhere and were not heard of again. Pakabva became a ruin. In time people called the site by a different name, Kachinva, meaning Kachina Spring, recalling how, long ago, the kachinas came to that place and were driven away.

VIII Maski, the Land of the Dead

WHEN PEOPLE DIED THEY WERE PUT IN THEIR GRAVES facing toward the rising sun, the direction from which it was said a certain white brother would arrive bringing harmony and well-being to the Hopis. If an important person died he was sometimes buried sitting up, looking toward the east, so he could greet the Bahana whose coming had been prophesied. But though the dead ones had been waiting there a long time, the Bahana had not yet appeared.

There was a young man in Oraibi, the son of the chakmongwi or crier chief, who sometimes went down to where the dead were buried. He spoke to the dead, saying, "Are you people still there? I do not hear anything. I do not see anything." And one day he asked his father about these things. He said, "All those dead ones that have been placed in the ground, are they still living there?"

The chakmongwi answered, "What we have buried in the earth is only the stalk. The breath has gone elsewhere and lives on."

The young man asked, "Well, now, how can it be that we know they are elsewhere? Who has ever been there to verify it?"

His father said, "My son, it has been told to us that way by the old people. When a person dies, his body is placed in the earth and there it rests. But the breath of life goes on."

The young man said, "So we have been told. But how do we know that when the stalk dies the breath also does not die?"

And the chakmongwi answered: "Yes, this question has been asked many times in the kivas. But the learned ones among us always give us the same reply. When a person dies, his breath departs from his body and goes to Maski, the residing place of the dead. Only that much is known, because, as you say, no one returns from that place to let us know what it is like."

The young man brooded often about the nature of death. He sometimes sat at the edge of the village looking into the distance and wondering: "When a person is dead, is there anything left of him? Does his spirit go on to another land as the old people tell us? Are the rain clouds that come from the west really a gift from the dead ones in Maski?"

His father, the chakmongwi, saw in the young man's face that something was taking hold of him. He said to his wife, "Our son is gripped by something. He does not do what the other young men do. He often sits at the rim of the mesa looking off into the sky. It is as if he is not really there but away on a long journey. What he sees I do not know."

The chakmongwi talked to other men in the kiva about his son. He said, "My son will not leave it alone. He wants to know the answer. He says, 'Who knows for certain about Maski? For no one has ever returned from there to tell us about it.' He says, 'When the dry husk is put in the ground, how do we know that the breath of life is not dried up also?'"

They replied to the chakmongwi one way and another, but the answer was nevertheless the same: "It is true that the dead go to Maski. Our fathers have told us this. But what happens there we do not truly know, except that the spirits of the dead residing there send us clouds to water our fields."

The young man was sitting at the edge of the mesa one day looking into the western sky. He noticed a shadow on the ground beside him. He saw a person standing there. The man's face was painted in the ancient style. His hair was decorated with feathers that hung down all around, and two mountain sheep horns were fastened to the top of his head.

The person said, "I have heard your thoughts. If you wish to travel to Maski I will help you."

The young man answered, "Yes, I wish it."

The person gave him something, saying, "Here is a powerful medicine. Tonight when you are ready to sleep, put some of this medicine on your tongue. You will become as one who has died. Your father must prepare you as the dead are prepared. Then your spirit will be able to go on the journey to Maski. When you have arrived at that place, do not linger too long. After you have seen everything, return again quickly." The person then moved away and disappeared.

The young man went to his house. He told his father, "An ancient person came to me out on the mesa. He said, 'I have heard your thoughts. Here is the medicine that will take you to Maski. When you lie down to sleep, put the medicine in your mouth. Your spirit will depart. Let your father dress you as one dresses the dead. You will go to Maski. You will see what is there. You will return.' "

The young man's mother said, "No, do not do it. Who has ever been to Maski and returned?"

But the young man answered, "I have to go. I cannot be forever without knowing."

And his father said, "Yes, he must do it. A good spirit has put this in his mind. A man must find answers to his questions."

The young man prepared to sleep. He lay on his blanket and put the medicine in his mouth. He slept. The breath went out of his body. His mother cried, saying, "Our son has gone from the land of the living." The chakmongwi dressed his son's body. He painted the lower part of the young man's face black, and put a small bit of eagle down on his forehead. Around his son's waist he fastened a white kilt. After that the chakmongwi and his wife sat nearby, looking on the body of their son.

At first the young man saw nothing. Everything was dark and silent as though he were truly dead. Then he found himself walking on a trail toward the west. He passed through a vast cactus field and came to a place where the trail ended at the edge of a steep bluff. He wondered how he could go on.

And while he was standing there the ancient one with the

mountain sheep horns on his head appeared again. He said, "You have come."

The young man answered, "Yes, I have come."

The ancient one said, "Take off your kilt and spread it on the ground. Lie on it. It will carry you across the chasm. When you arrive in Maski do not touch anyone. If you do you cannot return."

The chakmongwi's son removed his kilt and lay on it. It lifted into the air and carried him across the chasm, descending where the trail continued to the west. He put his kilt around him again and resumed walking. He came to where a man was sitting at the edge of the trail.

"At last someone has arrived," the man said. "Carry me a distance of four steps."

The chakmongwi's son said, "No, I cannot. Otherwise I will not be allowed to return. Why is it like this with you that you cannot go by yourself?"

"It is because in life I did something that was not good," the man said. "I did not listen to my ceremonial fathers. I did not respect the ceremonies. Therefore I cannot go to Maski all at once. I wait for other dead ones to come along the trail. I ask them to carry me four steps. Slowly, slowly I proceed, and the place to which I am going is still far away."

The chakmongwi's son went on. In the distance he saw a column of black smoke rising in the air. He came to a woman who was carrying a heavy metate on her back. But instead of a leather forehead strap she used the cord from a hunting bow. It cut deeply into her skin and gave her much pain.

She said, "Ah, someone has come. Carry my metate for me for a while."

He answered, "No, I cannot do it, else I cannot return where I came from. But why do you carry that way, with a string instead of a strap against your forehead?"

She said, "Why, in life I did things that were not right. I behaved too freely with many men and brought misery to my family. For this reason I must carry this way to the end of the trail."

He went on toward the west, coming to the place where the trail ascended a high sand dune. His feet sank in the soft sand. The walking was hard. He saw a man walking ahead of him, slowly,

slowly. When the chakmongwi's son overtook the man he saw him wearing a heavy necklace made of vulvas.

The chakmongwi's son said, "Why do you wear such things?"

The man answered, "I am compelled to do this. In my life I showed no discretion. I had intercourse with many women, whoever would lie with me, even the wives of other men. As this was forbidden, now I am made to suffer this way."

The young man passed others on the trail, all going in the same direction. Some were wearing clothing made of cactus leaves, whose thorns cut deeply into their skin. Some carried heavy stones, their feet sinking deeply in the sand. Some were completely naked and had to go forward that way without anything to cover them.

As he approached the column of black smoke, the chakmongwi's son came to a fork in the trail. A One Horn priest and a Two Horn priest were standing there.

The Two Horn priest said, "Well, you have arrived. We have been expecting you."

"Yes," the young man said, "I have come."

The Two Horn priest said, "You have seen them, all those people along the trail. Some of them died long ago, but because of the evil things they did in life they have to travel slowly, slowly, and so they have not yet reached this place. When they arrive here we decide which way they go. The trail to the right is the way to Dark Canyon and the deep pit of fire. The trail to the left goes to the village where the spirits live on. The Dark Canyon is without any bottom. The fires within it rage endlessly. It was from this burning pit that Masauwu escaped in ancient times."

The young man said, "But who knows for certain whether a person has done good or evil in his life?"

The One Horn priest said, "Everything a person does in his life is known here. Here we stand. I am the strict one. The Two Horn priest is the lenient one. If a man has done evil things, I condemn him. If he has done good things, the Two Horn priest speaks for him. A good man goes on swiftly to the village. An evil man without virtues takes the Dark Canyon trail. Those who are neither all good nor all evil, we discuss the matter. I recall their bad actions, and against those things the Two Horn priest balances the good things they have done and asks for leniency. In this way the judgment is made. Come with me now and I will show you the Dark Canyon."

The chakmongwi's son followed the One Horn priest along the trail. They came to the rim of the canyon in which the fire was burning. The young man shielded his face with his arm. He saw two men of the One Horn Society standing at the edge. As a dead spirit arrived at that place they seized him and threw him into the fiery pit. Another dead spirit arrived, and him also they threw into the fiery pit.

The One Horn priest said, "These are persons whose evil deeds in life were too great to forgive."

Then they returned to the fork in the trail where the Two Horn priest was waiting. He said, "Now let us go the other way and enter the village."

Close by the trail were children playing in a field. The children cried out, "Look, a dead spirit has arrived." They ran forward and looked at the chakmongwi's son. They said, "No, he is not a dead one, he is living." And they ran away in horror. The young man and the Two Horn priest then came to a place where boys and girls were having a rabbit hunt. Seeing the chakmongwi's son, the young people fled, saying, "A living one is here. The smell of his body is too much."

The young man asked, "Why am I loathsome to them?"

His guide answered, "That is the way it is here. These people have discarded their bodies and left them behind where they were once living. To them, bodies of the undead are not clean. They look upon you just as you, back in the land of the living, look upon dead spirits."

They went further on. They passed a field in which a man was weeding corn. The One Horn priest said, "Over there is a person from your village. Do you recognize him?"

The young man answered, "Yes, he was our crier chief not long ago. He was an old man and he died. Now he looks younger."

They passed another person in the field. The chakmongwi's son said, "Him also I recognize. When he was alive he was the war chief in our village."

The Two Horn priest said, "Ahead of us is where the people are living."

The young man said, "Why it looks very much like Oraibi."

"Go through the plaza," the Two Horn chief said. "There on one side you will see the houses of your people, the Bear Clan."

As the young man went through the plaza people looked at him from the roofs. They said, "Here, someone is coming. But he is not truly a dead spirit."

The young man said, "It is true that I am not dead. I have come to Maski to see how it is with the people in this place."

People came down the ladders from the rooftops to talk with him. Some of them he remembered seeing long before when he was a small boy. He said, "I have made this journey from Oraibi."

They said to him, "Well, that is a long journey. Come up, come into the house and eat something." They went up one of the ladders, but when he tried to follow them the rungs broke because they were made out of sunflower stalks. The people laughed. "The living ones are too heavy," they said. "We who reside in this place have no weight at all. Wait down below and we will bring you some food." They brought him a melon and some other kinds of food, and while he ate they watched him and were amused. They said, "It is strange to see a living person eat, for he eats the outer substance of things. Here we eat only the spirit of food and the substance is thrown away."

The young man said, "I did not believe that there was such a place as this. I thought, 'When a man dies, his spirit surely dies with him and lies with his body in the grave.' Now I understand how things are."

An old man who was the Bear Clan chief in the village said to him, "Yes, that is the way things are. As you see, here we live surrounded by fields of flowers. Things are not bad for those of us who led good lives before we died. But sometimes the living forget us. Remind the people to make pahos for us at the time of the Soyal ceremonies. In exchange for these pahos we can do things to help the people of Oraibi. We will send clouds to water their fields."

The young man said, "Yes, I will tell them everything I have seen and heard in Maski."

"Now you must return," the Two Horn priest said. "You are the first living person to come here. Go back to Oraibi and say, 'The

people in Maski, I have seen them. Those who were good in their
lives go on forever. People who died only in recent days are residing
there side by side with the ancient ones.' Tell the people to respect
virtue so that they may come to this village and share it with us."

So the young man began his return journey. On the trail he
met the same ones that he had seen before, the ones dressed in cactus
clothing, the naked ones, the ones carrying heavy loads, and all the
others. At the place where he had come down from the high bluff he
lay on his white kilt and it carried him up above to where the trail
resumed. He continued through the cactus fields and went on.

At a certain place he saw Gogyeng Sowuhti, Spider Grandmother, waiting for him. She said, "So, my son, you have been
there."

He answered, "Yes, I have journeyed there and now I am returning."

Spider Grandmother said, "Now that you have come back you
are contaminated with death. You cannot go back to Oraibi that
way. You must be purified."

He said, "Help me, then, Grandmother."

Spider Grandmother prepared a large earthen vessel of water,
and put secret things into it. She made the water boil, and then
she instructed the chakmongwi's son to get into the vessel. There his
skin was boiled. When he got out, Spider Grandmother inserted the
thorn of a Devil's Claw cactus through his scalp. She twisted it, and
the young man's skin split at the bottom of his feet. As Spider
Grandmother continued twisting the cactus thorn she drew the
skin upward over his head, finally removing it entirely. Then she
threw the skin into the fire, where it was consumed. She said, "Now
the contamination of Maski has been removed. You may return
home."

The chakmongwi's son went on. He came to Oraibi. He entered
his house. He saw his body lying there on the blanket. He saw his
father and mother sitting silently nearby. He lay down and his
body and spirit again became united. He slept.

His father said, "Look, he breathes!"

His mother said, "Yes, he is returning from a night of death!"

The young man stirred. He sat up, saying, "I have come back."

He stood up. His father led him into the kiva. The priests and old men of all the societies were there.

The chakmongwi said, "Here is my son at last. He died and went to the place in the west of which we have been speaking. Now he has returned. He will tell us what he has seen."

The young man sat down with the others. "Just as the grandfathers told us," he said, "there is a place called Maski. I took a medicine offered to me by an ancient one. I died, and my spirit went on a long journey. My kilt carried me across a great gorge. On the other side I saw many dead spirits on the trail going slowly, slowly. They could only go a little at a time because when they were alive they did something that was not good. Some carried heavy loads with only a bowstring across their foreheads, and they suffered greatly. Some were naked and some wore clothing of cactus. A man wore a heavy necklace of vulvas that bent him down, because he had acted freely with other men's wives. A woman suffered because she was licentious in life. Some who were punished this way had done one thing, some had done another.

"I came to where a One Horn priest and a Two Horn priest stood at a fork in the trail to meet those who were arriving. The One Horn priest condemned people for their evil acts, and the Two Horn priest recalled their good deeds, and thus each person who arrived was judged. One branch of the trail went to the Dark Canyon filled with fire, and there I saw the evil ones thrown into the flames. The other branch of the trail went to the village where the dead spirits live on. I saw persons who once lived here in Oraibi. They said, 'Yes, here we live, surrounded by flowers.' They said, 'Those who are alive should not try to come here, for this way of living is not for them. But all those who respect the ceremonies and the kachinas, who listen to the wisdom of the old people, who do not injure others, who share food in time of hardship, and who honor the Hopi virtues—they will have a home here with us when the time comes.' They also said, 'Let the people make pahos for us at the time of the Soyal ceremony. We shall be grateful to them. We shall send rain clouds in return.'"

The chakmongwi's son continued: "I have been to Maski, I have seen it and I have returned. It is out there toward the setting sun. That is where each of us will travel when the sun of his life goes down. I know now what I could not accept before, that when the dry stalk of a person's body goes into the earth, it stays there and the flesh falls away. But the breath of his life takes the trail to the west. And now I have told you everything that I learned."

In the kiva the men listened with silence. When the chak-mongwi's son was finished they said, "We have heard you. It is just as our grandfathers told us. Now we know for certain how it is, and no living person need ever go there again."

This is how the existence of Maski was verified.

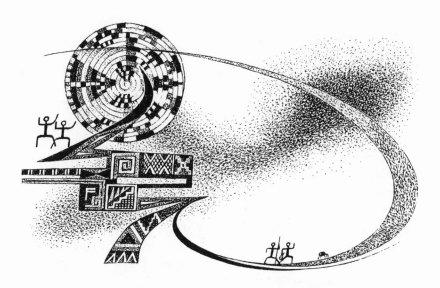

IX The Lalakon Dance at Shongopovi

SOMEWHAT NORTH OF WHERE THE PRESENT VILLAGES are, the warrior brothers Pokanghoya and Polongahoya were living with Gogyeng Sowuhti, Spider Grandmother. When the boys were not hunting to keep their house supplied with meat they were often going here and there exploring the mesa. The place at which they lived was at the edge of the wilderness, and so they rarely encountered human beings.

One day the two of them were playing nahoydadatsia and pursuing their buckskin ball when they came to a field of tall grass. There was a breeze blowing across the mesa and it made the grass sway, first one way and then another. The boys stopped and became silent. They watched the grass moving.

Pokanghoya said, "See, the grass is dancing. The heads are bending this way, then that way, then this way, then that way."

Polongahoya answered, "Yes, I see it. The grass is singing. It is saying, 'Ss, ss, ss, ss.'"

They remained there watching the grass dance and listening to it sing.

Pokanghoya said, "See that tall one there with the long hair, he is the singing chief."

Polongahoya answered, "Yes, they are calling the rain. The clouds are gathering up above."

After a while the brothers left that place and resumed their game of stickball, and when the sun began to go down they returned home.

Spider Grandmother said, "It is late. Where have you two boys been?"

The brothers said, "Yes, we are late because we have been to the dance. We wanted to see everything and so we remained there for a while."

Spider Grandmother said, "What dance are you talking about? I did not hear that there was to be a dance anywhere today."

The brothers said, "Why, we did not hear of it either. But while we were playing nahoydadatsia we came to where it was going on. There was a large crowd there."

Spider Grandmother said, "What kind of dance was it?"

Pokanghoya said, "We don't know about that. They danced like this, moving their heads from one side to the other."

Polongahoya said, "We did not understand the words, but they were singing, 'Ss, ss, ss, ss.'"

Spider Grandmother said, "What kind of costumes were they wearing?"

The boys answered, "Why, their costumes were brown, and the people had tassels in their hair."

Spider Grandmother said, "You two, what are you telling me? Those were not people. You were watching the grass out there on the mesa. You are teasing."

The boys said, "Yes, it was the grass. But it was a very good dance."

Spider Grandmother replied, "Well, now, I have heard that there will be a real dance four days from now at Shongopovi. The women will dance with basket trays. That is a dance worth seeing. And while the dance is going on, the women give out trays to the people. Why don't you go there. Perhaps you can bring me a tray or two."

The boys said, "Yes, we will do it. We will go to Shongopovi and get you some coiled trays."

On the fourth day they prepared to go to the dance. Spider Grandmother made them wash themselves well, and she gave them clean clothes to wear. She said, "You must look respectable when you arrive at Shongopovi." The boys took their nahoydadatsia sticks and their buckskin ball and started out, playing as they travelled. They followed their ball wherever it went, running through sand, gullies and mudholes. And when they reached Shongopovi they were very dirty. They were sweating and splattered with mud. Their hair was dishevelled and their noses were running. The people in Shongopovi were clean and well dressed for the Lalakon Dance, but Pokanghoya and Polongahoya looked filthy and unkempt.

The women were already dancing in the plaza, and there were many spectators sitting around the edges and up on the roofs. From time to time the dancers threw coiled trays for the spectators to catch. Pokanghoya and Polongahoya tried to catch the trays, but they could not do it. The men always pushed them aside so they could get the coiled trays for themselves. Many people received trays in this way from the dancers, but the two brothers got nothing, and they said things to the men who were jostling them. The men also became angry. They said, "You dirty ones, go somewhere else. Return to your own village, wherever that is."

But the brothers stayed on, vainly trying to catch the coiled trays. They grew hungry. They saw that other visitors to Shongopovi were being invited into the houses and given something to eat. But no one invited Pokanghoya and Polongahoya. They were ignored.

Pokanghoya said at last, "Is this the way to treat strangers from another place? They refuse to offer us food. They refuse to let us catch a coiled tray. These are miserable people living in this village. Let us go home."

But before they left they ran forward and snatched two trays from the hands of the dancers. Then they went running toward the north. Some of the people saw the brothers take the basket trays. They said, "Those dirty ones have stolen the Lalakon trays. Let us punish them." So a number of young men began to pursue them. When Pokanghoya saw them coming he put a certain medicine in his mouth and chewed it. He also gave Polongahoya some of the medicine. And when the pursuers were about to catch them, the brothers turned and spurted medicine on their pursuers and turned them to stone. The stones are standing there yet, just a short distance north of the village.

The warrior brothers arrived home. They were tired and hungry. Gogyeng Sowuhti gave them food and they ate. They said, "Here, we have brought you two coiled trays from Shongopovi. We had to take them from the hands of the dancers, because no one would let us catch them when they were thrown. The men kept pushing us away, saying, 'You dirty ones, get out of the village.' We were very hungry. People gave something to eat to other strangers who were there, but they looked over our heads and offered us nothing. And when we took our coiled trays and left, men came after us to punish us. Therefore we turned them to stone."

After he had finished eating, Pokanghoya said, "Those people are not generous. They do not treat travellers well. They do not deserve everything that we have done for them. The salt beds we made for them are too close. The people take their salt for granted, they think that the salt made itself. But it was the two of us who went out, while the people were still at the sipapuni, and created the salt at different places. We placed salt over there near Muyovi, the Rio Grande, for people who would live in the eastern villages. Those people who live in Koechaptevela and Awatovi, they have not offended us, and they can continue to get their salt at that place, where the Zunis live. But as for the people of the western villages who get their salt north of Moencopi, they are not going to be able to find it there any more. Hereafter when they go for salt they will have to travel through hard country. They will meet Utes, Paiutes and Navajos on the way, and when they have found their salt they may have to fight to keep it from their enemies. This is the way it will be from this time on."

Spider Grandmother said, "Where are you going to put the salt?"

Pokanghoya replied, "We are going to place it near where the people emerged from the Lower World. To reach it the people will have to pass by the sipapuni. Then perhaps they will remember where they came from and what was given to them in the Upper World."

Spider Grandmother said, "Very well, I will go with you on the journey."

The next morning the two brothers and Gogyeng Sowuhti went westward until they came to the spring called Moenavi, close to where the present village of Moencopi stands. They went north of that spring to the place where Pokanghoya and Polongahoya had created the salt bed in ancient times. The two brothers scooped up all the salt that was there and put it in a small bag, which Polonga-hoya carried in his belt. After that the three of them made a trail westward. After travelling for some time they stopped to rest, and at this place the brothers marked a totolospi pattern on the rocks and played that game together. They said, "Hereafter, when anyone comes this way he will stop here and play totolospi with us. If he loses the game to us he cannot have any salt and will have to turn back."

They went on. After a while Spider Grandmother grew tired. She said, "Well, you boys go on. I will have to stay here."

Pokanghoya said, "Yes, if that is how it is, we will make a place for you to rest."

The brothers then scooped a trench out of the solid rock. They told Spider Grandmother to remove all her clothes and to lie in the trench they had made. When she was lying on her back, Pokanghoya squirted medicine on her and turned her to stone, with her vulva plainly visible.

Pokanghoya said, "Whenever men come this way for salt they must copulate with Grandmother, and on their return journey they must bring her gifts. This will remind them that nothing in this world is without obligations."

The brothers went on. They arrived at another place. Pokang-hoya took the bag of salt from Polongahoya. He said, "You, my younger brother, remain here, so that whenever men come this way they will remember who created their salt." Thereupon he sprayed medicine on Polongahoya, who turned to stone.

He continued the journey into the great western canyon. At a certain place where the descent was difficult he created giant steps in the rocks, and going down these steps he came at last to the Little Colorado River. He passed a cave in which Masauwu, the Spirit of

Death, sometimes lived. He arrived at the sipapuni through which mankind had emerged into the Upper World. It was just as Gogyeng Sowuhti had left it, covered with water so that it resembled a pond. He said, "Here men will pause to ask once more, 'Who are we? Where did we come from? Why are we in this world? Where are we going?' "

He went on. He passed the place where the Colorado and the Little Colorado meet. There he went deep into the gorge, and he went around touching the rocks and canyon walls with his hands. Everything he touched turned into salt. He emptied the salt bag they had brought from the old salt bed north of Moenavi, spreading its contents on all sides. Then Pokanghoya ascended partway up the canyon wall, where he turned himself into rock.

In time some of the men of Shongopovi and Oraibi and other western villages went to the old place looking for salt. But they found that all the salt was gone from there, except just a little that the brothers had spilled on the ground. They said, "What has happened? Our salt has disappeared. Where are we going to get the salt that we need?" They discovered a trail going west, and on that trail they found stone footprints left by Pokanghoya and Polongahoya. They said, "These footprints are a sign. Let us follow them." They came to the place where the brothers had played totolospi. They found the spot where Spider Grandmother had been turned into stone. They found where the younger brother had been turned to stone. They came to the giant steps and the place where Pokanghoya had transformed himself into stone. Below in the bottom of the canyon they discovered Masauwu's cave and the sipapuni. At last they discovered the new salt deposit created by Pokanghoya.

After reaching this place, the men returned to their villages and discussed the meaning of everything that they had seen. They came to understand the signs that the brothers had left for them along the trail. From that time on, whenever men went along the salt trail they stopped at certain spots and placed pahos there. At another place, called Tehtuvani, they put their clan marks on the cliff walls to show that they had made the long journey for salt. Where the brothers had stopped to play totolospi, they stopped and played a game against the invisible warrior gods, arranging the playing sticks in such a way that they would win, guaranteeing good fortune on the trip. Where Gogyeng Sowuhti had been turned to stone, the men mounted her and had intercourse, promising to bring her a present of salt on the return journey.

Arriving at the place where Polongahoya had been turned to stone they said, "Yes, this is the younger of the brothers who turned mud into rock at the beginning of things, and who carried the salt away from the old place and brought it here." Coming to where Pokanghoya had transformed himself into stone they said, "Here is the elder brother who made the trail and guided us on the way. It is he who turned the earth and rocks in the canyon to salt, so that the Hopis would never be without it."

And going down still farther into the gaping jaws of the canyon they left pahos at Masauwu's cave. Arriving at the sipapuni they scooped out a little clay to be used in the village ceremonies. Leaving pahos there also, they went on to gather the salt they needed. Having accomplished that they returned the way they had come, not forgetting to leave a present of salt near the exposed vulva of Gogyeng Sowuhti.

It is said that the salt deposit in the canyon was the last of the great creations of Pokanghoya and Polongahoya. It is also said that although the figures of the brothers and Spider Grandmother are there in stone, the three of them really returned to their home on the mesa and went on living.

X The Dispersal from Sikyatki

THE COYOTE, FOX AND FIRE CLANS coming from the south had settled
a few miles northeast of Koechaptevela and built a village they called
Sikyatki. With the passage of time their village grew large, and their
fields of corn spread out on all sides, excepting only that side that
was in the direct shadow of the mesa cliff. The people considered
Sikyatki to be the end of their migrations, and they built their houses
to last. Their pottery fires were burning almost every day, and the
granaries in the houses were stacked with dried corn ears.

At that time the marauding tribes such as the Utes, Paiutes and
Navajos had not yet arrived in the vicinity of the mesa. Nevertheless,
sometimes strangers came to the edge of the cliffs above Sikyatki and
shot arrows or hurled stones into the village. The people said, "We
need a guardpost on the top of the mesa to warn us of enemies." So
they built another settlement up above on two large mounds that
are still visible. They built houses and kivas there, and a little to
the south where the finger of the mesa was very narrow they built
a wall extending from one edge to the other to give them security
from the Koechaptevela people. They cut steps in the cliffside also,
so that they could go from the lower village to the upper without
difficulty. Their guardpost on the heights was called Koekuchomo.
From that spot the whole valley to the east, the south and the west

could be seen. Sikyatki went on growing. Other clans arriving in small groups of people settled there, some coming from the small villages around Awatovi on Antelope Mesa. Sikyatki became larger than Koechaptevela.

In Koechaptevela the Bear, Snake, Horn-Flute, Water, Sand and other clans were living. The people of Koechaptevela were uneasy about Sikyatki. Sometimes there were quarrels between the villages over the springs, or about the gathering of firewood on the mesa top. And for a while the wall that the Sikyatki people had constructed across the narrow part of the mesa created hard feeling. Nevertheless, the lives of the two villages became intertwined. When there were ceremonies in Koechaptevela, the Sikyatki people came to watch. When a special occasion occurred in Sikyatki, Koechaptevela people came to participate. Sons and daughters of Koechaptevela married daughters and sons of Sikyatki.

They were having a Niman, or Home-Going, Dance in Koechaptevela one time. It was the last appearance of the year for the kachinas, who were about to return to Tokonave. Many visitors came from Sikyatki to join the festivities. Among them was the nephew of Sikyatki's chakmongwi, or crier chief. Along with other young men, he stayed on until late afternoon, for it was a custom that the marriageable girls could not show themselves in the plaza until the last kachina dance of the day. The young men sat waiting on the roofs of the surrounding houses. Just before the last dance began, the girls came in with their ova marriage shawls around their shoulders and sat at one end of the plaza. The nephew of the Sikyatki crier chief was attracted to a certain girl because of her beauty.

His friends saw him looking at her. They said, "Oh, no, she is not for you. She is the daughter of the chief of Koechaptevela."

He answered, "Why do you say that? I was just looking."

But when he went home with his friends to Sikyatki he could not stop thinking about her. The next day he went back to Koechaptevela. He found the chief's house. He heard the sound of grinding within. He looked through a small window and saw the girl on her knees grinding corn on a metate. He watched her without speaking, but he shut out the light and the girl knew that someone was standing there. She turned toward the window, saying, "Why have you come?" Because he was shy he did not answer her, but left the place at once. The next day he came again. This time they talked a little through the grinding room window. On the third day they talked a great deal. And on the fourth day she said, "Let me see your hands. He put his hands through the opening and she felt the callouses on them. She said, "Yes, you are a hard worker. I think you would make a good husband." He returned to Sikyatki. He told his friends he was going to marry the daughter of the kikmongwi of Koechaptevela.

Most of his friends were pleased. But among them was another young man who, like the chakmongwi's nephew, had not been able to get the girl out of his mind. He said nothing, but he thought, "Why should I leave the girl to my friend? For she pleases me as much as she pleases him."

And so the next day he went to Koechaptevela and found the girl there in the grinding room. He stood at the window and spoke to her as though he had no time to lose. But the girl did not care for him, and she covered the window with a large coiled tray. He went home angrily. That night he could not sleep. The next day he returned to Koechaptevela and again he tried to talk to the girl through the grinding room window. She said, "No, there is no use. I have already made a choice." He persisted, coming again on the following day. Once again she covered the window with a coiled tray.

He went home. His heart was bitter. He felt a strange sickness, and that night he could not sleep. The next day he did not go out to work in the fields with his father or his uncles. He wandered about. He lay on the roof of his house. When his friends came looking for him he ignored them. Darkness fell over the village. He took his bow and some arrows and went to Koechaptevela. He went to the grinding room window, and by the light of the fire he could see the girl working at her metate. She turned, and when she recognized who was at the window she took a handful of ground corn and threw it at him.

Now the young man felt a great blackness enter his heart. He placed an arrow in his bow, and aiming through the window he released the string. The arrow struck the girl and she fell against the wall. The young man fled back to Sikyatki. He hung his bow on a peg and lay down on his mat. He did not speak, he did not eat, he did not drink, he did not sleep. He merely lay there with his eyes open.

Back in Koechaptevela the kikmongwi's wife did not hear the sound of the metate in the grinding room. She went to see what was the matter and found her daughter lying against the wall. The kikmongwi also came. They felt her body, but the breath of life had gone out of it. The word went around the village that the chief's daughter was dead. The girl's brother came. He removed the arrow from her body and examined it closely. He said, "The person who killed my sister is from Sikyatki." His parents said, in grief, "What kind of person could do such a thing?"

The next day they buried her. After that the kikmongwi brooded. He spoke little. His heart was too heavy. He spent much time in the kiva, sitting there as though life had departed from him also. But one day he left his house and went to Sikyatki to speak with the chief of that village. They sat together and smoked. Then the Koechaptevela chief said, "My daughter was killed by a person from your village."

The Sikyatki chief answered, "That she is dead we all know. But who knows the person who killed her? I do not know in what village he lives. If he lives in Koechaptevela, how will you find him? If he lives in Sikyatki, how shall I find him?"

The Koechaptevela chief said, "The people say that the nephew of the crier chief came often to see her."

The Sikyatki chief answered, "Yes, that is so. He intended to marry her. He spoke to us about the matter. But the day your daughter died he was far away in Shongopovi."

The chief of Koechaptevela said, "Very well. It was not he. Yet the arrow that killed my daughter was made in Sikyatki. Therefore you have a great responsibility."

The chief of Sikyatki replied, saying, "To lose one's daughter, that is a bad thing. But who will come forward to say, 'I am the one'?"

The Koechaptevela chief said, "The chief of the village is father to all the people. Do you not know which of your children could do such a thing?"

The Sikyatki chief fell silent. The kikmongwi of Koechaptevela arose and went home.

Arriving there he sent for his son. He said, "My son, there is something to be done. It has to do with the killing of your sister."

His son said, "I will do it. Instruct me."

The chief said, "I want you to prepare for a certain kachina race."

The young man said, "Where is the race?"

The chief said, "I will let you know when the time comes. Meanwhile, strengthen your legs. You must learn to run beyond running. Tomorrow morning when the sun shows itself, run toward the large butte out there to the south, the distant one on the other side of Huckyatwi. Go as far as you can without stopping, then return."

His son said, "Yes, I will do as you tell me."

The next morning at dawn he began running toward the southern butte. When he was only halfway there he had to stop, and he returned home. He told his father, who said, "It is a good beginning. Tomorrow run again." The next day the young man ran a little farther. Every day he went running, and each day he improved. It was winter when he began this training, and one day early in the spring he was able to run out to the butte, circle around it, and return to Koechaptevela without stopping.

His father praised him, saying, "Now you are truly a fine runner. You are ready for the kachina race."

The young man said, "What kachina race are you speaking about?"

The kikmongwi replied, "We will discuss it tonight in the kiva."

That night, in the kiva, the chief and his son sat together and smoked. After a while the chief put his pipe aside and said: "I have sent a message to Sikyatki that four days from now our kachina runners will appear there to race against the best runners of that village. You will go to Sikyatki with the others and join in the races. Take baked corn and red and yellow piki with you for presents. When you have completed the last race, enter the village as usual. The young women and girls will be watching from the roofs of the houses. Among them will be the daughter of the chief of Sikyatki. You have seen her. You know who she is." The chief went on giving his instructions, and his son listened silently.

The day for the races came. The Koechaptevela runners prepared themselves. They dressed in kachina costumes and put on their masks. They carried roasted corn, piki and other presents to be given to the winners of the races. The chief's son was dressed as a Himsung or Hair-Cutter kachina. They went across the top of the mesa, following a trail near the edge of the cliff. They crossed the stone wall built by the Sikyatki people and came to Koekuchomo. There they descended the cliff on the steps that had been cut into the rock wall and entered Sikyatki.

There was great excitement in the village. All the people came out to see the races. The Sikyatki runners were ready, and soon the races began. A Koechaptevela runner and a Sikyatki runner raced together. The Sikyatki runner won, and he was given corn and piki as a prize. A second race was run, and this time a Koechaptevela runner came in first. He also received a prize. When his turn came, the son of the kikmongwi of Koechaptevela raced against a fleet-footed young man from Sikyatki. But the Koechaptevela runner had trained for many months and his legs were very strong, and he won his race easily. At the end he stopped and waited for his opponent to arrive. Because the son of the Koechaptevela chief was impersonating a Himsung kachina, he took out his knife and cut a lock of hair from the other young man's head. Now, for a person to have his hair cut in this manner was not considered a good thing. But this was a prize that could not be denied to a Himsung.

There were other races. The son of the Koechaptevela chief won many times, and each time he cut some hair from the head of his opponent. The sun moved into the west. Some of the contestants were tired and could not run any more. But the best runner from the village of Sikyatki had seen the Himsung kachina cut the hair of many of his friends, and he wished to avenge what had happened to them. So he challenged the Himsung to a last race and put down some roasted corn, piki and other things as a prize. The two young men raced. But the young man who was the son of the chief of Koechaptevela left his opponent far behind. When he reentered the village he took out his knife. The spectators said, "Now he is going to cut more hair."

But he did not wait for the other runner to arrive. He looked up to see where the girls and young women were standing on the roofs of the houses. He swiftly went up a ladder to the place where the Sikyatki chief's daughter was watching the races with her friends. He approached her. The young women huddled in a group against the wall. The young man pushed them aside and took hold of the daughter of the Sikyatki chief. He grasped the pumpkin blossom whorl of hair on the side of her head. The young women thought, "The kachina is going to cut her hair."

But the young man did not do that. He cut off her head. He went to the edge of the roof and waved the head to the people standing below. Then he went to the other side and jumped to the ground and ran toward the cliff. People began to cry out that the girl had been killed. The Sikyatki men, some of whom had been in the races, hurried to their houses for bows and arrows. They pursued the Himsung kachina, who was now going swiftly up the cliffside steps. When he reached the top he paused to wave the head at those coming up from below. By the time the Sikyatki men reached the upper level of the mesa the young man was a long distance ahead of them, running southward. They continued to pursue. The young man came to the gap in the mesa, which is a short distance north of where the village of Walpi now stands, and there he descended on the east side. He came to Gogyengva, Spider Spring. Here he removed his mask and placed it on a large rock. After that he continued running, going around the point of the mesa, and finally arrived at Koechaptevela.

The Sikyatki men arrived at Gogyengva, and there they saw the mask on the rock. They said, "This is the place where we must stop. If we pursue past this point, the whole of Koechaptevela will come down and make war on us. We cannot go any farther." So they turned back at that place, returning to Sikyatki.

In Sikyatki the village chief was stricken with sadness. He said, "Who could have done this terrible thing?" The people began to discuss what had happened. They began to understand that it was revenge for the murder in Koechaptevela. The body of the chief's daughter was buried. And four days later the kikmongwi went to Koechaptevela to talk with the chief of that village.

The two men sat together in the kiva. The Sikyatki chief said, "We welcomed your young men in our village. Yet one of them killed my daughter. How can it be?"

The kikmongwi of Koechaptevela said, "We welcomed your people here also. Yet one of them killed my daughter. Koechaptevela has lost a daughter, Sikyatki has lost a daughter. We consider the affair even, one for one. But if Sikyatki does not see the matter this way and wants to make war against us, let it be that way. The villages can make war or they can live on. Or the people of Sikyatki can go elsewhere and find another home. It is for you to decide. But the evil events that occurred began in Sikyatki. Therefore your village is fated to die. The cliffs at Koekuchomo will break off. The rocks will fall and bury the spring that lies below. Nothing will ever be the same."

The chief of Sikyatki returned to his village. His heart was heavy for himself and his people. He did not want war with Koechaptevela, and he said to the people, "Let us live on." So they lived on, but after that there was much bitterness between the villages, and nothing was quite the same. Sikyatki's corn did not grow as well as it had in the beginning, and rocks began to fall from the cliffs into the spring. The rains favored Koechaptevela's fields and often forgot to fall at Sikyatki. At last it became clear that Sikyatki would have to be abandoned.

The people prepared to leave. On a certain morning they departed, taking with them whatever they could carry. They went southward toward the large buttes. At first they travelled in a line along a winding trail. It is said that there were more than a thousand men, women and children who went down from Sikyatki. In the afternoon of that day they began to break up into small groups, some going one way, some another. They built small temporary settlements out near the buttes, and sent expeditions back to Sikyatki from time to time to bring supplies of corn from their storage rooms. After all the corn was consumed, the people abandoned their temporary villages and went on. Some of them, feeling that life in Hopi country was too hostile, migrated eastward toward the Rio Grande where, the old people said, their ancestors had lived long ago. Some reached the village of Hemis, in what is now New Mexico, but many disappeared and were never heard of again. One group made a settlement on the top of Huckyatwi, the butte directly south of the mesa. Others moved slowly westward, living through the winter at one site, then going on to another.

In time the Coyote, Fox and Fire clan people, who had gone south and west, circled around until they were within sight of Oraibi. They asked if they could settle in that village.

The Oraibis asked them, "What can you bring that we do not already have in our village?"

The Coyote, Fox and Fire people replied, "We have many things. The Coyotes are fierce and brave warriors. They will defend Oraibi from its enemies. As you see, we wear foxskins as the symbol of our courage. We also have many kachinas that Oraibi does not know about. They will bring rain and make the corn grow."

The Oraibis replied, "Yes, you have valuable things. Therefore you may enter the village and build your homes there. We will give you fields for your corn."

So the Coyote, Fox and Fire clan people from Sikyatki entered Oraibi and settled, though in later years some of them moved on and lived in other villages.

As for Sikyatki, it stood there empty. The walls crumbled, the rooms and kivas filled with drifting sand, and the village merged with the landscape out of which it had been created. The cliff continued to fall away, and Koekuchomo, the guardpost on top of the mesa, also became a ruin.

XI The Flight from Huckovi

ABOUT THREE MILES WEST OF ORAIBI was the village of Huckovi, and just a little beyond was the village of Pivanhonkapi. In those villages the people had been living many years.

In Pivanhonkapi was a young man who was very devoted to the ceremonies of his people. And in Huckovi was a young woman who wanted the young man's attention. But he did not care for her and avoided her whenever he could. He had been initiated into the important societies, and he was also one of the men who played a part in the Spruce Tree Dance that took place every year.

It was time for the Spruce Tree Dance to be performed, and all those involved in the ritual began four days and nights of purification ceremonies in the kiva. Before entering the kiva on the first day, the young man of Pivanhonkapi went out on the mesa to gather firewood for his parents. The young woman of Huckovi also was out there gathering firewood. When the young man saw her he tried to turn away, but she called to him.

She said, "Why are you running away? Am I a masauwu, a dead spirit? I am only an ordinary person." The young man did not answer her, and she said, "Do I look like a sowuhti, an old woman?"

He answered, "No, it is not like that. You look like a young woman."

She said, "Very well, then. If I am not a dead spirit or an old woman, why are you avoiding me? I have been expecting you out here."

He said, "Yes. I am gathering firewood for my parents."

The young woman said, "Yes, that is easily seen. But now let us put the wood gathering aside and lie down together in the tall grass."

He looked away, saying, "Yes, that would be something worthwhile. But I cannot do it. We are getting ready for the Spruce Tree Dance. The prayers are already being said in the kiva. Until the rituals are over I am not permitted to lie with a woman."

They talked this way, back and forth, but he could not be persuaded, and at last the young woman of Huckovi angrily returned to her village.

The Spruce Tree Dance always took place at the very rim of the mesa. Four round holes had been chiselled out of the ground, which was solid rock, very close to the edge of the cliff. Into these holes the people set four tall spruce trees, with some of their branches removed, and made them tight with wedges. In the dance four men dressed as kachinas climbed into the trees, sang kachina songs, and then performed courageous tricks, leaping from one tree to another without showing any fear of the death that awaited them if they lost their footing.

Now, the young woman of Huckovi who wanted the young man's attention was a two-heart, that is to say a powaka, who could perform acts of sorcery. She was greatly angered that the young man rejected her. She decided to destroy him. Using her art of sorcery, she caused a fault to appear in the rock where one of the spruce trees was placed, so that when the dancing took place the tree would fall over the edge of the cliff along with the performers.

But that night Gogyeng Sowuhti, Spider Grandmother, came into the kiva where the men were preparing for the ceremony. She said, "A two-heart person in Huckovi is angry because one of our dancers would not lie with her. She has made a crack appear in the rock where one of the spruce trees is placed. Take this mortar made of cornmeal and repair the damage." She gave them a handful of wet cornmeal, and they went to where the trees were enplaced. They removed all the trees and found the hole in which the fault had been created. They mortared it with Spider Grandmother's corn-meal, which became as hard as the rock itself. The crack was com-pletely healed, and after replacing the trees the men returned to the kiva.

The next day Spider Grandmother came again to let them know the young woman of Huckovi had caused a crack to appear in another hole. Again she gave them cornmeal mortar. Again they went to the cliff's edge and removed the trees. They found the hole which had been cracked, repaired it, and returned to the kiva. The same thing happened on the third day and the fourth. After they had repaired the fourth hole, the trees stood securely.

The dance began in the early morning. All the people of Pivanhonkapi came to watch, and there were also visitors from Huckovi. First the kachina dancers sang, asking for rain. Then the four men who were the Spruce Tree Dancers, dressed and masked as kachinas, climbed into the trees. Mounting to the treetops they swayed back and forth, sometimes above solid ground, sometimes beyond the edge of the cliff, singing while they did this. The men at the foot of the trees played musical instruments—a drum, a notched stick scraper, and gourd rattles. Two at a time the tree dancers made leaps in the treetops, going from one tree to another and passing each other in mid-air. The trees sometimes bent far over the cliff, but they did not break, and the holes repaired with Spider Grand-mother's cornmeal held firmly.

When the sun was overhead, the dancers and their counsellors, who were older men, left the place of the spruce trees and entered the kiva to rest and pray. Now, while the dancing was still going on, the caretaker of the kiva had gone out to collect some bird feathers for the making of pahos. And while he was away the two-heart woman of Huckovi, seeing that Spider Grandmother had undone her evil work, caused one of the overhead beams in the kiva to crack. So all the dancers and their counsellors were now sitting in the kiva un-der the cracked beam, singing prayer songs. Suddenly the beam broke and the heavy ceiling caved in, killing everyone including the young man whom the Huckovi woman wanted to destroy.

There was a great commotion in the village. The people tried to save the men trapped down below under the stones and earth, but they could not do it. Every family in Pivanhonkapi lost someone, and there was much sadness everywhere. But in Huckovi the people were not sad. Some of them were even amused. They said to one another, "Well, now those people over in Pivanhonkapi will stop saying, 'Come and see what our Kachina Dancers can do in the trees.'" This was how things were in the two villages.

That night a man of Pivanhonkapi was sitting on his roof thinking about the tragic event that had occurred. In the darkness of the night he saw a walking fire coming toward the village. It turned away and moved in another direction, then it turned again toward the village. It circled all the houses, then it entered Pivanhonkapi and went into the plaza. Now the man on the roof could see that what at first appeared to be a walking fire was really a tuwakomoviki, a fierce female spirit who owned and ruled the wild animals in the wilderness. She was terrifying to look at, and the man on the roof was afraid. The tuwakomoviki went to the shrine in the center of the plaza. She sat on the shrine and howled:

Ah   neh!   It - i - ta - ku - ah!

At this, all the dogs in the village began to bark or howl. The tuwakomoviki turned her face toward the man on the roof, saying: "You, on the house up there, come down. I want to talk to you. Do not be afraid. I have just arrived from the Little Colorado River. I want to help the people of Pivanhonkapi."

The man went down. She said to him, "Out there where I live, my messengers brought me news of the tragedy in Pivanhonkapi. They told me everything. The kiva was caused to collapse by a po-waka in Huckovi. They are evil people in that village. They are glad of what happened here. That is why I came. I want to help Pivanhonkapi. I am going to get rid of those people for you. To-morrow bring four pahos for me and leave them at this shrine. Then I will begin." After saying this she left the plaza and went out into the night. Her fire disappeared and everything was darkness.

The man went around the village telling everyone what had happened. The men made pahos that night, and in the morning they

placed them at the shrine in the plaza. That night the people of
Pivanhonkapi stood on their roofs instead of going to sleep. After
a while they saw a walking fire going toward Huckovi. It went one
way and then another way, passing around the entire village. It
entered Huckovi. In the plaza of Huckovi the tuwakomoviki began
to grind corn on a metate, and while doing this she sang:

The people of Huckovi were frightened. They decided to
catch this terrifying being and destroy her. So they gathered at the
trail where she would depart from the village, and there they
waited. Soon they saw the tuwakomoviki coming. She was lighted in
the darkness as though she were a fire. The people saw her sunken
eyes and her lips drawn back as on a dead person. Fright overcame
them. They turned away and fled.

The tuwakomoviki came again the next night, and the third
night and again on the fourth. It was then that the people of
Huckovi realized that the spirit did not intend to leave them alone
but would continue to torment them. They decided to abandon
the village. And so, taking whatever they could carry, they went
out of Huckovi and camped near a spring on the open mesa. They
had not yet decided where they would go. That night the tuwakomoviki appeared in their camp, terrifying them anew. The tuwakomoviki pointed toward the west, so in the morning the people
travelled westward. The tuwakomoviki followed them, driving them
onward whenever they lagged. Every night she appeared like a
walking fire in their camp, and every day she drove them on to the
west. She drove them as far as the Little Colorado River, and at
that place she disappeared.

But the Huckovi people did not remain there. They crossed
the river at a shallow place and continued westward. In time they

arrived at a spot near what is now called Redlands, in California. There they made a village and settled. Huckovi, the village that they had abandoned, became ruins.

Because a powaka in Huckovi was angry at a young Spruce Tree dancer she killed many people in Pivanhonkapi. And this is the reason why Huckovi no longer exists.

XII Judgment by Fire at Pivanhonkapi

FOR A LONG TIME AFTER THE HUCKOVI people departed, all went well in Pivanhonkapi. The springs were full of water, there was rain, there was corn. But because life was so good to them the people forgot to be grateful for the kindnesses of nature. They drifted away from virtuous things. Just as it had been in the Lower World, just as it had been at Palatkwapi, people did pleasurable things instead of what was right. They neglected the ceremonies, the children and the corn. They no longer paid respect to their elders and the kachinas. They did not bring pahos to the shrines. They preferred to use the kivas for gambling games rather than for rituals. Weavers were hardly ever at their looms, and women baked their pottery carelessly. Men and women became promiscuous and there was brawling almost every day, even in the village plaza. The people had forgotten the Hopi way of life, and the kikmongwi of the village, who was an old man, brooded on the evil circumstances that had fallen on Pivanhonkapi.

The kikmongwi had a son named Sikyatiti, and the young man had a wife called Yachakpa. Now, during these bad times in Pivanhonkapi it was not safe for a woman to go places alone, because there were many young men who were ready to take women by force. But one day Yachakpa had to go out for water. She took her water jug and went to the spring, which was some distance away from the village. While she was filling her jug, a young man dressed as a kachina approached her and asked for a dipper of water. Because of the way he was dressed, the young woman did not recognize him.

She said, "No, take your own water."

But he persisted until at last she filled the dipper and gave it to him.

Then he said, "Well, let us take a little walk over there."

She said, "No, I don't know you, so why should I walk over there?"

He said, "There is something over there for you to see."

She said, "No, I don't want to see it."

But he kept after her until at last she left her jug at the spring and went with him, thinking to return quickly. She kept saying, "Where is the thing you want me to see?" And he kept saying, "Over there, just a little farther." And in this way he managed to get her far away from the spring. At last they reached a place where there was a hole in the ground like the entrance to a kiva.

He said, "There it is, down below."

She went down first, and the man followed her, pulling a large rock over the opening to seal it.

When Sikyatiti, her husband, returned from working in the field he did not see Yachakpa. He went around the village asking for her. Finally someone said, "Yes, I saw her going out with her water jug to the spring."

So the kikmongwi's son went to the spring looking for his wife, but all he found there was her water jug. He searched for a long time. After that he went back to the village to get some of his friends, and then all of them went searching together, but they could not find Yachakpa. The next day many people of the village joined in the search, but they found nothing. After several days of looking for Yachakpa people said, "She is not anywhere. Every place on the mesa where a person could be, we have been there. There is no other place to look." And so they gave up the search.

But Sikyatiti did not stop looking. He hardly ate, he hardly slept. He went out searching every morning, and every night he came back alone. One day when he was wandering from place to place he saw a coyote sitting there. Instead of running away, the coyote spoke to him, saying, "I know you are looking for something. Follow me." Sikyatiti followed the coyote. They came to a house out there in the wilderness. Gogyeng Sowuhti, Spider Grandmother, was standing at the doorway. She welcomed them into the house.

She said, "My messengers told me that you were out there looking for something."

Sikyatiti answered, "Yes, Grandmother. I have been looking for my wife. She went to the spring for water. She disappeared."

Gogyeng Sowuhti said, "Yes, let us find her."

Now, Gogyeng Sowuhti was a povoslowa. She had a large quartz crystal that could reveal things to her. She took the crystal from a buckskin bag and placed it on the floor. She sat down and looked into it. She saw Yachakpa going to the spring. She saw Yachakpa talking to the young man dressed as a kachina. She saw Yachakpa go walking with the man. She saw them descend into the hole in the ground. She saw everything.

She said to Sikyatiti, "Well, this is not a good thing. The man who took Yachakpa belongs to a society of powakas. They all live there in Pivanhonkapi but they are not recognized for what they are. It is they who hold Yachakpa a prisoner. They go there to that underground place and abuse her whenever they want. They are evil people. Very well, let us go there and find Yachakpa."

Gogyeng Sowuhti, Sikyatiti and the coyote went out together. They went to the spring where Yachakpa had left her jug. And because Spider Grandmother had seen everything in her quartz crystal she knew where to go from there. They arrived at a certain place, and Spider Grandmother said, "Here it is. They are here, down below." But the rock that covered the entrance to the underground place was very heavy and they could not move it. So Spider Grandmother turned the coyote into a large bear, and he began digging with his front feet. He dug beneath the rock and made an opening. They entered. The young woman was there. Also, the powaka who had abducted her was there. Seeing Sikyatiti coming in, the powaka turned himself into a wildcat and sprang at him. But the coyote who was now a large bear fought with the wildcat and killed him.

They took Yachakpa out of the cave. At the spring Spider Grandmother and the coyote, who had resumed his own form, departed. Sikyatiti took his wife home.

When the kikmongwi heard the story of what had happened to his son's wife, he decided that something must be done. He went to the village where the Yayaponcha People lived. The Yayaponchas were feared, for they were sorcerers with special powers over the forces of nature, and they were wild in appearance, having long, unkempt hair. The Yayaponchas could make the north wind blow, call down storms, and make the lightning strike. They could kill people and revive them, cause landslides by pointing their fingers at cliffs, and control fire. The kikmongwi of Pivanhonkapi went to the Yayaponcha kiva. They received him, and they all sat in the kiva a while and smoked to bring harmony. When the time was right, the Yayaponcha chief said, "Why are you here?"

The kikmongwi said, "There is a thing I must speak about."

The Yayaponcha chief said, "Yes, let us talk about it."

The kikmongwi said, "The spirit of my village is sick. The people have become dark-hearted. They care nothing for virtue. They behave in evil ways. Respect for the things that deserve respect, it is not there any more. People do not observe the ceremonies, they laugh at the kachinas, and they have forgotten the songs. Instead of making pahos they gamble in the kivas. Instead of weaving and making good pots, the men and women roll around on the ground together, one man's wife with another woman's husband. Well, now, this has been an unbearable thing for a long while. Yet it has become worse. Now there is a society of evil ones in Pivanhonkapi who take women to a place where they can abuse them whenever they want. My son's wife, they had her there for many days and she could not escape until Gogyeng Sowuhti found her. All this evil must come to an end. I want to call down the fury of nature to bring judgment on Pivanhonkapi."

The Yayaponcha people pondered on what they had heard. They discussed the matter. Then their chief said, "Yes, if that is the way it is, we will help you. You yourself shall choose the manner of judgment. Shall it be water, storm, lightning, wind or fire?"

The kikmongwi said, "Let it be fire."

It was agreed that in four days there would be a dance at Pivanhonkapi and that the Yayaponchas would take part. The kikmongwi then left the Yayaponcha village and returned home. There he let it be known that the people should prepare for the dance.

The day of the festivities came. Different groups of kachina dancers performed in the plaza, each doing its own dances and songs. One group of dancers departed from the plaza, another appeared. The dancing went on all day. The last to appear were the Yayaponchas, who filed into the plaza silently. Four of them carried prayer offerings of cornmeal, and on top of each offering was a spark of fire. They began to dance. They sang:

> *"Houses will be wrapped in a red cloud*
> *Coming from the south.*
> *Enveloping first one place and then another,*
> *Here it will arrive at last."*

The people of Pivanhonkapi did not understand the meaning of the words. But they were alarmed because the Yayaponchas seemed to speak of a mysterious disaster yet to come. When the dance was over, the prayer offerings, each with its spark of fire, were distributed. The kikmongwi of Pivanhonkapi received one, which he took to his house. One was placed at the shrine in the plaza. The Yayaponcha chief carried one back to his own village. And the fourth prayer offering, surmounted by a spark of fire, was given to a Yayaponcha runner to carry southward to Neuvatikyao, the distant sacred peaks now known as the San Francisco Mountains. When he arrived at Neuvatikyao, the runner left the offering at a certain Yayaponcha shrine, after which he returned to his village.

Although the appearance of the Yayaponchas in Pivanhonkapi had alarmed the people somewhat, they soon began to forget. They went back to doing what they found pleasurable, and many of them descended into the kivas to gamble and play games.

The next night a few persons who were not in the kivas noticed a red glow in the sky above Neuvatikyao. They called into the kivas, saying, "The clouds are red above the southern mountains," but what they said aroused no interest down below. The next night it seemed as though the San Francisco Mountains were aflame. Again people called into the kivas, saying, "The mountains are burning," but the ones down below were too busy to pay any attention. On the third night the whole southern sky was alight, resembling an enormous red cloud, but the people in the kivas only laughed when they heard the news.

By the fourth day the great fire had reached the foot of the mesa and the sun was dimmed by smoke. People cried out. They ran this way and that, not knowing what to do or where to go. As the fire raged through the grass and brush, the inhabitants of Pivanhonkapi fled for their lives. Many were trapped in their houses and in the kivas, and there they died. Sikyatiti and his wife, Yachakpa, were among those who escaped. But the kikmongwi himself refused to come out of his house, and there he perished with the others. Those who survived were scattered, and in time they sought shelter in other villages.

Pivanhonkapi was smoke-blackened and deserted. Its walls began to crumble. The village became a ruin.

Now, the village of Oraibi lay directly in the path of the great fire, but Oraibi was not destroyed. When the people of Oraibi saw the flames in the south they went to their chief with the news. He climbed to the highest roof to see for himself what was happening. Then he went to the place where Gogyeng Sowuhti, Spider Grandmother, was living. He said, "The fire coming from the south is destroying everything. Soon it will reach Oraibi. How can I save my people?"

Spider Grandmother instructed him to make two arrows decorated with bluebird feathers. This he did. Spider Grandmother then took him to a little knoll west of the village and said, "Thrust one of your arrows in the ground here." The kikmongwi pressed the point of the arrow into the earth. They went to another knoll somewhat east of the village. Spider Grandmother said, "Place your second arrow here." At that spot the kikmongwi placed the second arrow. And when that was done, Spider Grandmother spun a web between the two arrows. After that she moistened the web with water.

The fire arrived, but it could not pass through Spider Grandmother's web, so it turned and went another way, leaving Oraibi unharmed. This is how Oraibi was saved from destruction even though Pivanhonkapi perished.

XIII The Antelope Boy of Shongopovi

IT WAS A TIME NOT AT THE BEGINNING and not at the end, when the villages were standing there just as they are now. And in those days, it is remembered, there lived in Shongopovi a man and his wife and one daughter. The girl was old enough to marry, but she did not want it. She met with a certain young man of the village sometimes, but mostly she kept to herself. Her parents wondered about it. They said to each other sometimes, "She is really a young woman now. Why is she always alone? Does she want to live forever without a husband?"

One day the village crier went through Shongopovi announcing that there would be a rabbit hunt the next morning. And so the un-married girls began at once to make somiviki. They ground blue corn into a fine meal, wrapped it in cornhusks and boiled it. But the girl who lived so much alone did not make any somiviki.

Her mother said, "How can you go on the rabbit hunt if you have no somiviki to give to the boys?"

The girl answered, "I do not think I will go on the rabbit hunt."

Early the following morning the young people began to gather at the edge of the village, and the girl's mother said to her, "Well, now, all the others are going out there to have a good time together, and you are staying behind like an old woman. This is not the way it should be."

The girl replied, "All right, I will go then. But I have no somi-viki."

The mother said, "Last night when you were sleeping I ground the blue corn. It is ready. The water is boiling. We can make the somiviki quickly."

So they wrapped the ground corn in husks and put it into the boiling water. When it was cooked they took the somiviki out and let it cool. The young people were at the edge of the village waiting impatiently for the stragglers. The crier chief kept saying, "Not yet, not yet. Wait until everyone is here." The girl came with her somi-viki just as they were starting to go down to the foot of the mesa on the west side.

They arrived at the valley below. They began hunting. Whenever a boy saw a rabbit he chased it and tried to knock it down with his stick. If he found a rabbit hole he wet the end of his stick, poked it into the hole and twisted it to catch in the rabbit's fur. Each time a boy caught a rabbit he held it up by its hind legs, and the girls raced to see who could get there first. The boy gave the rabbit to the first girl to arrive, and she would give him somiviki in exchange. The rabbit hunters went on this way from place to place.

The girl who had been reluctant to participate in the rabbit hunt had won two rabbits and given away most of her somiviki. But she was not feeling well and was going along slowly. She fell behind the others. She could hear their voices in the distance but she could not see them. She stopped to rest. She felt pains in her stomach. She found a secluded place among the rocks and lay down. And while she was lying there she gave birth to a baby. She worried greatly. She thought, "I cannot take this baby home. My parents will be angry with me." And so, after staying there for a time, she arose, wrapped the infant in a piece of her clothing, and placed it in an abandoned badger hole. Then she returned to the village.

Her parents said, "What happened to you? The others returned a long while ago."

She said, "I was tired. I rested. Then I came home slowly. Here are the two rabbits I won."

Now, after all the young people had finished with their hunting, a female coyote came out of hiding and began to look for food. Because she was old she could not run fast enough to catch game. She had watched the hunters, thinking that they might overlook some wounded rabbits and leave them behind. And so she went here and there where she had seen them using their sticks. She did not find any food. But she heard a sound coming from a badger hole. She approached the hole and looked inside. She saw the baby there and drew it out gently with her teeth. She thought, "This young one is hungry. If I were younger I would nurse it, but now I am dried up. I have no milk." She thought about the Antelope People living some distance north of Shongopovi. She thought, "Yes, I will bring it to them. They will take care of it."

Holding the baby carefully by its cloth wrapping, the old coyote went to the north. She came to the kiva of the Antelope People and set the baby down by the entrance. As was the custom, she stamped on the ground above the kiva, calling out, "I am here. Is there someone below?"

An antelope person called back, "Yes, we are here."

The old coyote said, "Come up. I have brought something."

So the antelope person went up the ladder to where the coyote was waiting. The coyote said to him, "Here is a male child I found out there in a badger hole. He is hungry, but I have no milk to give him. So I have brought him to you. One of your young women can feed him."

The coyote went away, and the antelope person took the baby down into the kiva and placed it near the fire. The antelope men gathered around. The chief of the Antelope People went to an adjoining room in the kiva. The women were staying there. The chief said, "A human baby has been brought to us. Who will take care of him?"

An antelope woman replied, "Yes, I will take care of him. Give him to me." She came to where the baby was lying. She picked it up, cleaned it and wrapped it in a blanket. Then she nursed it.

Because the baby drank antelope milk it grew as rapidly as an antelope. In four days he could walk a little. When he was four weeks old he was allowed to go out of the kiva to run with the antelope children. At first he was slow, but in time he could run as fast as the others. And thereafter he went out with the antelopes every day and did whatever they did. In the kiva the Antelope People resembled humans. But when it was time to go out they took their antelope skins from the wall, put them on and became antelopes. At night when they returned they removed their skins and hung them on the wall again. While the boy was an adopted son of the Antelope People he was not an antelope. He did not have a skin to put on when they went out together. He alone ran on two legs.

A man of Shongopovi went out one morning to search for game. He went to the north. He saw antelopes grazing there. He approached them silently. He saw the older antelopes. He saw the young antelopes running together, and with them a young boy running as though he too were an antelope. The hunter did not hunt any more, but returned to Shongopovi to tell what he had seen. He entered the kiva where other men were sitting and discussing things. He said, "Out there in the north, I was hunting. I came upon a herd of antelopes. The young ones were running together and among them was a human child."

The others answered in doubt, saying, "This is hard to believe. A human child running with the antelopes? The antelopes are swift. No human, large or small, could run with the antelopes."

The hunter said, "What I have told you is the truth. I was there and I saw it."

The next day another man went to the north to see if a boy was there with the antelopes. He came to where the antelopes were grazing. He saw the boy with the young antelopes. He saw them run together. He returned to the village to report what he had seen. He said, "It is true. There is a boy among them, and he runs as swiftly as the others."

The following day a third man went out to scout the antelopes, and the next day still a fourth man. They too saw the boy among the antelopes. The matter was debated in the kivas. Messengers went through Shongopovi to find out if some family was missing a child. They went also to the villages of Shipaulovi and Mishongnovi. But no one had heard of a missing child. In the kivas the people discussed what to do. Some said, "Do nothing. If the boy chooses to live with the antelopes, surely he has a reason." Others said, "No, it is not right for a boy to live among the antelopes. We must capture him and bring him to the village." So a hunt was organized to capture the antelope boy. The people of Shipaulovi and Mishongnovi were invited to participate. The next morning, parties from the three villages went to designated places in the north. As each party arrived at its starting place it lighted a fire. When three columns of smoke were visible, the people spread out and arranged themselves in a great circle around the antelope feeding grounds.

The chief of the antelopes was the boy's ceremonial uncle because he had taught him the knowledge and secrets of the antelope kiva. That morning, while the villagers were taking their positions for the hunt, the antelope chief said, "Wait, let us not go out yet. Something is happening today and there is something that must be done." He called the boy to sit with him in the kiva.

The boy said, "My uncle."

The chief said, "My nephew. Today the villagers are having a great antelope hunt. But it is you they are looking for. They say it is not right for a boy to be living with the antelopes. They mean to capture you and take you back with them. It is true, they are your people. Therefore you must return with them. Whoever captures you will take you as his own. So it is important for you to know who among them are your parents. When we go out today do not run with the young antelopes. Stay close to me. I will tell you who is your father and who is your mother. When the time comes I will let you know what to do."

The boy said, "My uncle, I do not want to go back to the village to live. The antelopes are my people."

The antelope chief said, "It is true, you are like one of our own. If things do not go well for you in the village, if they treat you badly, you can come back to us. But as for now, today you will have to go with your parents to Shongopovi."

Then the Antelope People prepared the boy. They washed his hair and cut it above his eyes in the Hopi fashion. They put a fluffy white eagle feather in his hair. They powdered his face with white cornmeal and painted his legs yellow. Around his waist they wrapped a white kilt, and around his ankles they fastened ankle bands. When this was done the Antelope People took their antelope forms and went out to their usual grazing place.

The people of the villages were waiting. They surrounded the antelopes. They moved in closer, making the circle smaller. The antelopes sought to escape. But if they went one way, there were people there. If they went another way, there were people there also. So they kept going around in a circle, and as the people came closer the circle became smaller and smaller. And at last the antelopes were confined in a very small space.

The antelope chief said to the boy, "Look carefully. That young woman standing over there is your mother. And over there, that man by the rocks, he is your father. Do you see them?"

The boy said, "Yes, I see them."

The antelope chief said, "The next time we pass this way, go quickly to your mother. Otherwise someone else may take you."

When they had gone around the circle one more time the antelope chief said, "Go now. Go swiftly."

The boy left his place among the antelopes. He ran swiftly to his mother. He put his arms around her, saying, "My mother." People gathered around. He said again, "My mother."

At first the young woman said nothing. She was thinking, "How can this be? He is mistaken." But remembering at last how she had put her baby in the badger hole, she placed her arms around the boy, saying, "My son."

The young woman's uncle who had been standing nearby said to her, "Is it true? Is this boy your son?"

She answered, "Yes, he is my son."

Her uncle asked, "Where is the boy's father?"

The boy went to where his father was standing. He took his hand. He said, "My father."

His father replied, "My son."

The young woman's uncle was angry. He said, "Why have you deceived us?"

The young woman said, "I was afraid. I tied my belt tight so that no one would notice. I went on the rabbit hunt and the baby was born there. I was afraid to bring him home, so I wrapped him in some of my clothing and left him in a badger hole."

Her uncle said, "It was a bad thing you did. If the antelopes had not taken care of your son he would have died." He came forward. He pulled down the hair whorls from each side of her head. He straightened her hair and tied it in a knot the way it is worn by married women. He said, "Take the boy home. His father will join you there."

She returned to her parents' house, taking the boy with her. After a while the boy's father came and lived with them there, as is the custom. They went on living. The mother loved the boy. The father loved him also, but he felt restless about the way things had happened. He scolded the boy and spoke to him sharply. He loved him but he could not manage to speak to him except in hard words. He neglected him as well. He did not provide him with moccasins like other boys had. He did not make a bow for him and teach him how to hunt.

The boy was unhappy. And one day after his father scolded him sharply he went out of the village and travelled north until he came again to the place of the Antelope People. He entered the kiva. He said to the antelope chief, "My uncle."

The chief said, "My nephew."

The boy said, "As you told me to do, I went to Shongopovi. But I cannot live there any more. My father is angry with me. He does not want me. Therefore I have come back. You are my people. I will live here."

His antelope uncle said, "Yes, live here. From now on you are one of us."

The Antelope People washed his hair and fixed it in the antelope style. They dressed him in the antelope manner. His uncle gave him an antelope skin, and a name. He named him Yuteu. The boy became an antelope.

Back in Shongopovi they missed the boy and searched for him everywhere. His parents went to Shipaulovi and Mishongnovi to see if he was there. They looked in the fields on all sides of Shongopovi.

His mother said at last, "There is no use looking for him any more. He has returned to the Antelope People who were kind to him."

The young woman's father, the boy's grandfather, considered what could be done. While others slept, he stayed up all night making pahos. And in the morning he went north to the country of the Antelope People. He saw the antelopes, but there was no boy with them. He waited all day but he did not see his grandson. So he left the pahos where the antelopes would find them, then he returned home. He said, "I went there, but it is too late, for he is an antelope now."

The boy's father was filled with remorse. He wanted his boy. He went north to the antelope country. He watched the antelopes, hoping to catch sight of his son. But he did not see him. Day after day he went to watch the antelopes, forgetting to take care of his fields. But there was no boy there, only the antelopes, nothing more.

XIV The Races Between Payupki and Tikuvi

WHEN THE CASTILLAS ARRIVED AT MUYOVI, which is the Rio Grande, they inflicted themselves on the people who were living there in the villages. They subjected them to great cruelties and indignities. They profaned the religious ceremonies, took women as they pleased, killed people and destroyed villages. For these reasons, many of the people abandoned their homes at Muyovi and went elsewhere. Some went out into the wilderness and disappeared. Others travelled westward to find sanctuary among the Hopis. There were those who arrived at Antelope Mesa. They came from Acoma and Laguna and other Rio Grande villages. The village of Awatovi received many of them, but others built new settlements nearby, including people who had come from Payupki. Some of the Payupki people went farther west, however, and settled on the mesa top a little north of the present village of Shipaulovi. Close by was another Hopi village called Tikuvi. These people from Muyovi called their village Payupki. They planted corn, and they lived on.

It is said that the Hopis were not too happy that the Payupkis had settled there. Sometimes there were frictions and disputes. Nevertheless the troubles between the villages were not great. Sometimes the kikmongwis of Payupki and Tikuvi exchanged visits. And when there was a kachina dance in one village the people of the other village came to watch.

One day the chief of Payupki was visiting in Tikuvi. He saw a man with a belt of bells going around from one place to another announcing that there were to be races on the following morning. He went to each kiva in the village, leaving out none, inviting all of Tikuvi's runners to participate in the event. When the kikmongwi of Payupki returned home he was thinking about the Tikuvi races. Because Payupki was a very small village it did not have many good runners. But the chief sent for a certain boy and said to him, "Tomorrow there will be racing in Tikuvi. I would like to know how good their runners are. As you are the best runner we have, I want you to go to Tikuvi. If you are invited, join in the races. Do not try to win. Merely run with them. Then return and let me know what you find out about things."

So the next day the boy waited until he saw the Tikuvi people going down to the racing grounds. He also went down, and when he arrived there he was invited to compete along with the others. He said, "Yes, I will do it. Over in Payupki we do not have many good runners, but I will try."

The runners stood in a line, and when they were given the signal they began to run. At first the Payupki boy was far behind. But as the race went on he moved forward. After a while there were only two runners ahead of him, and then only one. He desired to win, but he remembered that he had been sent to get information and not to defend Payupki's reputation. So he did not try to pass the runner in the lead. That was the way it was in the other races also. He ran on the heels of the leaders but did not try to win. When the racing was ended for the day the Payupki boy returned home.

He said to the kikmongwi, "I went to the Tikuvi racing grounds as you instructed me. Though I finished behind the leaders, I am sure I could have won. But I did not press on."

The kikmongwi said, "Good. You have told me what I wanted to know. Some day we will run against Tikuvi. Meanwhile, train yourself and make your legs strong."

The boy did what the chief wanted him to do. Every day he went running across the mesa. He practiced running through gullies, through sand, and over the hills. He felt himself grow stronger.

Then one day the chief of Tikuvi came to visit the chief of

Payupki. They sat in the kiva and smoked for a while. When the tobacco was consumed, the Payupki chief put the pipe away. He said, "I am glad you have come. What is in your mind?"

The Tikuvi chief answered, "I came to tell you that four days from tomorrow we will be having races again. We would like your runners to come and compete. Bring whatever you want for prizes. We shall do the same."

The chief of Payupki said, "Well, we are a small village. We have only one good runner, whom you have already seen. But he will compete in the races. And we shall bring something for the betting."

The Tikuvi chief said, "Yes, that is good." And in this way the competition between the villages was arranged.

On the night before the races were to take place, the men of Tikuvi went into a kiva to discuss the contest.

One man said, "The boy from Payupki, can he beat our runners?"

Another answered, "He ran against us before. He could not win then. Why should we be concerned?"

Still another said, "Yes, we can bet whatever we please. There is nothing to fear from the Payupki boy."

They went on discussing the matter, and while they did so Gogyeng Sowuhti, Spider Grandmother, began to descend into the kiva with her medicine bag.

Some of the men called out, "What is it you want, Old Woman?"

She said, "I have come to give assistance to the Tikuvi runners. I have brought medicine to put on them."

But the men did not want her. They said roughly, "Go away, Grandmother. Return to your house and sleep. Our runners don't need your help."

Spider Grandmother said, "When you are in trouble you send for me. Now you say, 'We don't need you, Grandmother.' Very well. I heard you. Therefore I shall leave."

She went up the ladder and out of the kiva. She went to her house out on the mesa and gathered her things together. Then she left that place, and from there she walked to Payupki. The people in that village welcomed her and took her to the kiva where the men were discussing the race. As she descended the ladder the men welcomed her.

They called out, "Come down, Grandmother, come down."

The chief gave her a pipe to smoke. She smoked energetically, blowing great clouds of smoke out of her mouth. The men smiled, thinking, "Spider Grandmother is old. She takes in too much smoke. In a few minutes she will become dizzy and fall over." But Spider Grandmother did not fall over, and after blowing out more clouds of smoke she returned the pipe to the kikmongwi.

He said, "You are welcome here. Why have you come?"

She answered, "I went to the kiva in Tikuvi to give help to their runners who will race tomorrow. But the men laughed at me. They said, 'Go away, Old Woman.' So I left them. The house I lived in out there, I do not want to live in it any more. I have come to your village. Because I have been well treated here I want to help your runner."

They brought the boy runner into the kiva. Spider Grandmother took a bowl from her bag. She put a medicine powder in it. She added water and stirred with her finger. She said, "This is to protect the boy against sorcery." Spider Grandmother rubbed the medicine on the boy's legs. Then she said, "In Tikuvi they will sit up all night talking. Here in Payupki we should sleep."

The chief said, "Spider Grandmother speaks wisely. Let us sleep."

The people found a room in the village for Spider Grandmother. They brought blankets for her, and something to eat. They put a fire in the fireplace. Then the village slept.

When the sun was overhead the next day, the men and boys of of Payupki went to the Tikuvi racing grounds.

The Tikuvi chief asked, "Are your runners here?"

The Payupki chief replied, "Our village is only a small one. We have only a single fast runner in Payupki. He is here. He is the same one that ran in your last race."

The Tikuvi people laughed. They said, "Why, yes, we recognize him. The last time he was here he did not win anything. Is he going to compete against all of our runners?"

The Payupki chief said, "Yes, that is the way it will have to be."

People from both villages put before them on the ground all

the things they had brought for betting—moccasins, belts, shawls, kilts, and bows and arrows. Then the racing began.

The boy from Payupki won the first race. He won the second race. He ran against Tikuvi's fastest runners, and he won every race. When it was over, the men of Payupki collected all the things they had won from the Tikuvi men and carried them home. They gave some of their winnings to Spider Grandmother, which made her contented.

That night the Payupki chief again sent for the boy runner. He said, "Things are warming up now. You must learn to run as you have never run before. Tikuvi is angry and wants revenge. We will be challenged again, and the weight of the outcome lies on you."

So the boy trained hard, running, running, running all the time. One day when he returned to his house, his sister was there grinding corn. She said, "Well, I was out there. I saw you running, but you do not run fast enough."

He said, "I do the best I can. Is it not good enough that I beat all the others over there in Tikuvi?"

She replied, "Tomorrow when you go out to practice I will come along. I will show you something."

He said, "Corn grinding, you can show me something about that. Running is something else."

But the next day when he went out to practice his sister came with him. He said, "You are going to race with me? Very well. Go on ahead of me. You can start where the cottonwood tree is standing. Run to the sand hole out there in the south, go around it and return to the village."

She went to where the cottonwood tree was standing and then they began to run. The boy was greatly surprised. Instead of closing the distance between them, he fell farther behind. While he was still on the way to the sand hole his sister passed him on her way back. By the time he made his turn she was far ahead of him. When he was halfway back, she had already finished. He returned to the village. There he found his sister grinding corn.

He said, "How can you grind corn now after so much running?"

She answered, "The running, it was hardly anything."

Again the next day they went running together. This time they started even, from the same place, but the girl was soon far ahead.

She ran around the sand hole and passed her brother going the other way. She taunted him, saying, "Run, brother, run." But he could not catch up with her. She finished running and went on to the village. When the boy arrived there his sister was grinding corn. He said, "How can you grind corn after a long run like that?" She only laughed. They went running again on another day. This time the boy started ahead of her at the cottonwood tree, but even before he reached the sand hole his sister passed him. She left him far behind, finished and returned to the house. The boy arrived. He went to the kikmongwi's house. He said, "I am not the fastest runner in Payupki. My sister is the fastest." The kikmongwi listened in silence. He reflected on the matter.

In time the chief of Tikuvi came again to visit with the Payupki chief. They smoked. Then the Tikuvi chief said, "Four days from now we will race at the usual place. Bring your best runner so that he can race against our people."

The Payupki chief answered, "Yes, we will do it. But things have changed. Now our best runner is a girl."

The Tikuvi chief was surprised. He said, "Well, then, let it be that way."

He returned to his village and reported what he had heard.

The night before the race the men of Tikuvi went into a kiva to make plans. Because their village had been beaten before and had lost many things in the betting, they now intended to use sorcery. So they sent a messenger to find Spider Grandmother. He came back without her. He said, "I went to her house on the mesa. But she was not there. Here house is empty. No one at all is living there. She has gone away, and I could not find her." The men were concerned. However, they knew of other persons who had a knowledge of sorcery, and they devised a way to win the running contests.

In the kiva at Payupki, also, there was planning. Spider Grandmother put medicine on the legs of the girl runner. She said, "The people of Tikuvi are bad-hearted. They intend to win by sorcery. So when the girl runs I will take on my other form and become a small spider. I will sit on her ear and tell her what to do."

The night passed and the day of the race came. Everyone gathered at the racing grounds. This time the women as well as the men of Payupki were there because it was a girl who was going to represent the village. Both villages had brought many things to bet—blankets, bows, moccasins, turquoise beads, shawls, even pottery and grinding stones. The girl from Payupki tucked her skirt into her belt and prepared to run.

The first race began, and the Payupki girl won it. The Tikuvi people paid the articles they had lost in the betting. The second race was won, and again the Payupki people received their winnings. The girl won the third race and the fourth. By now the Tikuvi people had lost everything they had brought to bet.

It was time for the last race to start. The Payupkis wanted the betting to go on, but the Tikuvis said, "We have nothing more." They were sullen. The men were ready to leave. But the Tikuvi women looked at the piles of winnings on the Payupki side. They did not want to leave. They said, "Let us go on with things. We have a proposal. If our runner wins this last race, you will give us everything you have collected there, everything that you brought from your village and everything that you have taken from us. If your runner wins, all of the women of Tikuvi will belong to Payupki."

The Tikuvi men did not like it. They argued about it. At last, however, because they planned to use sorcery to win the final race they decided to do what the women wanted. The Payupkis also agreed.

So the final race began. Spider Grandmother now changed herself into a spider and sat on the girl runner's ear. Her opponent was the swiftest runner the Tikuvis had in their village. At first the two of them ran together, neither one ahead of the other. After a while the girl took the lead. Spider Grandmother urged her on, saying, "Run, daughter, run!" Suddenly there was a whirring sound and a white dove flew past them. Spider Grandmother said, "You see what they are doing. They have transformed the boy into a bird." The dove was far ahead when they reached the turning place. So Spider Grandmother called out to a hawk that was sitting on a tall rock. The hawk swooped down and struck the dove to the ground. The girl runner passed him. But soon there was the whirring sound again, and once more the dove was in the lead. Again Spider Grandmother called on the hawk to strike, and once again it swooped down and knocked the dove to the ground. The girl took the lead, but when they were almost in sight of the finishing place the dove passed them for the third time. Again the hawk struck the dove down, and after that it struck once more. At this moment the girl runner ended the race. The people of Payupki applauded her, but the people of Tikuvi were silent.

The men and women of Payupki picked up all their trophies and started home. The women of Tikuvi followed them. They arrived at Payupki. There Spider Grandmother talked to the kikmongwi, saying, "Well, now, the village of Tikuvi has fared badly. But the women of Payupki whom we won in the betting are not prizes of war. Instruct all the men that they are to leave the women alone. We do not yet know how things will go. Perhaps in time they will become wives to Payupki men. But now they are not to be molested. Find places for them to live in the village, and treat them well."

The kikmongwi said, "Yes, that is the way it will be." The Tikuvi women were found places to live. Each family in Payupki took one or two of them, and treated them well.

As for the men of Tikuvi, they were bitter. They went to their village and brooded. They had to take care of the things their wives and daughters formerly had done for them. They had to grind corn and make bread and make pottery, and they did these things badly. They became more and more angry about what had happened to them. At last they decided to make war on Payupki and reclaim their women. They said, "We will destroy that village and drive the Payupkis out. We will not leave anything standing in that place. We will take everything of value from Payupki. We will leave nothing but stones there." They prepared. They made arrows. They planned how they would attack.

Spider Grandmother heard about what was going on in Tikuvi. She called all the Payupki people to their kiva. She said: "In Tikuvi they are preparing for war. They are smoothing their arrows and bending their juniper saplings to make bows. They will attack at night when Payupki is sleeping. They plan to kill and destroy, and to drive us into the wilderness. In Tikuvi there are many warriors, while in Payupki there are few. Therefore there is only one thing that we can do. We must leave this village and go to another place.

I can guide you to a place of safety where the corn will grow and where there is running water."

The people of Payupki discussed the matter. They agreed that they must leave. So Spider Grandmother continued: "We have no time to waste. You men, tomorrow in the gray dawn before the sunrise, go out and round up all the horses and cattle and place them in corrals. The women will prepare food for you to carry. Drive the cattle to the east wall of the mesa. Descend there and cross the low ground. Go up the slope to the south until you are again on the plateau, and travel eastward until you reach the canyon. Go down, follow the canyon to the end. There you will find water for the cattle. After that, go east again. The women will follow you."

So early in the morning the men and boys brought all the cattle in from where they were grazing. Then, taking the food the women had prepared for them, they drove the cattle, among which there were a few horses, eastward to the eastern rim of the mesa. They descended there to lower ground, and proceeded somewhat to the south until they had climbed again to the mesa top, after which they went toward the east. They passed not far from the village of Awatovi and came to the canyon that is now called Keams Canyon. They drove the cattle to the far end of the canyon and there, as Spider Grandmother had told them, they found water. After resting a while they went again to high ground and travelled eastward.

Back in Payupki the women prepared to follow the men. They took what food they could carry, some of their clothes and only a few pots. Their grinding stones they left behind because they were too heavy. They carried everything on their backs with the aid of straps braced against their foreheads. Spider Grandmother said, "It will be a long and hard journey. With loads such as these we shall never arrive at our destination. Therefore something more must be left behind." She brought out a large storage jar and set it down. She said to the women, "Place all your jewelry and ornaments in this jar. We shall bury it safely, and someday we may be able to retrieve it." So one at a time the women came and dropped their most valuable possessions into the jar—turquoise and coral beads and all manner of such things. Spider Grandmother sealed the jar and buried it in the ground. Then the women left Payupki following the route that the men had taken. They stopped and rested whenever they had to, and thus they travelled more slowly than the men. But some time later they found the men and the cattle near a spring a considerable distance to the east. From that point on, the Payupkis, along with the women who had come from Tikuvi, travelled together.

Now, after they had been going eastward for a number of days they saw a lone stranger driving a herd of cattle. When he was close enough he called out to the Payupkis, but they did not understand his language. He came closer and spoke to the chief, but the chief also did not understand him. Spider Grandmother said, "This man is a Castilla. He wants to know who we are and where we are going. I will talk to him." So Spider Grandmother, who spoke all languages, talked with the Castilla. After that she said to the chief, "The Castilla wants to gamble with us, his cattle against ours."

"No," the chief said, "that is not possible. These cattle are all that we have left."

Spider Grandmother said, "Unless we gamble with him he will not let us pass."

"Can he prevent us?" the chief asked.

"Yes," Spider Grandmother said. "He carries a magic killing stick called a musket."

"Very well," the chief said. "If we have no choice, we will do it. What is the contest?"

The Castilla pointed to a dead tree standing in the distance. Spider Grandmother said, "It is this way: He will shoot his weapon at the tree. One of our men will shoot at the tree. Whoever splits the tree wins the contest."

The chief called to a man who was known as the strongest bowman among them. He said, "You will shoot for us. May your arrow fly straight and hard so that we do not lose our cattle."

The Castilla tried first. He raised his magic killing stick and pointed it at the dead tree. There was a loud noise and black smoke came out of the stick. The bark splintered, but the tree remained as it was.

Now it was the turn of the Payupki bowman. Spider Grandmother asked the chief to call for the best medicine man among them, and the chief did so. Spider Grandmother instructed the medicine man what to do. As the bowman placed his arrow against the string, the medicine man called out, "Place your arrow in the bow." Instantly a dark cloud began to form in the sky. As the bowman drew back his bowstring the medicine man said, "The bow is bent." When he said this the storm cloud grew larger. As the bowman released the arrow the medicine man said, "The arrow flies." There was an earsplitting clap of thunder, and a bolt of lightning came down from the sky. The dead tree glowed as though it were on fire, then it fell in many pieces.

The people went to where the tree had stood. They saw the arrow sticking in a fragment of wood. The Payupki chief said, "Well, now, the thing is done. We did not want it, but the Castilla insisted. So it has come to this. He must give us his cattle."

The Castilla turned his eyes away, thinking that he would not pay the bet. But he looked again at the shattered tree and at the dark storm cloud still hovering overhead. At last he said, "Take my cattle. You have won. Never before did I see such a thing."

So the Payupkis took his cattle and added them to their own, and after that they continued their way eastward. They travelled many days, and in time they came to a place of clear running water. It was Muyovi, the Rio Grande. Spider Grandmother said, "Here along this river you can make a good life. Build your villages and live on." Then Spider Grandmother left them and returned to the west. Some of the Payupkis moved on farther and settled in the land of the Zunis, but most of them built their houses close by the place where they had last seen Gogyeng Sowuhti. Their village is still there and it is now called San Felipe. Sometimes the Payupki women urged that an expedition be sent back to Payupki for the turquoise and coral things that were buried by Spider Grandmother, but it was never done.

As for Tikuvi, the men of that village were surprised and perplexed when their war party went to Payupki and found it deserted. They lived on in Tikuvi for a while, but because there were no women in their village they soon began to drift away to other places on the mesa. Some went to Shongopovi, some to Shipaulovi, and some to Mishongnovi. In this way Tikuvi was abandoned, and it also became a ruin.

XV The Castillas at Oraibi

THE FIRST CASTILLAS TO MAKE CONTACT with Oraibi were soldiers, and in the beginning there was often fighting. Hopis and Castillas were killed in those times, but after a while they accepted one another in peace. The Castilla priests came and asked permission to build a house in Oraibi and live there. So the Oraibi authorities gave them a place north of the village. The priests got busy at once building their house, and they had much help from the Hopis. Then they started building their church or assembly house, and they made the Hopis help them put up the walls and gather the building materials. The Hopis hauled stone from different places on the mesa, but they had to travel a great distance to get the great timbers that the priests wanted. They went all the way to Kisiwu, about sixty-five miles northeast of Oraibi, to cut trees and drag the logs back. Sometimes they went a hundred miles south to Neuva-tikyao, the San Francisco Mountains, to get timber. After a while the priests received some oxen from Santa Fe, and these animals were used to drag the timber. That is the way the big trees were brought to Oraibi. In some places the stone floor of the mesa was worn into deep grooves from the dragging of so many logs.

When the church was finished it had a tall tower. In it were large bells that had been sent from Santa Fe. The Hopis had thought that when they were through building the church the Castillas would be happy and leave the people alone. But that was not the way it turned out. There was always something more that the Castillas wanted. They demanded one thing and another. They rang the tower bells to call all the Oraibis to the church. Then they said all the people should have their heads washed. If someone asked, "Why do you want me to wash my head?" they said, "No, you do not have to do it, we will do it for you. It will bring you good fortune. It will protect you." So quite a few of the people said, "Very well, we will let them do it." Then the priests poured water on the heads of the Oraibis and baptized them. They said, "Now you are Christians." People said, "No, we are still Hopis." The priests said, "Well, you are Hopi Christians now. You are not savages any more." Many Oraibis did not like that, and after having their heads washed they stayed away from the church.

Now that the church was done the priests spent a lot of time on other things, but they still had work they wanted the people to do. Sometimes they paid the Hopis in woolen clothes sent from Santa Fe. But sometimes they did not pay anything. They said that because the people had been baptized they should not expect any rewards for their work. They said the work was for the God of all the people. And there were quite a few Hopis who were afraid of the Castillas and did whatever they told them to do. One thing the priests were always doing was to send people long distances to bring water. There were good springs around Oraibi, but the priests did not like that water. They kept sending expeditions west to Moencopi to get water from there. The Oraibis protested against going so far, but the Castillas said the water from Moencopi was holy and could be used in the church rituals. The men who were sent on these water expeditions did not want to go to Moencopi any more. After a while they would start out toward the west as though they were going to Moencopi, but then they would turn off the trail and go to some other springs not so far away. They would rest there about two days and then come back. The priests thought the water was all right until they found out it didn't come from Moencopi, and then they were angry about it and tried to punish people. Later on they got the Oraibis to build some cisterns for them. After that there weren't so many water expeditions to Moencopi.

It went on this way, and all the time the Castillas were intruding into everything in the village. They demanded that the Hopis attend the church meetings every Sunday. They tried to stop the ceremonies in the kivas, and told the people they must not have any more kachina dances. Some of the things they saw in the dances made them very angry. The Koyamsi kachinas jumped around and played pranks which the priests said were indecent and should not be seen by anybody. But they didn't like anything about the kachinas. They said kachinas were devils working against God. So whenever they could they prevented the kachina dances. The old people kept the ceremonies going in the kivas, but it was very difficult because the priests would often force their way in and disrupt the rituals.

The Castillas demanded food offerings constantly, and many families had to give up a share of their corn, squash and melons. By this time the priests had a lot of sheep that had been sent to them from Santa Fe. They made the Oraibis build large stone corrals for them. The Hopis had a few sheep, the Castillas had many. The people became discouraged about the way life was going. They did not plant as much as in the old days, and some of them neglected their fields. They were tired of the heavy work they had to do for the Castillas. They were tired of hearing the priests say that the kachinas were something bad. And they grew angry when they discovered that the Castillas were taking Hopi women into their house and abusing them. Talking together in the kivas at night they said, "Something must be done. We cannot go on living this way."

From time to time groups of people from the Muyovi villages near Santa Fe arrived in Hopi country, looking for a place to live where they would not be harassed by the Castillas. There were Acomas, Lagunas, Payupkis and others. Some of them made villages on Antelope Mesa. Some settled on Black Mesa not far from Oraibi and Shongopovi. From these people the Oraibis heard reports of how their eastern cousins were faring. They heard that some of the Pueblo villages had resisted the Castillas and were severely punished.

The old men talked together in the kivas, saying, "These

Castillas think we are their slaves. They tell us, 'Do this,' or 'Do that.' What they don't want us to do, they say, 'Stop it.' They wish to bring our ceremonies to an end. Things are very bad with us. Because we listened to the Castillas and stopped our kachina dances the rain is diminishing year by year and our corn dries up in the fields. Because we are abandoning the Hopi Way, the land Masauwu gave us is becoming a withered woman. If we are to live we must have rain. Let us not neglect the kachinas any longer."

So they repaired their kachina costumes and painted their masks afresh. They held kachina dances in the plaza. They resumed their ceremonies in the kivas. They made pahos and placed them at the shrines as in the old days. The priests did not like it. They threatened people. They went to the old men and argued with them. They appeared at the kachina dances and tried to stop them. They took the prayer feathers away from the shrines.

And now the Hopis sent emissaries to Muyovi to find out what was going on in the villages there. Among them were representatives of Oraibi, Shongopovi, Koechaptevela and Awatovi. They found the people of Acoma, Laguna, Zuni and the other Rio Grande villages in distress. They heard that a Tewa named Popay, from the village of Santa Clara, was trying to organize a rebellion against the Castillas. Popay was then in the northern village of Taos, and the Hopis followed him there. They told him the Hopis, like the people closer to Santa Fe, could no longer tolerate the Castillas. They were ready to join in a rebellion. It was arranged that on a certain day all the villages would attack the Castillas. Every village was given a string with a number of knots in it. Every day one knot was to be untied. The last knot in the string represented the day of the rebellion. The Hopi emissaries received their string, which they carried home with them, untying a knot each day as they travelled. They reached Awatovi and informed the chief of that village. They informed the chief of Koechaptevela, then the chief of Shongopovi, and finally the chief of Oraibi. Thus all the villages received the news.

Each morning in the chief's kiva at Oraibi a knot was untied. When at last only one knot remained, the Hopis knew that the next day they would strike at the Castillas. Now, in the Rio Grande villages someone had revealed the conspiracy to the Castillas, and because of this the rebellion was launched several days earlier than had been planned. On August 10, 1680, the Eastern Pueblos, led by Popay, rose up and attacked the Castillas. On a certain rock in that country there are marks showing that the Pueblos had many losses, but that more than five hundred Castillas were slain. The Pueblo warriors drove the Castillas out of Santa Fe and back into Mexico.

On the morning that the last knot was untied in Oraibi, the Hopis did not yet know of what had happened in the eastern villages. As they prepared, they believed that the Zunis, the Acomas, and Tewas and the others were doing likewise. It happened that some of the priests of the Oraibi mission had gone south for supplies. Only two remained at the church, along with some Indian assistants and a few soldiers. The Oraibi leaders met in the chief's kiva.

The village chief said, "Well, now, today it will be taken care of."

The kalatakmongwi, or warrior chief, said, "Yes, now it must be done. Who will take the lead?"

The Badger Clan chief said, "We Badger people will take the lead."

The Badger Clan warriors painted their chests and legs and put on kachina masks. Then they took their weapons and went to the house of the priests. They struck the door with their bows and called for the priests to come out. When one priest perceived that a crowd was outside, he opened the door just a crack and told the people to go away. But the Badger Clan warriors pushed the door open and forced their way in. They seized the two priests who were inside, along with several Indian church assistants, dragged them outside and threw them on the ground. There they quickly killed them all by cutting their throats. Other warriors broke into the place where the Castilla soldiers stayed. The soldiers tried to fight back but they were so few that they were soon beaten to the ground. They were killed in the same manner as the priests. The Oraibi warriors, led by the Badger Clan men, dragged the corpses by their legs to a place outside the village and threw them into a gulch. After that they rolled stones into the gulch to cover the bodies.

What went on at Oraibi was also going on at Awatovi, Koechaptevela and Shongopovi. Any Castilla priests who were in those villages were killed. People went through the mission buildings to collect all the food that was stored in them, most of which the Hopis themselves had provided from their fields. The sheep and cattle in the church corrals were taken and divided among the clans. Then the people began the razing of the church buildings, taking them down stone by stone.

In Oraibi they destroyed the church to its very foundations and scattered the rubble to the four directions. The great beams they had been forced to transport from Kisiwu and the San Francisco Mountains were dragged away and stored for repair of the kivas. The large bells from the church tower were taken out of the village and sealed up in a crypt. The steel lances of the Castilla soldiers were taken by the One Horn Society and put away in a secret place.

At Koechaptevela the church was dismantled in the same way. The bells were buried below the mesa at a place of drifting sand. On top of the mesa a line of stones was laid out to point at the burial place of the bells. For many years after that, old men went to the stone marker and, following the line with their eyes, looked at the valley below to see if the drifting sand still covered the bells. It was also like that at the other villages. In Awatovi the church was torn down and totally destroyed, though some of the smaller buildings were left standing and converted into living quarters.

Now that all this had been done, the people waited, expecting a Castilla army to come and make war on them. They repaired their weapons, made new arrows and buckskin armor, and looked toward the southeast each day for sight of invaders. It was at this time that the people of Koechaptevela moved their village to higher ground to be more secure. At first a few families from Koechaptevela went up the crest of the mesa and built houses at the southern point. Others followed them, and finally the ancient site of Koechaptevela was abandoned. The new village was called Walpi, The Gap. From its western side the people could look down and see the remains of their original Black Mesa settlement.

Though the Castilla armies returned to the Rio Grande and reestablished their control over the Eastern Pueblo villages, they did not come back to Hopi country for many years.

XVI The Arrival of the Tewas

Somewhere, somewhere
Far away, Sibopay.
What was I at Sibopay
When I was born?
Where did I come from?
Where am I going?
What am I?
That is what I was asking
At Sibopay.

We emerged
From the First Mother somewhere.
That was Sibopay.
We went to Oga'akeneh.
We went to Shokugeh.
We went to Tewageh*.
That is what our fathers told us.

*Most frequently spelled and pronounced Tsewageh, though sometimes the name is given as *Chekwadeh.*

THE TEWA PEOPLE SAY they did not emerge from the sipapuni, through which the Hopis came from the Lower World. The Tewas say, "We emerged from our mother, the first mother, somewhere." That is the meaning of Sibopay, the place of the beginning. From

Sibopay they went to Oga'akeneh, a great body of water. They crossed over the great water and arrived at Shokugeh, meaning Slippery Point. There they remained for many years. Then, in time, they travelled again until they reached the Rio Grande, which the Hopis call Muyovi, and there they settled again. Thus the Tewa villages of Tesuque, Pojoaque, Nambe and Tewageh came into being where once was only wilderness.

Other peoples as well came roaming through this river valley, and often the Tewas had to fight to protect their crops and their families from the enemy. They had to fight the raiding Utes, Kiowas and Comanches, and sometimes the Tewa women as well as the men fought in defense of their villages.

Now, the Hopis also were being attacked by raiding tribes. Utes, Paiutes, Chemehuevis and Comanches preyed on the villages, killing, stealing women and looting corn from the granaries. The village of Walpi was suffering from the attacks. Because many Hopi men had been killed in the fighting their numbers were reduced, and with each raid the village became weaker. The leaders of the Bear and Snake clans, which were the ruling clans in Walpi, seeing that Walpi's strength was diminishing, decided that they would have to get help from somewhere. After many discussions in the kivas it was agreed that they would invite the Tewas of Tewageh, whose bravery was widely known, to come and settle nearby.

So messengers were sent to Muyovi carrying pahos. They arrived, after a journey of many days, at the river. They went across, and on the east side, close to where San Juan and Santa Clara now stand, they came to Tewageh. They went into a kiva with the Tewageh village chief and the clan chiefs, and they smoked together. At last the Tewa leaders said, "Yes, you are welcome here, cousins. But why have you come?"

The Hopis answered: "Here, we have brought these pahos for you. May you and your people flourish. As for us, Walpi is besieged by Utes, Paiutes, Chemehuevis and Comanches. They steal our food, our women and our children. They come and they come again. You people of Tewageh, we have often heard of your courage. Our people invite you to come and build a new village on our mesa. If you are there the enemy will be discouraged and turn back. We will give you land for your corn. We will live side by side. You will be our brothers."

The Tewas listened. They said, "This is a big thing. We will consider it."

The messengers returned to Walpi. Time passed. The enemy went on raiding, but the Tewas did not come. So messengers again went to Tewageh carrying pahos. They inquired whether the Tewas were going to come. The Tewa leaders said, "It is a big thing. We are still discussing it."

So the messengers returned to Walpi and reported what they had been told. More time passed. Every morning when the Walpi people arose they looked out on the valleys around them, wondering, "Will the enemy come today? Will they come tomorrow?" The raids against the village continued, and Walpi was suffering. So messengers were sent to Tewageh a third time. They asked, "Are our Tewa brothers going to come?"

The Tewas answered, "You ask our people to leave their homes and fields. Now, that is not a small thing. We do not know yet if we can do it. Nevertheless, we have not forgotten the matter."

A season passed, but the Tewas did not arrive at Walpi. The clan chiefs said, "We must try once more. This time if they put us off we will surely know that they are not coming." And so Walpi's messengers went to Tewageh for the fourth time. They said, "Brothers, we are not strong enough to turn back the Utes, the Paiutes and the Comanches. If the Tewas do not come, how shall we survive?"

This time the Tewageh chief answered, "Yes, we have thought about the matter. Any Tewa warriors that wish to go to your country with their families may do so." And he had it announced throughout the village that whoever wanted to make the journey to Walpi should make himself ready. First one man and then another said, "Yes, I will go."

The chief said, "You people who have chosen to go, assemble in the plaza." Many persons went to the plaza, and others were going toward that place. Seeing that so many people were willing to leave the village, the chief said, "Well, now, that is enough. Half of the village may go, but half must remain here so that we can defend ourselves and keep Tewageh living."

There were somewhat more than eight hundred people in Tewageh at that time, and those who were going to Walpi numbered about four hundred. They gathered all the belongings they could carry. The women prepared food for the journey and the men saw to their weapons. When everything was ready they went out of Tewageh toward the west.

It was a long march. When they came to the place now known as Canoncito they halted and made a temporary camp there. After resting for some days they continued on and in time arrived at Awpimpaw, meaning Duck Spring, not far from the present town of Grants. Here again they remained for some time to give the women and children a rest, and then they went on to Bopaw, Reed Spring, near where the town of Ganado stands today. They made a temporary camp there and remained for a while. After that they continued their journey, going west and north, at last reaching Kwalalata, the Place of the Bubbling Water, somewhat to the northeast of Walpi. That was their fourth stop, and now they built a temporary village on top of the mesa and awaited word from Walpi about where their permanent village would be.

Much time had elapsed since the Hopis had sent their first messenger asking for help. Now the Tewas had arrived. But the people of Walpi were not certain about things. They began to wonder if they had done well to invite the Tewas. The Tewas sent a message to Walpi to announce their presence. Even so, the Walpi people did not invite them to come any closer. They said among themselves, "How do we know the Tewas will protect us?" The Walpi clan chiefs delayed. They decided to test the Tewas. So they sent a message to the Utes, challenging them to come and attack Walpi. The Utes replied, "Yes, do not be impatient. We shall come." Then the Walpi chiefs sent a message to the Tewas telling them to be prepared because the enemy was on the way.

The leader of the Tewas who had made the journey was a man named Agayoping,* meaning Star Butte. He ordered the men to prepare for battle. They made arrows and repaired their lances, bows and shields. Agayoping said, "Four times they sent for us. Now that we have come, who knows whether we are welcome? They are testing us. They want to know if we have courageous hearts. Very well. Let us meet the enemy."

Agayoping sent scouts to the north. On the third night the scouts saw many campfires in the direction of Tokonave, Black

*The narrator indicated later that the Tewa leader's name more likely was *Agayotsay*, meaning Yellow Star.

Mountain. On the fourth day they saw the enemy approaching on horseback. They saw flashes of light reflecting from the mirrors worn by the riders and thus knew them to be Utes. They returned to report what they had seen, saying, "Brothers, the Utes come riding in great numbers."

The Tewas painted their faces. Agayoping said: "Let us do what we know so well how to do. The Utes, they are many, though there are few of us. The Hopis are not sure of our courage. Very well. We are Tewas. To be a Tewa is to have a brave heart. To die is not much, for all men die. To have a brave heart, that is to be remembered. Today we will fight the Utes. We will split into two parties. One party will meet the Utes in front. The other will go behind them."

A messenger came from Walpi announcing that the enemy were approaching.

Agayoping answered, "Yes, we are ready."

The women were told to remain at the encampment, and some men were assigned to stay with them in case the Utes should reach the ridge. The rest of the men went south to the gap, which is a break in the mesa top. From there they could see the Utes riding along Wepo Wash. They saw them dismount and go down into the wash to plan their attack.

Agayoping said, "Let us begin. Let one party approach the enemy from the front, the other from the rear. Strike them hard. Shoot first at their war counsellor. When you have killed him, another will take his place. Seek him out, strike him from his horse. A war party without a counsellor is like a body without a head."

The Tewas descended from the mesa top. Arriving below, they broke into two parties, one going one way, one another. The first party advanced standing up so the Utes could see them. The second went crawling unseen among the rocks. The Utes also were advancing. The battle began. The best Tewa bowmen were in front. They rained arrows on the Utes. The Utes charged their horses toward the Tewas. Dust rose from the ground and hung like a cloud around the battle. An arrow struck the counsellor of the Utes, and he fell from his horse. Another man took his place but an arrow struck him also. The Utes fell back, regrouped and charged again. But now the Tewas' second war party attacked from the rear and the Utes turned aside to avoid being caught in a trap. They retreated to a place still

called Tukchu, Meat Point, because it was there they had stacked
their pounded meat before the attack. At Tukchu the Utes tried
to hold their ground, shooting arrows from behind their meat bags.
But once again they were caught between two Tewa war parties,
and so they had to retreat from that position. They tried to hold
their ground at still another place—now called Kwokwadeh, meaning Stone Wall—and this was their last stand. After that the Utes
had no place to stop, and the Tewas drove them through the valley,
which was now marked with the scattered corpses of men and horses.
The Utes signalled the Tewas to end the fighting, but the Tewas
would not stop. At last only three Ute warriors were left. One of
them tied a cloth on the end of his bow and waved it.

Agayoping called his men to a halt, and went forward alone
toward the survivors, one of whom spoke, saying, "Who are you
people? For we see that you are not Hopis."

Agayoping answered, "No, we are Tewas."

The Ute said, "My cousin, we did not know it was you. We
thought we were fighting the men of Walpi."

Agayoping said, "That is the way it is. Though you came to
make war against Walpi it is we, the Tewas, that you have had to
deal with. My cousin, why do you bring trouble to Walpi? The
people are peaceful. They do not make war on you. Why do you
attack them?"

The Ute replied, "We came only to get corn and other supplies."

Agayoping said, "The Utes have made a mistake, as you have
discovered. We are not going back to Tewageh. We are going to
stay up there on the mesa. If your war parties come again we shall
be waiting."

The Ute said, "No, we shall not return. Here is my bow as a
pledge. It is not made of wood, which rots. It is made of elkhorn
and will last forever. The peace between us will be as lasting as my
bow. Our war parties shall not come again."

Agayoping accepted the bow. He said, "I have heard your
pledge. Return to your people and tell them how it was when the
Utes met the Tewas."

The three Ute survivors of the battle departed. The Tewas
took the scalps of their slain enemies, and searched for the bodies of

four Utes who had shown great bravery. When they found them they cut open the breasts and removed the hearts from the bodies, and at a certain spot they buried the hearts in a common grave. Agayoping said, "Here the hearts of courageous men are buried. Let us remember this place and see what grows from the earth here in time to come." Years later a juniper tree grew out of the grave, and it is still there. The Tewas call the place Pintoy, and the Hopis call it Anangtana, both names meaning the Place of Hearts.

The Tewa warriors gathered the weapons of their dead enemies and returned to the gap. There they found the village chief and the clan chiefs of Walpi waiting for them.

Agayoping said, "It is done. The Utes are dead, all except three who returned to their homes. As you see, many Tewa warriors died also. But now it is finished. Here are the scalps. Take them."

"No, keep the scalps," the Walpi chiefs said. "They are yours. You have won them in battle. We are glad, cousins. Now your people can come and build their village over there on the north side of the gap."

Agayoping answered, "Well, now, Walpi is south of the gap, but you want us to settle north of the gap. How could we protect you? The enemy could be in Walpi before we would know of their coming. No, if we are to defend Walpi we must sit like a watchdog in front of your house."

The Walpi chiefs discussed the matter, and at last they said to Agayoping, "Very well, let it be that way. Build your village on the point of land just south of the gap."

Agayoping replied, "You ask us to live on a very small portion of earth. It is not enough. Our numbers are few now, but in time we will have more people. We must have room to grow."

So the chiefs of Walpi conferred again, and after much discussion they walked southward to a spot very close to their own village. They said, "Now, this is where you will build your houses. As for your fields, look out there to the east. You see Eagle Point. Look to the west of that. You see Big Water Point. The land between these points is reserved to the Tewa people. And may the Tewa people flourish."

"Very well," the Tewas said. "It is agreed."

Then the Bear Clan chief said, "Our lives are now bound together. So if a Tewa man wants a wife, let him seek her among the Hopis. If a Hopi man wants a wife, let him come to the Tewas to ask for her. In this way the bonds between us will grow strong."

But Agayoping replied, "It is too soon to accept such a thing. We do not yet know if we can live together forever. We came trustingly because you sent for us. The first time your messengers arrived at Tewageh we said among ourselves, 'Let us wait a little. Perhaps Walpi will change its mind.' When your messengers came a second time we said, 'it seems that Walpi still wants us.' After the third time we said, 'Yes, Walpi has made up its mind about this thing, and if they ask us a fourth time, why then we will go.' Your messengers came a fourth time, and so half the village of Tewageh left everything behind and came on the long journey. We rested there at Kwalalata, thinking, 'Soon the Walpis will come and greet us and give us a place to build.' But you let us remain out there on the ridge. You did not trust us. You did not invite us to come closer. Instead, you said to each other, 'What kind of people are those Tewas? How do we know that we want them here?' So you decided to test us and sent for the Utes. We kept our trust. We went out and drove the Utes away. But in the battle we lost many young men. So now we are thinking, what will the future bring? We do not know. For the moment let us speak no more of letting our sons and daughters marry each other. What if something should happen and you should ask us to go away? If we were to have sons, daughters and grandchildren living in Walpi it would be hard for us to leave. So let us wait. We will see how things go, and later on we can speak of this matter again."

The Walpi chiefs said, "Very well, let it be that way. Another time we will speak of it again. Meanwhile we will grow closer and learn to speak each other's language."

Agayoping said, "Well, now, that is something else." He took some roasted corn from a small bag tied to his waist and handed it to the Walpi chiefs. He asked them to chew the corn without swallowing it. This they did. Then he said, "Put what you have chewed into my hand." This they did also, whereupon Agayoping placed the chewed corn in his mouth and swallowed it.

The Walpi people said, "What does it mean that you swallow what we have chewed?"

Agayoping replied, "It means that the language that comes from your mouths, we shall swallow it and make it our own. We too shall speak Hopi."

The Walpi chiefs said, "Good. Let it be that way. Now you chew corn for us and we shall swallow it."

Agayoping and some of his men put corn in their mouths and chewed. While doing this they dug a hole in the ground, and when it was as deep as the length of an arm they spat the corn into it and covered it with earth and stamped it down.

The Walpi people asked, "What does it mean that you bury the chewed corn?"

Agayoping replied, "It means that what comes out of our mouths will never be in the mouths of the Hopis. We cannot share our language with you. It would give you power over us. You would learn the secrets of our kiva ceremonies, and you would forget where we come from and that we are Tewas. Our two villages must be able to communicate, and therefore we shall speak Hopi, but the Hopis shall never speak Tewa."

After saying that, Agayoping placed a large piece of petrified wood at the spot where the chewed corn was buried. He said, "Let this stone mark our boundary. We shall build our houses up to this mark and not beyond."

So all the Tewas moved from the place where they had been camping and built their new village. At the center, around the plaza, the Bear Clan built its houses. The Sun Clan built a little beyond, and beyond that the Cloud Clan built. The Corn Clan constructed its houses facing the eastern approach to the village. Around the edges the other clans built—the Tobacco Clan, the Green Corn Clan, the Parrot Clan, the Cottonwood Clan, the Stick Clan and the Shell Clan. The people of Walpi referred to the new village as T'hano, or simply Hano, believing that the Tewas were T'hano Toh'wa—that is to say, T'hano People like those living in Taos and Isleta. But the Tewas rejected this name and called their settlement Tewa Village.

Agayoping instructed that the record of the battle against the Utes be engraved on stone, and it was done. A picture of a Ute shield was cut into the cliffs near the gap, and next to it were cut many small marks to show how many Utes died in the fighting.

True to their word, the Utes did not come back again to attack Walpi. But there were Apaches to contend with, and the Tewas many times went out to turn them back. Another record on the cliffs near the gap shows how many Apaches died in a certain attack against Walpi.

In time other Tewas came from the villages on the Rio Grande to live in Tewa Village. They brought with them the sacred masks and ritual objects that Agayoping's people had left behind in Tewageh.

As the years went by there came to be trust between Tewa Village and Walpi, and the sons of one married with the daughters of the other. Now the villages are closely related. But Agayoping's prophecy proved true, because while all the Tewas living in Tewa Village speak the Hopi language, the Hopis have never mastered Tewa.

XVII The Destruction of Awatovi

FAR BACK IN TIME WHEN MOST OF THE CLANS were just coming in and settling at Shongopovi and Koechaptevela, Awatovi was already standing on Antelope Mesa. The paramount clan in Awatovi, from which the village took its name, was the Bow Clan. But there were others there as well, many of them having come from the Pueblo villages in the region of the Rio Grande, and a few from Palatkwapi in the south. Among them were the Tobacco, Rabbit, Blue Horn, Sun, Sand, Parrot, Bluebird, Strap and Corn clans. Awatovi was a large village, having, it is said, four rows of multistoried houses and, between them, three wide courts that stretched to the very point of the mesa. Also in the village were numerous kivas and shrines.

When the Castillas arrived in Hopi country they came from Zuni in the southeast. The first Hopi villages they saw were on Antelope Mesa, among which were, in addition to Awatovi, Chak pahu, Akokavi, Moesiptanga and Kawaika. The horses on which the Castillas rode were somewhat frightening, and people did not go out to meet the strangers. The Castillas arrived at Kawaika. They were all in armor except for one priest who rode with them. They announced that all the villages now belonged to the Castillas, but the Kawaikas did not accept them. So the soldiers drove the people out and set on fire everything that would burn. After that they arrived at Awatovi a little farther to the south. Now, the Hopis had been waiting a long time for the special Bahana who was supposed to come in fulfillment of a prophecy, bringing harmony, virtue and good fortune. At first they wondered if these Bahanas were the ones they were expecting. But when they saw the smoke going up from the Kawaika and heard what had happened there they said, "No, these cannot be the ones we are waiting for." Across the trail into the village they drew a line with cornmeal, which meant that the strangers were not to enter. Nevertheless the Castillas crossed the line as though it were not there. Some of the Awatovi men prepared to fight, but others said, "Wait. Let us have patience. They may go away." And it was decided that they would not fight. Instead, they gave presents to the Castillas. When at last the Castillas continued their journey to the other Hopi villages to the west, some Awatovi men went with them as guides, and people said, "Yes, perhaps now we are done with them."

But after some years the Castillas returned among the Hopis bringing missionaries with them. The missionaries began to wash heads in Awatovi. They would take children to a certain place and put water on their heads, and then they would ask men and women to come and have the same thing done to them. If a man asked, "Why should I do this?" the priests said, "It will bring you good fortune." And so some people let the priests do what they wanted. Then the priests began to build their church just north of the village, and they persuaded those with the washed heads, who had suddenly become Christians, to gather the building materials. The people went to a mountainous place in the east to cut the trees, and hauled them back and shaped them into beams for the church. They hauled and cut stones for the walls. The priests taught them Christian songs and washed more heads whenever they could. In this way a great many of the Awatovi people became Christians. The ones who were converted moved close to the new church and so the village was separated into two parts.

But as time went on the missionaries began to oppress the village. They were cruel. They turned brother against brother and clan against clan. They tried to stop ancient ceremonies. They went into the kivas and seized the altars and other paraphernalia they found there. If they found pahos at the shrines they took them away and burned them. They even destroyed some of the shrines, using the stones in the church walls. Seeing that they could do anything they wanted, they began taking girls and young women into the church compound and making them bed partners. They did not even hesitate to take a woman away from her husband. Thus one young man who had an attractive wife was sent to the Colorado River, a distance of many days, to bring back a vessel of holy water. When he was gone the missionaries took his wife into their house. The young man never returned, having been killed by Paiutes during his journey. It is said that other men of Awatovi who urged people to have nothing to do with the Catholics simply disappeared and were buried in a crypt beneath one of the church buildings.

By the time that the uprising against the Castillas occurred, half the people of Awatovi had been baptized. These people did not follow the old ways. They ridiculed the old ceremonies and abandoned the beliefs of their ancestors. They no longer felt responsible to their parents, their uncles, their ceremonial fathers, their clans, or the traditions that had been handed down from ancient times. Chaos came to Awatovi, and there were hard feelings everywhere.

After the Pueblo revolt against the Castillas, and after the great church in Awatovi had been torn down, the people of that village went on living. The ceremonies and the kachina dances took place once more when they were supposed to, but there was no harmony among the people as there had been before the coming of the Castillas. Outwardly Awatovi was following the Hopi Way, but there was dissension and anger, and sometimes one man would not speak to another of the same clan.

Then one day twenty summers after the destruction of the church the missionaries came again. Some wanted to turn them away before they entered the village, but those who had been baptized welcomed them. So the priests were in Awatovi again, and they began to rebuild the church on its old walls. They spoke also of returning to the other villages, and when this news was carried to Oraibi, Walpi and Shongopovi the people there were disturbed. They said, "Is this the way it is going to be? Will it now begin all over again?"

The return of the priests to Awatovi emboldened many persons in their disrespect for the old ways, and lawless people caused violence in the streets. Sometimes there was fighting in the plazas. Kwitamuh, or hooligans, roamed through Awatovi looking for excitement. They taunted and threatened the old, and pursued young girls. Out of fear of these kwitamuh, people stayed close to their homes and no woman went to the spring alone.

The kikmongwi of Awatovi saw how things were going. He said to his wife, "Well, now, it has gone so far that nothing can be saved." He went to Walpi, which was on the heights above the old village of Koechaptevela. He found the kikmongwi of Walpi and the two men descended into a kiva. They smoked for a while, and at last the kikmongwi of Walpi said, "You are welcome here. But I see something is troubling you. Why have you come?"

The chief of Awatovi answered, "Yes, my heart is troubled. Evil is in my village. The people are killing each other. The girls are being raped by the kwitamuh. It is worse now than it was before. What is happening must somehow come to an end. What shall I do?"

The Walpi chief said, "Speak what is in your mind."

"Now it is like the Lower World," the chief of Awatovi went on. "The Castilla sorcerers are among us again, washing heads and causing the people to turn against one another. They are causing the young to despise the old and to ridicule the ceremonies and the kachinas. Awatovi has broken into pieces. It has lived out its life."

The kikmongwi of Walpi said, "What do you want of me, my brother?"

The kikmongwi of Awatovi answered, "It is a big thing I am going to ask you to do. I want you to send your warriors to bring Awatovi to an end."

The Walpi chief closed his eyes and reflected silently. Then he replied, "Yes, I see how bad things are in Awatovi. But what does that have to do with my people here? We are people of peace. Our young men know how to be courageous. If the Paiutes attack us we fight. If the Apaches attack us we fight. But we do this only in self-defense. That is our way. We cannot make war on another Hopi village. That would be an evil thing. No, I cannot agree to it. What you are asking is too much."

So the kikmongwi of Awatovi departed from Walpi and went

westward. He passed Mishongnovi, Shipaulovi and Shongopovi and arrived at Oraibi. There he found the kikmongwi of the village at his house, and the two men went into a kiva. After they smoked for a while the Oraibi chief said, "You have had a long journey. What has brought you so far?"

The Awatovi chief said, "You are my friend. I need your help. My people are out of control. The Castilla missionaries have returned and they are preparing to stay forever. The village is in chaos. The young insult the old, women are raped, the shrines are desecrated. The ceremonies are ridiculed, contempt is shown for the kachinas, and the kwitamuh run wild. Thus the evil that followed us from the Lower World has torn us into pieces. Awatovi must be destroyed. Its people must be scattered and its houses razed to the ground."

The chief of Oraibi said, "You are speaking of your children. Does one destroy one's own children?"

"It is a hard thing," the Awatovi chief answered. "But my people have already been broken by evil. All that is left is for Awatovi to be swept clean, for it is a pollution on the earth. Awatovi's fate will be my own fate, I will not avoid it. You, my brother, help me now. Let Oraibi's warriors accomplish the destruction. When Awatovi's life comes to an end, take the young women. They will help Oraibi to increase. Take our fields and gardens and grow your corn there."

The Oraibi chief considered everything. At last he said, "Yes, I will help you. We shall provide warriors, but it is too big a thing for us alone. Other villages should be involved."

The Awatovi chief said, "In Walpi the kikmongwi has already told me, 'No, it is not our way.' "

The Oraibi chief said, "Well, let us go there together and see what can be done."

So they went to Walpi, but this time they did not visit the kikmongwi but the kalatakmongwi, the war chief, who was of the Reed Clan. After they smoked, the Awatovi chief told his story. Then the chief of Oraibi said, "We in Oraibi are going to help our brother from Awatovi. He says, 'Take the young women, take the land.' We will take the young women, they will help Oraibi grow. But the land is too far from us. We will leave it to the Walpis."

"Yes," the kalatakmongwi said, "since Oraibi is going, my Reed Clan warriors will go also." He went to the kikmongwi of the village and said, "The chiefs of Oraibi and Awatovi have asked my help in this affair. Oraibi says, 'Take all the land, it is too far from us.' Very well, I have agreed to it."

The kikmongwi replied, "This is not a good thing. It is not the Hopi Way. I do not want a part in it. I will not tell the people, 'Go over there to Awatovi and kill your cousins.' However, you are the war chief. If this is the way you want it to be I cannot stop you."

The kalatakmongwi said, "Yes, I have decided. We shall join in this affair with the Oraibis."

So the war chief of Walpi and the village chiefs of Oraibi and Awatovi made their arrangements. The war parties would have four days to prepare, and on the fourth night they were to arrive at a certain rocky place near Awatovi and remain in hiding until the people were asleep. When it was time to attack, the Awatovi chief would signal them from the entrance to the village. After they were through talking, the kikmongwis returned to their homes. The warriors of Oraibi and Walpi prepared themselves. They rehearsed what they would do. They made new arrows and repaired their bows.

Now, in Awatovi there was a priest of the One Horn society who had three sons—Sakieva, the eldest, Momo'a, the second, and Pakushkasha, the youngest. On the night of the same day that the Awatovi chief was in Walpi a gang of kwitamuh from the converted portion of the village caught the three brothers, killed them, rubbed their bodies with cornmeal, and threw them into a fire in a corn-roasting pit. The cornmeal on the bodies meant, "What is planted here shall not grow," signifying that the old way of life was doomed to perish.

The next day was the first of the four before the attack. And on that morning the One Horn priest whose three sons had been murdered wandered through the streets of Awatovi in his ceremonial dress. He carried a rattle in his hand and he sang as he walked. His song was about his dead sons:

> "Aha-ay-hay! Aha-ay-hay!
> Ha-oh, ha-o-oh!

Ha-oh, ha-ah-oh!
Listen to me! Listen to me!
Someone said that we must not live here!
Someone said that we must go away!
That is what Sakieva says from the pit of fire!
That is what Pakushkasha says from the pit of fire!
That is what Momo'a says from the pit of fire!
Soon everyone will be crying and mourning!
Let us all go and leave no one behind!
That is what Sakieva says!
Ai-ai-ah!"

The One Horn priest was in the streets again the next day singing out the message from his dead sons. He was there again on the third day and the fourth. Though there were many who made

jokes about his song, there were also those who understood. Among
those who understood the message were the leaders of the Tobacco
and Bow clans. In the darkness of night the Tobacco Clan people
took their Two Horn altar and their other sacred objects from the
kivas and carried them out of Awatovi. These things they sealed
up in a cave on the mesa somewhere north of Walpi. The Tobacco
Clan chief led his people to the narrow place between cliffs that is
now called Keams Canyon, and there he kept them in hiding. The
Bow Clan chief also led some of his people away in secrecy.

On the fourth day the war party from Oraibi set out. Down
below Walpi they were met by the Reed Clan warriors. The combined forces then continued on to Antelope Mesa in the east, finally
stopping at a place not far from Awatovi where they could not easily
be seen. Darkness came. Some of the men slept, while others ad-
justed their weapons. In the early hours of the morning they went
forward silently to the outskirts of the village.

The village was quiet. The people were asleep in the houses
and the kivas. The war parties wanted to go on, but their leaders
restrained them, saying, "No, we must wait for the kikmongwi to give
the signal." After a while they saw a light. It was a firebrand held
by the Awatovi chief. He waved the firebrand several times. Then
he threw it down, went along the trail into the village, and descended into a kiva.

The war chiefs gave their final instructions, and the war parties
went forward. Passing through the stone gateway of the village
they went at once to the kivas and pulled out the ladders so that
none who were down below could escape. Then they ran through
Awatovi, dragging people from the houses and setting fire to everything that would burn. Some of the Oraibis and Walpis stood at
the edge of the village and killed all who tried to get away. A few
tried to go down the gullies at the mesa's edge, but they were
either killed by arrows or seized and thrown over the cliff. Meanwhile, the Walpi and Oraibi warriors who guarded the kivas threw
burning wood and cedar bark through the openings. They found
strings of chili peppers hanging in the houses and threw them into
the kivas also. The burning chilies caused stinging fumes to mix
with the smoke of the burning wood. At first there were shouts,
screaming and coughing down below, but soon there was only

silence. Having killed all who were in the kivas, the war parties renewed their search for those who might still be hiding in the houses.
Young women and children were herded to a place outside the
village. Any men and old women who were found were killed.
When daylight came, Awatovi was already a smoking ruin, but the
war parties stayed on a while longer to devastate the village further.

After that they began marching their captives to the west. Now,
there were some Awatovi men who had found hiding places during
the night. When the war parties departed, the Awatovis who had
escaped death hunted through the ruins and found some bows,
arrows and lances. Though they were not numerous, they followed
the Oraibis, the Walpis and their captives, and near the place now
called Five Houses they attacked, trying to free the women and
children. But they were overcome by the Walpis and Oraibis, and
all of them were killed. Their heads were cut off and thrown in a
pile. The place where this happened was thenceforth called Maskoteu, meaning Skull Mound.

The war parties continued on, until they came to the wash
just a little to the east of where the village of Polacca now stands.
They rested there. They began to argue. The Oraibis had been
promised all the young women taken from Awatovi, and for this
reason they had relinquished Awatovi's lands to the Reed Clan people of Walpi. But the Walpis also had taken many female prisoners.
The Oraibis said to them, "It was agreed with the chief of Awatovi
that all the women would belong to us. The women you have,
therefore, belong to Oraibi."

The Walpi men said, "No, we never agreed to such a thing."

The Oraibi men answered, "Yes, that is the way it was. The
women are ours."

The Walpis were angry. They said, "We also were at Awatovi.
We did our part. Before we give you the women we captured we
will kill them." And without discussing it any further, they turned
on their prisoners, killed a number of them and cut their heads off.

The Oraibis said, "Why do you stop? We will help you." And
they also killed a number of women and decapitated them. They
threw the bodies into a gully. This spot is now known as Mastoeki,
Place of Dead Persons.

The war parties then proceeded to a place near Wepo Wash, on the west side of Walpi, where they stopped once again and killed still more prisoners. This place came to be known as Masjumo, Dead Person Hill. After this they did not kill any more of the captives, but divided the ones that remained. Oraibi took the largest share. Six women and girls and six boys were taken to Walpi, and six of each sex were sent as a present to the village of Mishongnovi.

On the following day some members of the war parties from Oraibi and Walpi returned to Awatovi to make certain that there was no person still alive in the village, and to destroy whatever remained standing upright. They found smoke still rising from the kivas and houses, but except for their own voices, Awatovi was a dead and silent place.

Now, when the chief of Awatovi went back into the village after giving the signal at the gateway, he had no thought of living on. He entered a kiva knowing that he would not again come out of that place. His purpose was to obliterate Awatovi and all the evil that was in it. And as he was the chief and the father of the people, he chose to die with the others.

Some of the people of the Tobacco and Bow clans who had left before the attack found sanctuary with the Navajos. The Tobacco Clan chief and those who had hidden with him in the canyon, and some of the Bow Clan as well, some time later went to Walpi and were received there because they had the Two Horn Ceremony and the Wuwuchim Ceremony and knew all the songs that were in the Laguna or Kawaika language. In time these ceremonies spread to the other villages, but the Two Horn altar remained in Walpi.

The captives taken at Awatovi were warned that they must never return to the place of the destruction. It is said that some of the women brought to Oraibi were not well treated and were considered as outcasts and prostitutes. Others were taken as wives by Walpi, Mishongnovi and Oraibi men, and it is from them that many of the Bow and Tobacco Clan people in these villages are descended.

The fertile fields in which the Awatovis grew their corn were taken under the control of the Walpi Reed Clan, but the Reed Clan people today avoid those fields and leave them to the Navajos.

The Hopis do not like to speak of what happened at Awatovi. They feel it is something not to be remembered.

XVIII The Navajo Attack on Oraibi

WHEN THE RAIDING TRIBES FIRST CAME to Hopi country they were mostly Utes, Paiutes, Comanches and Chemehuevis, but after the Navajos arrived it was they who worried the Hopis most. Sometimes the Navajos attacked one Hopi village, sometimes another. What they wanted was sheep and corn. If they could get the sheep from the corrals and the corn from the fields without fighting for these things they would do so. But if they could not get these things in this manner they fought their way into the villages, where they took not only food but women and children as well. They made the women their wives and raised the children as Navajos.

In Oraibi one night the men were in the kivas preparing for a ceremony. While they were occupied in this way, Gogyeng Sowuhti, Spider Grandmother, entered the chief's kiva. The chief said, "You are welcome, come in and sit with us."

But Spider Grandmother said, "No, I only want to tell you that the Navajos are coming from the north."

The men said, "Well, then, let us prepare to drive them away."

Spider Grandmother answered, "This time it will not be easy. The last time the Navajos came there were not many of them. It was only a small food-gathering party. This time it is different. They are travelling in great numbers."

They thanked Spider Grandmother for warning them. Then the chief sent scouts to a place on the mesa from which they could see toward the north. When they returned they said, "In the distance are many campfires. The Navajos are plentiful. That is the way it looks to us."

The kalatakmongwi, or war chief, said, "We must know more about how strong they are. Who will go to the edge of their camp as scouts?"

The leader of the Coyote Clan said, "That is for us. We shall send a scouting party." So four men of the Coyote Clan painted their faces and fastened their foxskins behind them, after which they went off toward the Navajo encampment.

The other Oraibi men prepared for battle. They painted their faces. They wrapped tough buckskin around them as armor, tested their bows and made more arrows. As the first gray light of day came, the Oraibis took their weapons and went to a place on the mesa some distance to the north. There they spread out in a long line across the mesa, some taking cover behind rocks while others remained in the open.

The Coyote scouts had not yet returned, but soon the Oraibis saw dust rising from the flat ground to the north, and they knew from this that the Navajos were riding horses. The war chief said: "Well, this is the way it will be. They will be on horses and we will be on the ground. They will charge forward to see who is waiting for them here, then they will go back. The next time they will come closer. When they are in range of your arrows, shoot. The Navajos are good horsemen. They will slide down to the sides of their horses to avoid your arrows. If you cannot hit the riders, shoot at their horses. Let us hold fast here like a wall to protect Oraibi. Do not let them break through. If it seems they will overrun our position, fall back and form another wall."

So they waited, and after a while they saw their scouts coming back, running swiftly. The scouts arrived. They said, "The Navajos are all mounted. They are very numerous. Their bodies are painted. They carry battle-axes, lances and bows. We hid among the rocks, but a Navajo warrior saw us and came forward, saying, 'Do not try to defend the whole mesa. There are too many of us. Defend the village instead.' We said, 'Why do you tell us this?' He replied, 'I am Nuvakwahu, Snow Eagle. I was born a Hopi in Oraibi, but I was stolen by the Navajos when I was small. Now I also am a Navajo.' He departed quickly and we did not see him again."

The war chief said, "How can we trust him? He is a Navajo. We will meet them here. If they break through at this place we can fall back. If they break through at the village we have no place to go."

Soon they could see the Navajos coming on their horses, their war chief in front. He wore a red cloth cape and had feathers in his hair. His horse's mane and tail were decorated with strips of colored cloth. Seeing the long line of Hopis stretching almost from one cliff to another, the Navajos stopped. They held a council. Then a small party headed by the war chief galloped directly at the Hopi line, drew up suddenly, shot some arrows, and wheeled and galloped back again. After that the main party attacked. Like the Hopis, they were now stretched out abreast, and they charged at the whole Hopi line at once. But they had not perceived that many Oraibis were concealed among the rocks. As the Navajos approached, the hidden men stood up and began shooting. Some of the Navajos were hit, and the others turned back and formed for a new attack.

The second time they charged, the Navajos struck at one end of the Hopi line. They had shields, but the Hopi arrows came at them from different directions and a good many Navajos were hit during this charge and some horses were also wounded. So they pulled back and held a council about what to do next. On their third charge they began their attack at one end of the Hopi line, then swerved and rode parallel to the line shooting arrows and striking with their battle-axes and lances as they went. This time a number of Hopis were hurt, but because of their buckskin armor only a few were killed. If a Navajo fell from his horse, the Hopis would run forward and kill him and capture the horse if they could. Although the Hopi line was pressed back in several places, the Navajos did not break through except for a few men who, seeing that they were almost alone, quickly rode back to join their companions.

After numerous charges the Navajos began to withdraw toward the north to disengage from the fighting, but the Hopis now went forward and pursued them. So the Navajos made one more charge, after that withdrawing again. There were many Navajo bodies and some dead horses scattered over the battlefield by this time, so the Hopis decided to continue their attack. They followed the Navajos to the north and to the east. At a certain place the Navajos began to go down from the mesa to the valley below. As the Hopis approached this spot a Navajo warrior rode toward them waving his bow. He called out, speaking Hopi, "I am Nuvakwahu. I was born in Oraibi. I was captured by the Navajos when I was a child. Now I am a Navajo, but I am still your brother. Therefore listen to what I am saying. Do not pursue any farther, for a large Navajo war party is arriving in the valley." After saying this he wheeled his horse and rode down from the mesa.

The Hopis stopped to discuss the situation. They saw that they also had lost many warriors. Dead or dying Oraibis were lying here and there mixed with the Navajo dead. But their war chief advised them to continue the pursuit in the hope of destroying the whole Navajo expedition. So they followed the Navajos down into the valley. There they found the enemy drawn up in a formation waiting for them. At this place they fought again, first one side attacking, then the other, and when the sun began to go down both the Navajos and the Hopis withdrew to safe camping sites for the night.

Before the sun rose the next morning the Oraibis were positioned for the battle. They sent Coyote Clan scouts out to discover what the Navajos were doing. The scouts returned a little after sunrise, saying, "The Navajos are greatly reinforced. The new war party that has arrived is twice the size of the first one, and every man has a horse."

The main force of the Navajos appeared on high ground ahead of them and began its attack. This time the Navajos broke through the center of the Hopis, breaking them into two parts. Many Hopis fell at this place. Those who survived returned to the top of the mesa with the Navajos in pursuit. They were able to pause for a while at a place called Shonoteka and defend themselves among the rocks. But the Navajos were now coming up to the mesa top at different places, and so the Hopis returned to Oraibi to avoid being cut off.

When they arrived at the edge of the village, Navajo raiders were already there driving sheep out of the stone corrals and loading horses with corn taken from outlying houses. The Hopis drove these raiders away. But they found that the people had already abandoned half the village and had blockaded themselves on the other side. They had piled up heavy logs and beams at the entrance to the plaza to prevent the Navajos from coming through.

Hopi stragglers kept arriving at the village until a large part of the Hopi war party was there, excepting those who had been killed or so badly wounded that they could not return. From the housetops the people could see bands of Navajos gathering not far away and preparing to attack the village. Oraibi women and children, carrying all the corn they could and driving a few sheep ahead of them, were leaving the village by back trails to find places of safety. At the same time, the Navajos were again in the other part of the village, and soon they were able to tear down the barricade at the plaza. Oraibi warriors shot arrows at the invaders from the housetops, but everything looked very hopeless at this time, particularly when scouts came in to report that a very large Navajo party that had been resting just to the north was now riding toward the village.

Only a few Hopis were on the highest rooftops from which the advance of the Navajos could be seen. And only these few were spectators to what happened at that moment to turn the battle. What they saw were the warrior gods, Pokanghoya and Polongahoya, going out toward the enemy with lightning arrows in their bows. The warrior gods shot their lightning arrows. There was a great flash and a sound like thunder, and many Navajos who had been riding a moment before were now lying scattered and lifeless on the battlefield. The warrior gods released two more arrows, and again there was a flash and a thunderous noise, and now Navajo bodies were lying everywhere. The main Navajo war party turned away and rode northward. Seeing this, the raiders looting in Oraibi abandoned the stocks of corn they had piled up, mounted their horses and departed.

When the Navajos were gone the Oraibis went out to gather their wounded and dead. They went all the way to the place where the Navajos had turned them back. They first collected their wounded, many of whom died before reaching the village. Then they brought in their dead and stripped the Navajo corpses of weapons and silver ornaments. Among the Navajo dead they found the body of Nuvakwahu, Snow Eagle, who twice had warned them not to fight in the open. They brought his body back to Oraibi and made inquiries throughout the village to see if any of his relatives could be found. An old woman of the Bear Clan claimed him, saying he was her grandson. She cut his hair in Hopi style and washed the Navajo war paint from his body, and he was buried as a Hopi.

The Navajos had to abandon many of their dead, but some they were able to take away with them on horses.

This is how Oraibi was saved by the warrior gods, Pokanghoya and Polongahoya, when it was almost overcome. The village had lost many brave fighters, and so its strength was diminished. The people wondered how it would be if the Navajos returned. But the Navajos did not come back to Oraibi because of their experience with the warrior gods. Whenever they carried out raids thereafter they went to other villages instead.

XIX The Founding of Moencopi

ABOUT FIFTY MILES WEST OF ORAIBI on the trail to the salt-gathering place made by Pokanghoya and Polongahoya is Moencopi, meaning Running Water. At this spot there are good springs and running streams. In ancient times many migrations passed through this place. After the people came into the Upper World the Bear Clan, the Bluebird Clan, the Spider Clan and other related clans journeyed through Moencopi and left their marks there on the rocks and cliffs. Some of them built small villages nearby, the ruins of which can yet be seen. A number of the clans went northward from here, eventually travelling east and south again to gather on the lands given to the Hopis by Masauwu.

Because their clans had left marks on the rocks around Moencopi, many families in Oraibi claimed the land there and planted fields of squash and corn. But there was not yet a village at that place, only a few summer houses, nothing more. And so, it is said by the old people, whenever it was time for planting or weeding or harvesting at Moencopi, the men and boys of Oraibi would go there in work parties. They would gather at the edge of Oraibi in the darkness before dawn and run all the way to their fields around Moencopi. They would work in their fields, and after that they would

return to Oraibi the same day, running all the way, arriving as darkness fell over the land.

This is the way it went on for generations, with no permanent
settlement at Moencopi, until a certain Oraibi man named Tuvi, of
the Short Corn Clan, built a winter house at Moencopi and remained
there all year around. Why Tuvi departed from Oraibi is not remembered. But it is said that he was involved in some kind of dissension
in the village and left it to be at peace. It is said that his original
name was something else, but that after he went to Moencopi people
referred to him as Tuvi, meaning the outcast, or the rejected one.
After he built his house near the running water, other people of his
clan followed him, and then came people of different clans. Thus
the village of Moencopi was created and grew larger. The men who
lived there no longer had to run all the way from Oraibi to work
their fields. Because Moencopi was an offspring of Oraibi it was considered a Bear Clan village. But the first kikmongwi of Moencopi
was a woman of the Short Corn Clan, who held her position in
trust for the Bear Clan. Her name was Mashilaywi. After Mashilaywi
there were other Short Corn Clan chiefs.

Mormon missionaries came to Moencopi during the time of
Tuvi, and because there were Paiutes nearby, Tuvi asked the Mormons to establish a mission there, believing that this would make
the settlement more secure. The Mormons set up a mission
and built their first school. Then they built a new school at a place
called Koechaktewa, meaning White Sand. Later the white people
changed the name of this place, calling it Tuba City in honor of
Tuvi.

The first government school for the Hopis was at Keams Canyon, about eighty miles east of Moencopi. Then the government took
over an old trading post at Blue Canyon and made a school out of
it. It was much closer to Moencopi than Keams Canyon. Some of the
Moencopi children went to school there, at the trading post, but
some were in the Mormon school. In 1904 the government told the
Mormons to leave Tuba City. It offered them four hundred fifty
dollars for their mission building and their orchards. But the Mormons said it was not enough. They refused to take the four hundred
fifty dollars and went away empty-handed. Not many Hopis became
Mormons, only the young ones who had been in the mission school,

and most of them went back to their own religion after the Mormons were gone.

Moencopi and Tuba City were surrounded by Navajos after a while. The Navajos took over large sections of traditional Hopi land. Once the Hopis had many sheep and horses all around Moencopi. But the Navajos pressed in. They crowded the Hopis and sometimes fought with them over the livestock. Hopis once had many sheep in Coal Canyon, but today there aren't many left. The Navajos control much of the land between Moencopi and Oraibi. But as the marks on the rocks show, it was the Hopis who claimed the land in the beginning.

XX The Breakup of Oraibi

THE WHITE MEN SAID, "Things must change here in the villages. You must follow the new ways."

The Hopis answered, "You people, we do not tell you to live one way or another. Why do you tell us to do this and to do that?"

Nevertheless the Bahanas kept coming and telling the people what to do. Soldiers came and chased children through the villages. When they caught them they took them to the government school in Keams Canyon. Missionary men told the people: "The kachinas are only ordinary persons wearing masks. Masks cannot bring rain. If you need rain pray to Jesus Christ. He owns all the rain."

Some of the Hopis said: "Well, now, the whites are smothering us with advice. Do they understand the old ceremonies? No. Do they know anything about the history of our people? No. They say to us, 'Old men, your ways are foolish. Send your children to the school and let them learn something, then they will not be ignorant.' First they give the Navajos our grazing lands, then they take the children and teach them not to be Hopis. This is a bad thing they are doing."

There were some other Hopis who said: "Yes, we truly know the secrets passed on to us by the ancients. But the Bahanas also know something. Look at their windmills. Did we ever know how to make windmills to bring water up from the ground? This is really something. When all the clans were arriving in the old days, our chiefs said to them, 'What can you do?' And they replied, 'Why, we have the knowledge of how to bring rain.' Our chiefs said, 'Yes, it is a good thing to know how to bring rain. Therefore come into the village and live with us.' Now the white man comes. He has the knowledge of windmills. Do we say, 'Yes, that is a good thing, for the windmill brings water from under the ground'? No. Some of us complain. The white man makes glass to cover the house windows. It keeps out the cold winter winds. Is that bad? Let us look at the matter this way. If our Zuni brothers offer us a new kachina do we say, 'No, we don't want it'? If our Kawaika brothers offer us a ceremonial song do we say, 'No, we already have ceremonial songs'? If the white man has something good for us, let us accept it. If it is something not good, let us refuse it."

Some people thought one way, some another. In all the villages there was constant argument about these things. In Oraibi at that time the chief was Loloma of the Bear Clan. It seemed to him that the Hopis must live fraternally with the Bahanas. He said, "Let us send some of our children to the white man's school. They will bring something back to us." Those who opposed Loloma said, "This is a bad thing. We want to initiate our children into the societies. We want to teach them the right way of living. How will we do it when they are away eating the white man's food, wearing the white man's clothing, and learning ways that are not good for us?"

Because he was determined to make peace with the Bahanas, Loloma decided to allow some missionaries to enter Oraibi, and he chose the Mennonites. This made feelings in the village more bitter. Those who were hostile to the white man's ways said to Loloma, "Have you already forgotten what happened when the Catholic missionaries were here? This is a bad thing you are doing."

The chief of the Mennonites who came to Oraibi was a German named Voth. It is said he was chosen because he was a firm and stubborn man who would know how to discipline the Hopis. He did not have any respect for the Hopi Way. If he was not wanted at a ceremony, nevertheless he intruded himself, even pushing into kivas where sacred rites were taking place. Once when he was stopped by a Two Horn priest from entering a certain place, Voth kicked this person out of his way and entered. Everything he saw and heard he wrote down in a little book, and he took photographs of priests and kachina dancers doing various things. Afterwards he went away and revealed to the whites all the secrets he had learned. At a certain museum in the east he displayed numerous sacred things he had either taken of his own will or induced certain Oraibi people to part with. Some of this paraphernalia had come from the kivas, and there were many Hopis who had never seen these things with their own eyes. What Voth was doing made many persons bitter. They said to Loloma, "Well, now, this is what you have accomplished by inviting the Mennonites into the village. You are leading the people to disaster."

By this time Oraibi was split into two factions. Those who supported Loloma called themselves Friendlies, because they wanted to get along with the Bahanas. Those who were against Loloma called themselves Hostiles. Loloma was an old man, and when he died Tawakwaptewa, also of the Bear Clan, became chief. Tawakwaptewa, like Loloma, thought the people should send their children to the school at Keams Canyon. But black soldiers had to come and get the children of the Hostiles. Bitterness made the Friendlies and Hostiles grow further apart.

The leader of the Hostiles was Yukioma, chief of the Fire Clan. He said: "The Fire Clan is the defender of the Hopi Way. It was we who received fire from Masauwu in the Lower World. We were the first to emerge from the sipapuni. We are thus the firstborn among the Hopis. Because we are the custodians of the Hopi tradition and the firstborn, we are as an elder brother to the clans. We were not properly acknowledged when we arrived at Oraibi. For this reason evil times have come to the people. Some who do not know what they are doing want to live the white man's life. As for the Fire Clan, however, it will remain faithful. The village is divided. Therefore you others who do not want to live as Hopis, it is time for you to go away. Go out into the wilderness. Migrate again and build yourselves another village somewhere."

The Hostiles were greatly outnumbered by the Friendlies in Oraibi, and so Yukioma sent messages to the Fire and Water Coyote clans in Shongopovi and Shipaulovi asking for reinforcements. He also asked the help of other clans. Hostiles began arriving in Oraibi, whereupon Tawakwaptewa asked for Friendlies to come from Moencopi and elsewhere. Tensions rose in the village. Leaders of one group would not speak to leaders of the other. It came time for the Niman ceremonies, but the Hostiles and the Friendlies would not join one another in the kivas. The Friendlies had one Niman Dance and on another day the Hostiles had their own Niman Dance. The fraternal societies of Oraibi were broken down the middle and could not function any more.

Seeing how things were going, Tawakwaptewa said, "It has been bad in Oraibi ever since the Fire Clan arrived and demanded to lead us. Now it is worse. It cannot go on this way. The Fire Clan and its affiliated clans can return to the cliffs at Kalewistima from where they came. Let them take with them all the others who want to make trouble."

He went to Yukioma. He said: "Well, now, we have come to the end. Take all your people from Oraibi. We can no longer live together. The village is dying. You say you came from Kalewistima*. Very well. Return to Kalewistima and leave us in peace."

Yukioma replied angrily, "No, on the contrary, it is you and your people who will leave."

Four times Tawakwaptewa ordered the Hostiles to leave, and each time Yukioma declared that it was the Bear Clan and its followers that would have to go. Fighting broke out in the plaza, and it was ended only when some Bahanas intervened.

Tawakwaptewa decided that he could not delay any longer. Early on the morning of September 8, 1906, the Friendlies went from house to house rounding up all the Hostiles and taking them to a flat, rocky place just a little north of the village. The Friendlies said, "This is not your home any longer. Go back to Kalewistima."

But the Hostiles remained where they were, and Yukioma said, "No, we are not going anywhere. It is we who will stay and you who will go." He said, "Whatever is to be done, it will be done here where we stand. If you try to kill us we will try to kill you."

There was anger between them but there was also sorrow, for families were broken up, half on one side and half on the other. A man standing among the Friendlies could look across the flat place and see his brother among the Hostiles. And a father among the Hostiles could see his sons and daughters among the Friendlies.

The Bahanas in Oraibi kept urging the people not to fight.

*Most of the Hopi villages use the pronunciation *Kawestima*.

And at last Yukioma said: "Yes, I agree. Let no blood be spilled over this. Who is to go and who is to stay, we will decide it by a contest. You Bear Clan people and all who want Oraibi to go the white man's way, stand on one side. My people will stand on the other side. There will be no weapons. We will have a pushing contest. If you force us back, we will go away. If we force you back, you will go away and we shall remain in Oraibi."

There were other men still coming from the village to join either the Friendlies or the Hostiles and some of them carried clubs or guns. Both Yukioma and Tawakwaptewa said to these men, "No, take those weapons away." And the missionary Voth who was always in the middle of everything, he went back and forth urging the people not to fight each other. Yukioma scratched a line on the ground, then more lines until there were four parallel lines in all, and he said to Tawakwaptewa, "Well, now, let us come and stand here face to face, you and I, and our men will stand behind us. If you are pressed back across the last line on your side, or I am pressed back across the last line on my side, the matter will be decided."

And so Yukioma and Tawakwaptewa came to the center and stood facing each other. Yukioma placed his hands on Tawakwaptewa's chest, and Tawakwaptewa placed his hands on Yukioma's chest. The Hostiles crowded close behind Yukioma, and the Friendlies crowded behind Tawakwaptewa. The pushing began. The two chiefs were squeezed tightly in the center of the struggle. The breath was pressed out of them. Both of them had a hard time. Yukioma was not a heavy man, and sometimes he was squeezed upward so that his head was higher than the others. Tawakwaptewa also suffered by being at the center of the contest. The densely packed crowd moved forward then backward, a little bit this way, a little bit that way. There was grunting and shouting. But the Friendlies were more numerous, and slowly the Hostiles were pressed back. At last Yukioma called out, "Stop! It is done! I have been pushed across the last line!"

The struggle came to an end. Yukioma and his people went to their houses for their belongings. They took corn and other food, blankets, clothing, pots, whatever they could carry. Then they left Oraibi and camped out on the open mesa. When darkness fell, their fires could be seen from the highest rooftops in the village. Some of

Yukioma's people slept, but many sat up all night discussing what they would do next. When morning came the exiles left their camping place and moved on.

Two men who remained in Oraibi, Charles Addington and Robert Silena, carved a record of the pushing contest in the rock where the bitter contest had taken place. They marked a line on the rock and around it some mnemonics. And they inscribed the pledge of Yukioma: *Well it have to be this way now that when you pass me over this line it will be done. Sept 8th, 1906.*

So ancient Oraibi, which began its life as Ojaivi, had been broken into two parts. Those who supported Tawakwaptewa of the Bear Clan remained behind and tried to live on as though the village were still whole. Those who went with Yukioma included all of the Fire Clan and the Water Coyote Clan, and also people of the Sand, Bluebird, Spider, Badger and Reed clans. Some people of these latter clans also remained in the village, so that the clans were split. Families were broken up and the main ritual societies—the Wuwuchim, the Two Horn, the One Horn and the Flute—were shattered. When the Fire and Water Coyote people departed they left all their ceremonial objects behind in the kivas. The Oraibi people destroyed these things or allowed them to become lost. After this, initiations of the young could not be carried out properly, and certain old rituals could no longer be performed. Later on some Oraibis tried to revive some of the ceremonies but they were unable to do it.

Almost half the houses in the village were empty, and some people who remained there no longer found Oraibi a good place to live. They began to move down from the top of the mesa to a place called Kikoechmovi, meaning Old Ruins, on the eastern side, and in time Kikoechmovi became a village. Kikoechmovi, also known as New Oraibi, is alive today, but Oraibi is a dying village whose houses are mostly in ruins, with only a few families living on.

When the Hostiles departed from Oraibi they camped first at one place and then another. They came in time to the ruins of the old village of Huckovi and they stayed there for a while. It was expected by many that the Fire and Water Coyote clans would return to Kalewistima in the north, where the ancient cliff villages of Keet Seel and Betatakin are still standing. But instead of going to that place they travelled a little farther to the north and west, and there, only a few miles from Oraibi, they settled and made a new village which they called Hotevilla. The soldiers of the white men did not leave them alone. They demanded that the Hotevilla people send their children to the government school. But Hotevilla said, "No, we don't want it." So the soldiers arrested many of the men of Hotevilla and put them in prison. The village had a hard time then, and the people were hungry that winter because they did not have enough corn. But later on things became a little better.

Among the people who had left Oraibi with Yukioma were some who chose to leave only because they did not want to be separated from their clans or their families. And there were some who were not ready to make up their minds about whether Yukioma or Tawakwaptewa was right. After living at Hotevilla for a year they tried to return to Oraibi, but the Oraibis did not want them. So they built a village of their own just a little east of Hotevilla and named it Bakavi.

In Hotevilla the Fire and Water Coyote clans tried to carry on their ceremonies, but because the important ritual societies had been broken up, and also because most of the sacred paraphernalia had been left behind in Oraibi, they were greatly handicapped. Other villages say that the people of Hotevilla no longer have the knowledge of performing rituals properly. But in Hotevilla it is said that the Fire and Water Coyote clans took the knowledge with them and left the Oraibis without anything.

One of the important objects retained by the Fire Clan was the piece of the stone tablet made in ancient days at the edge of the sipapuni when the people had just emerged from the Lower World. Old men in the other villages acknowledge that this portion of the tablet still exists. The Fire Clan people are still waiting for a certain Bahana to appear with the other part of the tablet, as was prophesied in the beginning. But much time has passed and the Bahana has not come, and there are some who say it is already too late and he will not come at all.

Notes on Narrators and Informants

THE MYTHS, LEGENDS AND RECOLLECTIONS on which this book is based were gathered during three stays at the Hopi Reservation in 1968, 1969 and 1970. The narrations and explanations come from persons of different clans in the First Mesa villages of Walpi, Hano (Tewa Village) and Polacca, the Second Mesa village of Shongopovi, the Third Mesa villages of Oraibi and New Oraibi, and the western village of Moencopi. Narrators and informants were mainly older people, six of whom were in their seventies.

In general there is a Hopi reticence about discussing matters that could be considered ritual secrets or religion-oriented traditions. There is some distrust about the uses to which such information in the hands of outsiders might be put, and also a desire not to be identified within the community as a person who has, in effect, "given away" some of the Hopi heritage. (Hopi leaders were disconcerted and resentful early in this century when writings of certain ethnologists "revealed" some ritualistic matters that they felt should not have been brought into public view.) There is a feeling that the substance of Hopi beliefs is actually a kind of tangible cultural property that should not be dispensed to other people. Rather than seeing the takeover of various Hopi ceremonials by the neighboring Navajos as an implied compliment, some Hopis place it on a level with cattle stealing. There is also recognition that some information belongs to particular clans or fraternal societies and cannot be given out except by a qualified authority. In several instances informants hesitated to discuss certain matters without first consulting a senior member of the clan—an "uncle"—and on a few occasions I was brought together with such a person to get information or a narrative directly. Reticence on these various grounds is exacerbated by divisions in some of the villages between traditionalists and progressives. Traditionalists reflexively avoid anything that might seem to place them in the progressive camp. The villages are small. Little can happen that is not soon widely known, and most individuals are responsive to the strong currents of social pressure. For such reasons many information-gathering sessions with my informants were held outside the villages, frequently at Keams Canyon or Tuba City. Regretfully, a number of informants requested that their names not be mentioned in connection with their contributions. Under the circumstances I thought it best not to identify any except by village. It is my hope that in time all of them will agree to let their names be known.

Informant 1, Hano (Tewa Village)
Informant 2, Moencopi
Informant 3, Moencopi
Informant 4, Walpi
Informant 5, Walpi
Informant 6, Polacca
Informant 7, New Oraibi
Informant 8, Oraibi
Informant 9, Moencopi
Informant 10, Shongopovi
Informant 11, Oraibi

Notes on the Stories

I. The Four Worlds

THIS IS THE BASIC HOPI CREATION MYTH, unique in its details but containing elements shared with the Eastern Pueblos and with the neighboring Navajos. As told in various Hopi kivas, or in different villages, or by members of different clans, the myth has innumerable variations, but its basic outlines are similar in most versions. Descriptions of the first two worlds are not easily come by, and even when encountered they are so brief as to indicate that this portion of the myth is virtually lost. The main narrative begins in the Third or Lower World. The events that take place here and, after the emergence through the sipapuni, up above in the Fourth World are much like the statement of a theme in a symphony. Principles are established and prophecies made which are referred to again and again throughout the later legends and even in the "historic" contemporary narratives. The Hopi fate seems to be projected almost from the beginning. The way of life is sealed, and the endless migrations launched. The search for a Promised Land, aspiration toward a good life, flight from evil, all these elements persist in the subsequent narratives. And so, also, do the themes of dissension, separation and migration. Looking backward from much later events, such as the destruction of Palatkwapi, the massacre at Awatovi, and even the 1906 fragmentation of Oraibi, one sees their origins in the basic conditions and propositions established at the mythological time and place of the origin. The journeys from one underworld to another and finally to the Fourth

World set a pattern of migration and quest that is discernable throughout the whole restless history of the Hopis.

There can be little doubt that what we call Hopi traditions are an
amalgam of myths, legends and histories contributed by different clans
and different tribes that came together, in the end, to become the Hopi
people. The Hopis themselves acknowledge that different stocks have
been absorbed over the years. One Sun Clan member said he had been
told by his elders that his people had been "something like Chemehuevis." The Snake and Horn clans which came from the north, and which
figure importantly in Hopi tradition, are said to have spoken a dialect
related to the Paiute. The concentric movement toward what became the
center of Hopi life brought small wandering groups from all directions,
and with them came different histories, different explanations of life,
and sometimes conflicting cosmogonies. There is still an implicit understanding among the older Hopis that various clans have a particular
claim to certain gods. The Sun Clan, for example, claims the warrior
brothers Pokanghoya and Polongahoya. It also claims Gogyeng Sowuhti,
Spider Grandmother (literally, Spider Old Woman), though people of
the Bear Clan contend she belongs to them. Masauwu is said to belong to
the Fire (Firewood) Clan, and Huruing Wuhti, Hard-Substances Woman
or Sea Lady, to the Water Coyote Clan.

These various deities generally were assimilated without difficulty,
and their contradictions submerged. Huruing Wuhti is somewhat of an
exception. Her role in the creation or emergence remains in conflict
with that of Spider Grandmother. Huruing Wuhti is associated with the
myth that the Hopis came to their present world by a voyage across the
sea rather than through the sipapuni. Hopis have rationalized the con-
tradiction away by calling Huruing Wuhti the Deity of the West (the
direction of the ocean) and Gogyeng Sowuhti the Deity of the East.
They have spent long hours in the kivas discussing this question, and
one philosophical compromise coming out of such discussions is that the
two deities are really the same and represent Mother Earth, or the
Earth Mother, with Tawa, the sun, representing the Father. But the
conflict has never been really resolved—even though one ethnologist
tried to do the impossible by transposing the Huruing Wuhti myth into
the Third World, thus leaving Spider Grandmother unopposed in the
Fourth.

The myth of an arrival by an ocean voyage persists in various clan
traditions. The name of the Water Clan in Hopi is Patkinyamu, literally meaning Dwelling-on-Water (that is, Houseboat) Clan. The belief
is that before these people arrived at ancient Palatkwapi they reached
the present world after a long water crossing. Generally speaking, the
sipapuni story is centered in Walpi (which is modern Koechaptevela) on
First Mesa, while the water crossing story is heard most frequently in

Oraibi, on Third Mesa, but there are conflicts of view even within these villages. A member of the Coyote Clan in Oraibi stated that in his village the sipapuni story is told to younger children, and that later on they are given the water voyage explanation, which has been reinforced by infiltrating scientific views that Indians arrived in the New World via the Aleutians and the Bering Strait. More Hopis than not accept the version in this collection, and most agree that the location of the sipapuni has long been forgotten. However, some of the Third Mesa clans place the sipapuni in the Grand Canyon near the confluence of the Colorado and Little Colorado rivers, and they stop at this site ceremonially in the course of salt-collecting expeditions. (See the story, "The Lalakon Dance at Shongopovi.")

While the Huruing Wuhti and Gogyeng Wuhti myths have never been made compatible, Spider Grandmother is clearly the long-run victor. She is the first of the deities to appear in person among the people, and she reappears again and again to help villages, clans or individuals through their difficult trials. She is with the people on their migrations, often helping them make decisions on which their fate depends. She counteracts malevolent sorcery, makes impossible tasks possible, and intercedes when enemies or natural disasters threaten. While Huruing Wuhti's character has been lost in generalities or remoteness, Spider Grandmother remains close by, concerned for the people and involved in their affairs. Although she is frequently seen in her spider form, she is above all the human grandmother, wise in her knowledge of the forces of good and evil, tolerant of human foibles and weaknesses, and pliable in the hands of her grandchildren, the young warrior gods Pokanghoya and Polongahoya.

The young warrior gods, like their grandmother, have human qualities with which people can identify. They have a passion for games, particularly nahoydadatsia, a kind of field hockey, and when their help is needed men give them not prayer feathers but a buckskin ball. They are often unpredictable, willful and mischievous, indulging in humor that can be painful to others. They tease Spider Grandmother and play jokes on the villages. But they are nevertheless defenders of the people in times of duress. Time and again they appear with their lightning apparatus or lightning arrows to destroy predatory giants, monsters, Navajos, or Paiutes. (See the story, "Homolovi and the Journey Northward.")

The paramount deity, as the myth explicitly states, is Tawa, the sun. What is meant, Hopi informants state, is the sun spirit or the sun force, conceived as male in its attributes. The sun impregnates the earth, and the earth gives birth to living things. A distinction is made between the sun spirit, the supreme deity, and the sun that the people (with Spider Grandmother's advice and help) put in the sky to provide light and warmth in the Upper World.

Details of how the sun, moon and stars were placed in the sky vary from one account to another. In some accounts, particularly those heard on Third Mesa, Huruing Wuhti is credited with these accomplishments and Spider Grandmother has virtually no role at all. In the version of the myth given here the creation is shared. Tawa creates original life and, learning from trial and error, produces human beings. Spider Grandmother leads the people from one level of creation to another and finally into the Upper World, where she is primarily responsible for making the sun and moon. The warrior brothers, Pokanghoya and Polongahoya, create mountains, bluffs, salt deposits and other terrestrial attributes. And Coyote, almost as an afterthought, places the stars in the sky.

There is also the role of Masauwu, the Spirit of Death who "owns" the Upper World. Beyond giving the people fire, he performs no creative deeds, but he permits them to settle on his land, an act that is crucial to the outcome of the emergence. Though he disappears from the place of the original settlement, he is not far away, and he plays a part in many of the subsequent events. His existence and reality are believed in by many older Hopis today. On some ceremonial occasions he is represented as a kachina, and sparks or fires that are seen moving in the night are thought to be Masauwu in search of a person whom he intends to take away. He is portrayed as wearing a rabbitskin cape and having gruesome features—no hair, burn scars on his skin, and face and cape smeared with fresh blood. His appearance is explained by the story that he was once thrown in the fiery pit in the Land of the Dead (implicit evidence of his evil deeds), from which he managed to escape before being consumed. (See "Maski, the Land of the Dead.") How he came into possession of the Upper World is not quite clear, but it is indicated by some Hopis that Tawa, not knowing what to do with Masauwu after the escape from the fiery pit, simply said, "Well, then, live there in that place."

The importance of the Fire Clan in Hopi tradition relates to its claim of a special relationship with Masauwu. Because of this relationship the Fire People (not yet a clan) are allowed to emerge first from the Lower World, on the understanding that they are assuming the responsibility to lead the others to the final destination. Having once emerged, however, the Fire People are unwilling to carry out the responsibility, whereupon others (later to become the Bear Clan) take the lead. Bear Clan fundamentalists to this day tend to regard the Fire Clan and its affiliates as "troublemakers," and point to the events of 1906 as living evidence. (See the story, "The Breakup of Oraibi.")

Sources: Numerous informants contributed to this section, but primarily informants 1, 2, 5, 7, 10.

II. The Migrations

THE JOURNEYS DESCRIBED in this section represent only a fragment of the migrations, and relate primarily to the Bear Clan and its affiliates—the Strap, Bluebird, Grease Cavity, Gopher, Spider and Spruce clans. Other migrations are described in subsequent chapters. One informant's explanation of how the clans took their names is this:

"When the people first started out [from the sipapuni] they didn't have any clans. That is, they were not known by certain clan names. When they were wandering through the country they came to a dead bear. Some people looked at it and said, 'That bear hasn't been dead very long.' They said. 'Since we're one group of people, why can't we claim to be Bear Clan members? Let's call ourselves the Bear Clan.' They said. 'All right. That's the way we'll distinguish ourselves in case we meet other people. We'll tell them we're Bear Clan.' They said, 'The bear is close to that spruce. While we're here, who wants to become a Spruce Clan?' Someone said, 'I will, with my brothers. We'll become Spruce Clan.' They separated themselves to become Spruce Clan. After the people skinned the bear they began to make straps out of the hide. Years ago they used to use wide straps to carry their bundles. They called that pikoysa. Someone said while making it, 'Say, I want to become Pikoysa Clan.' People said, 'All right. If you distinguish yourself as Pikoysa Clan, go that way.' After they stayed there for a while, bluebirds came down to pick on the bear's fat. One fellow said, 'Say, that's a pretty bird there. I want to become Bluebird Clan.' The people said, 'All right. You want to be Bluebird Clan. Separate yourselves from the others as Bluebird Clan.' The carcass was still there, and after a while some fellow looked inside and saw it was fat. He said, 'Say, it's all so greasy. I better belong to the Grease Cavity Clan.' It's called Wikoshuwoma. While they were staying there, an old gopher made its mound right under the carcass. Somebody saw it and said, 'That's a gopher. I want to be Gopher Clan.' So there are your affiliations—your Bear, your Spruce, your Strap, your Bluebird, [your Spider] and your Gopher." (Informant 1) This description suggests that all the groups were present at the same time. Most informants indicate that the groups came and went on one at a time.

The ethnologist Jesse Fewkes, writing at the turn of the century, stated his conclusion that there were three main streams of migration to the Hopi mesas—from the region of the Little Colorado River in the south and southwest, from the north, and from the Rio Grande Valley in the southeast. Excavations have established Hopi connections in all of those directions. But there are ample evidences that the centripetal journeys, over a long stretch of time, were from just about every direction of the compass. Hopi tradition is explicit in saying that some groups, such as the Snake and Horn clans that came from Tokonave in the north, originated some distance to the west of the Colorado River.

Anthropologists generally agree that the Hopis, like the Eastern Pueblo peoples, are largely descendants of the Anasazis or Basketmakers who inhabited the San Juan Valley for many centuries. From the San Juan Valley they are believed to have migrated to Hopi and Eastern Pueblo regions around the thirteenth century. But the Hopi recollection is that the migrations covered a wide span of time, with some of the clans coming from as far away, possibly, as what is now called Mexico. And so the migrations, for many of the clans if not all, were anything but direct. The Hopi settlements on Black Mesa appear to have been a magnet that drew in people of differing linguistic and cultural stocks.

In connection with the legend that eagles are descended from Hopi children lost during the migrations, an informant said: "When [the ancestral Hopis] went through here they left some of the children, who turned into eagles. That's why the Hopis treat them just like babies. When they are going to go after eagles [for the post-Niman Ceremony sacrifices] they make those cradleboards. They get the eagles when they are small. They usually let someone down [from a cliff ledge] tied to a rope. They catch the eagles and put them in the cradleboards. They bring them in just like that. Then they wash the eagles' heads, just like humans. They give them names and put them on top of their houses. Then they feed them. You're not supposed to just feed them any kind of meat. You're supposed to give them rabbit, fresh meat. When they grow up, about that time there is the Home Dance [Niman Festival]. The kachinas bring the children dolls or bows and arrows, and they give the eagles that [special] doll, the flat one. So when the dance is over, the next day, they wash the eagles' hair again. Then they kill them and remove the feathers. They keep the feathers to make prayer sticks and things like that. They bury the eagles just like humans, and they put flowers on the graves.

"We don't just go out and get eagles from anyplace. We've got to go where it's ours, belongs to our clan. All this, way up to Lee's Ferry, that belongs to the Bear Clan. And then this [other] way, it belongs to the Kachina Clan. My father's people, they have a place over there where they get eagles north of Red Lake. This way it's ours [Bamboo Clan], down this ridge clear back about fifteen miles. It's about May when they go out to catch the eagles. The Home Dances are in July." (Informant 2)

Sources: Informants 1, 2, 7, 8, 10 and others.

III. The Lamehva People

THE SITE OF LAMEHVA, where, according to this Reed Clan myth, the creation of the Reed People took place, is just below Second Mesa (a spur of Black Mesa), a short distance from the extant village of Mishongnovi. The spring from which ancient Lamehva took its name is still in use, and in recent years has been lined with stone. The site of the upper village, Kaiotakwi, is close by, now used as a burial ground. The Corn Rocks are a conspicuous feature of the terrain at this place and are mentioned in other legends and tales.

Koechaptevela, sometimes called Koechapteka, was the original lower-ledge settlement on First (or East) Mesa, also a spur of Black Mesa. When Koechaptevela moved to the mesa top after the Pueblo revolt in 1680, the new settlement was called Walpi, and nowadays the original village is sometimes referred to as Old Walpi. The remains of Koechaptevela can be clearly seen from the heights above.

According to accounts given by most informants, the Bear and Snake clans were the earliest settlers in this village, followed by the combined Horn-Flute Clan, accounting for the fact that the chieftainship has been held, traditionally, by a Snake or Bear Clan member. There is no recollection that a member of the Reed Clan ever held the chieftainship. Nevertheless, the Reed Clan people claim to have been the original settlers in Koechaptevela, and the clan elder claims the right to "pull the chief's ear" if circumstances require it.

Adjacent to the old site of Koechaptevela is a second village ruin called Kisakovi. It is said by some to be an intermediary site to which people moved before going up to Walpi. But others believe that the two old villages were more or less contemporary, and it may be that one of them, or some other nearby site, was in fact originally settled by the people from Lamehva. Reed Clan people in the more westerly Hopi villages tend to regard the Walpi Reed Clan as a separate group with its own distinct history. One notable feature about the myth is the clan's claim to having been created by Spider Grandmother in the very heart of Hopi country, whereas other clans either emerged through the sipapuni or came from some distant place across the water. The Walpi Reed Clan acknowledges but a single migration, and that one of less than a dozen miles from the place of origin.

That some elements of the Reed Clan story are shared with other clans, however, is evident. The account of events in the kiva of the Dog People is very similar in some of the details to an episode in the Snake Clan myth, in which a boy from Tokonave chooses a wife in the kiva of the Snake People. In a good many Hopi tales people transform themselves into animals by putting on animal skins, and become human again by removing the skins. The Reed Clan story involves Dog People, the Snake Clan story (see Chapter VI, "Tokonave: The Snake and Horn People") involves Snake People, and other tales involve Antelope People, Bear People, and so on. The role that Spider Grandmother plays in this story is almost identical to her part in the Snake Clan myth.

This legend, in slightly shorter form and lacking one particular episode included here, appeared originally in Courlander, *People of the Short Blue Corn*, and is used by permission of Harcourt Brace Jovanovich.

Source: Informant 4.

IV. The Destruction of Palatkwapi

V. Homolovi and the Journey Northward

THESE TWO SECTIONS CONSTITUTE the traditional account of the demise of the ancient village of Palatkwapi (sometimes called Palatkwa) and the long journey northward through Homolovi to the place where the Hopis now live. It is primarily the story of the Water, Sand, Tobacco, Rabbit and Sun clans and their affiliated groups. The substance of the account given here was provided by members of the Sun, Tobacco, Spruce and Coyote clans. All the variants heard agreed on the essential story line, though some contained elements not included in others. All agreed that Palatkwapi was destroyed because of its corruption, echoing the theme set in the myth of the flight from the Lower World, and which appears time and again throughout the Hopi literature. Some of the episodes of the flight from Palatkwapi are free-floating motifs that appear now and then in different contexts. One version of the story of the crippled man and the blind man, for example, was told to H. R. Voth three-quarters of a century ago as something that happened at Oraibi. And some of the picaresque adventures of the warrior gods, Pokanghoya and Polongahoya, identified here as part of the Homolovi experience, on occasion are told as independent tales with their locale at Shongopovi, Oraibi or other Hopi villages. Another familiar element is the training of a boy or young man to become a good runner so that he can perform some unusual or crucial task. And the "Tu-ta-heh" song which the young man sings on the rooftops is encountered again in a later story, "The Flight from Huckovi," along with the mystical grinding of the corn, the meaning of which was not understood by the narrators.

Balolokong, the great water serpent, has the status of a god in the Hopi mythology. He has been referred to on occasion by non-Hopi observers as the "plumed snake" or the "plumed serpent," suggesting ties with the plumed serpent myth of Central America. The fact that he is horned, not plumed, is made evident in this narrative, even though the story may be based on snake cult beliefs indigenous south of the Mexican border. The actual site of Palatkwapi is not known, but most informed Hopis locate it far enough to the south to place it in what is now called Mexico.

Sources: Informants 1, 5, 7, 8, 9, 10.

VI. Tokonave: The Snake and Horn People

THE EPISODE OF THE YOUNG MAN'S JOURNEY down the Colorado River in a hollowed-out tree appears in virtually all tales about the origins of the Snake Clan. His experiences in the kiva of the Snake People—as mentioned earlier—are similar to those of the boy in the Reed Clan story ("The Lamehva People"). Both situations involve a quest in a country where people transform themselves into animals by putting on animal skins. In both stories the young protagonists must make a choice among the animals. In both stories Spider Grandmother assists the heroes in their quests, and in both there is a smoking test or ordeal which is surmounted with her assistance.

The journeys of the Snake and Horn clans from Tokonave in the north and of other clans from Kalewistima in the Kayenta region appear to be recollections of actual migrations. Kayenta is considered by anthropologists to have been one of the culture centers of the proto-Hopi Basketmakers or Anasazis (a Navajo word meaning "Ancient People"). Kalewistima was a complex of old villages, some of them cliff settlements, in which various clans lived before going on to the Hopi mesas. When in recent historical times the village of Oraibi was fragmented (see the story, "The Breakup of Oraibi") the First and Water Coyote clans were expected to go back to their ancient homes in Kalewistima.

The Flute Ceremony brought to Koechaptevela by the combined Horn-Flute Clan now takes place at Walpi (Koechaptevela's last incarnation) every second year, alternating with the Snake Ceremony, brought by the Snake Clan. In the Flute Ceremony of earlier years, the priests went out to Kwaktapavi and from there reenacted the arrival of the Horn-Flute People at First Mesa. Wearing white cloaks decorated with sunflowers, they retraced the last stages of the ancient journey, passing by the springs at Wepo, Kanelva and Gogyengva. Upon reaching Walpi they were stopped by a line of cornmeal at the entrance of the village. There they ceremonially identified themselves, after which the line of meal was brushed away and they were permitted to come in. In more recent years the ceremony appears to have become somewhat abbreviated. One informant said of the ritual:

"The Flute Clan Ceremony used to alternate with the Snake. This year [1970] is a Flute Clan Ceremony. Last year was supposed to be a Snake Dance but they didn't have any. This year Ned's [the chief's] gang is going to show themselves. There's no Bear Clan in Walpi any more. Ned, he is Horn Clan, he is acting for the Bear and Snake clans. His people are going to put on the Flute Ceremony. It's in commemoration of coming to Walpi [Koechaptevela]. They go out to Wepo Wash, they come with those white cloaks wearing sunflowers all over. They want to convince the Bear and Snake clans that they are good people and that they can bring joy and flowers to Walpi. That's what it symbolizes. . . .

"For the Flute Ceremony they have a race early in the morning. They race from Wepo Spring and then come up to the point, to Walpi, carrying the sacred water [from the spring] in a little gourd. At the Snake Dance they do the same, Flute Dance they do the same. This is the Flute Clan's year. If they are good people all through the year they might be blessed by the Great Spirit to 'rain on their children,' as they say." (Informant 1)

Sources: Informants 1, 5, 7.

VII. Pakabva and the Kachinas

KACHINVA'S RUINS LIE BELOW the edge of the mesa about seven miles east of Walpi. Its name is generally taken to mean that it was a Kachina Clan settlement at one time. Few of my informants knew about this site's tradition, other than that it had some connection with the Kachina Clan. The story given here contends that the village had another name, Pakabva, in the beginning, and that it came to be known as Kachina Spring only after its demise. I found no stories about Kachinva excepting this one. Voth (*Traditions of the Hopi*, pp. 63–65) has a quite similar story about the village of Kaotukvi, which his narrator located "somewhere east of the Pueblo Indians." This could be a displacement of the village of Kaiotakwi mentioned in the Lamehva story in this collection. In any case the theme of the rejected kachinas appears to be a free-floating motif attached to the tradition of more than one village.

Fewkes (*Seventeenth Annual Report of the Bureau of American Ethnology*, p. 589) says of the Kachinva site: "The ruin is located on a small foothill and has a few standing walls. It was evidently diminutive in size and only temporarily inhabited. The best wall found at this ruin lies at the base of the hill, where the spring formerly was. This spring is now filled in, but a circular wall of masonry indicates its great size in former times."

Source: Informants 1, 11.

VIII. Maski, the Land of the Dead

VARIANTS OF THE STORY of the journey to the Land of the Dead are known in all of the Hopi villages, but the tale is considered to "belong" to the Oraibis. This version is based on narrations by members of the Sun, Spruce and Coyote clans living on Third and First mesas, and conforms in its main story line, and in some details, to a text recorded by Voth (*Traditions of the Hopi*, 1905, pp. 114–19). It differs in some respects from a variant recorded in Courlander, *People of the Short Blue Corn*, 1970 (pp. 129–42, "The Journey to the Land of the Dead"). In that variant the young man goes to Maski in pursuit of his wife, who has just died, and a love story is interwoven with the basic theme. In the version given here, the young man goes on his journey out of a compulsion to learn and verify, much as the young man in the Snake Clan story ("Tokonave: The Snake and Horn People") makes his trip on the Colorado River to find out what is at the end.

What is particularly intriguing about the Maski legend is the possibility, or probability, that it had a non-Indian origin. The concept that the dead go to Maski is of course in conflict with the implied promise in the emergence myth that when people die they will return to the Third or Lower World. It is not the only conflict in Hopi legends and myths, but the very concept of Maski suggests that it derives from concepts of Hell introduced by Christian missionaries in the seventeenth century. The fate of the damned and the tortures inflicted on them seem to come right out of medieval Christian teachings. They relate to Dante's Inferno and Hieronymus Bosch's fifteenth-century painting, "The Last Judgment," much more closely than they do to Hopi tradition. If this legend did have a missionary origin, as it surely seems to have had, it would be notable as virtually the only distinctly recognizable instance of European intrusion into Hopi traditional literature. The fact that more European religious or secular motifs have not found their way into Hopi traditions is testimony to the resistance given by the Hopis to the "heresies" offered by the Christian missionaries in the period of contact with the Catholic Church.

Sources: Informants 1, 8, 11.

IX. The Lalakon Dance at Shongopovi

IN THE THREE MAIN EPISODES of this legend we see the young warrior gods first in their youthful innocence, then as resentful provocateurs, and finally in their mythological role of culture heroes. The story of the journey to Grand (Salt) Canyon to transfer the salt deposits to that place conforms to an account given in the 1930s by Don Talayesva of Oraibi, as recorded in Mischa Titiev's article, "A Hopi Salt Expedition" (*American Anthropologist*, vol. 39, 1937). That account contains detailed reference to all the shrines and sacred spots along the salt trail, and the ritual observances at those places. The legend primarily belongs to the Third Mesa villages—Oraibi, Hotevilla and Bakavi (Bacobi)—and to Moencopi, an offspring of Oraibi. In former times these villages sent expeditions to Grand Canyon to gather their salt. According to the belief of some Third Mesa clans, Grand Canyon contains not only the sacred salt beds and shrines, but the sipapuni through which mankind emerged from the Third (Lower) World. As Titiev paraphrases the description given by Don Talayesva:

"It was not long now before the expedition found itself approaching *the* Kiva, the original sipapu through which mankind emerged from the underworld. Its outlines are indicated by soft, damp earth and an outer circle of bushes called pilakho. . . . Pushing their way through the fringe of vegetation, the party stepped into the inner ring within which the Kiva is located. The sipapu is full to the brim with yellowish water, of about the same coloring as the surrounding earth, which serves as a 'lid' so that ordinary humans may not see the wonderful things going on beneath the surface."

The Walpis and other First Mesa people do not agree that the sipapuni is at that place, asserting that its location is no longer known. The salt myth given here is not part of First Mesa belief. Walpi customarily sent its salt expeditions to Zuni in the southeast. In recent years, of course, virtually all Hopi salt expeditions have been to the nearest trading posts.

Sources: Informants 8, 11, with some details taken from Voth version.

X. The Dispersal from Sikyatki

THIS IS ESSENTIALLY A FIRST MESA ACCOUNT of the events at Sikyatki, obtained from Spruce, Tobacco and Coyote clan members of Walpi Village and Tewa Village. Informants of some of the more westerly villages stated that the most authentic accounts would be found on First Mesa, because Walpi (that is, Koechaptevela) was directly involved in the Sikyatki affair. Nevertheless, a member of the Sun Clan on Third Mesa provided a version of the esoteric type that substitutes pure fiction for historical recollection. In that variant a race between a swallow and a hawk, sponsored respectively by Sikyatki and the village of Matovi (Machovi), is the central feature of the conflict, and Walpi (Koechaptevela) is not mentioned at all. According to this variant the swallow

wins the race much as the tortoise wins over the hare in many folktales—
by engaging a number of swallows who look alike. The outcome of the
race brings hard feelings between Sikyatki and Matovi, and as a con-
sequence the Sikyatkians decide to leave. This appears to be one of the
free-floating motifs in Hopi literature that appear in numerous stories.
But the prevailing explanation of the dispersal from Sikyatki is the one
given here.

All the evidence indicates that Sikyatki died before the arrival of
the Spanish, and quite some time before the destruction of Awatovi (see
the story, "The Destruction of Awatovi"), but recollections concerning
the two villages seem to have become confused with each other. In his
book of Hopi texts, *The Traditions of the Hopi,* Voth includes a variant
whose denouement, the destruction, is borrowed bodily from the Awatovi
legend. The narrator declares that Sikyatki was attacked, its people
scattered, and its buildings destroyed by the people of Walpi (Koechaptevela). It is my belief that the ethnologist Jesse Fewkes accepted the
explanation in the Voth text, without having access to any other version,
because he also speaks frequently of the "destruction" of Sikyatki. I
could not find a single knowledgeable informant among the Hopis
willing to suggest that Sikyatki had been sacked. All agreed that the
Sikyatkians departed because of the bad feelings engendered by the
double murder. Fewkes excavated many sites in Arizona, and in 1895 he
carried out this kind of investigation at Sikyatki. In summarizing his
findings he said:

"There appears to be no good evidence that Sikyatki was destroyed
by fire, nor would it seem that it was gradually abandoned." ("Archeological Expedition to Arizona in. 1895," p. 635.) These conclusions
support the testimony of the prevalent traditional account, that the village was abandoned suddenly but that it was not destroyed. The kachina
race and the beheading of the girl are generally accepted as the pre-
lude to the abandonment. One thing that is noteworthy here is the
choice of abandonment over war, a theme that repeats itself frequently
in Hopi traditions.

Sources: Informants 1, 5, 6, 7, 8, 9.

XI. The Flight from Huckovi

THE SPRUCE TREE DANCE, around which this story is centered, appears to
have been a speciality of the village of Pivanhonkapi. There is no recollection that it was ever performed in any of the other Hopi villages.
Some investigators have suggested that it was a local variant of the
Ladder Dance, known to Indians farther south and still performed on
festival occasions in Mexico. The holes in which the spruce trees were

placed are still visible at the mesa edge bordering the Pivanhonkapi ruins.

In some renditions the explanation of the young man's refusal to have sexual relations with the young woman from Huckovi is that he already had a sweetheart in his own village. The most persuasive explanation is the one given here, attested to by several older people familiar with the story—that it was a period of purification during which abstinence was mandatory.

Noteworthy is the recurring theme of an incident leading to the estrangement of neighboring villages and the departure of one of them to find a new home elsewhere. One informant said that the Huckovi people, having crossed the Colorado River, finally settled among the Mission Indians in California.

The song sung by the tuwakomoviki while she is grinding corn is the same as the one attributed to the chief's nephew in the story, "The Destruction of Palatkwapi." In neither case could informants provide a translation. The words are thought to have a meaning, but they are obviously archaic, or in a foreign language, or merely nonsense sounds.

Source: Informant 8.

XII. Judgment by Fire at Pivanhonkapi

THE MOTIF OF THE CHIEF who arranges for the destruction of his village because it has become corrupt echoes the Palatkwapi story and has close parallels in the developments yet to come at Awatovi ("The Destruction of Awatovi"). Just as the chief of Awatovi stays and dies with his village, so the chief of Pivanhonkapi remains and perishes in the fire. The theme is widely encountered in Hopi accounts of how certain villages disappeared in the struggle between good and evil. The missionary-ethnologist Voth (ibid.) quotes a Shipaulovi informant as saying: "This is the way chiefs often punished their children [people] when they became 'bewitched.' That is one reason why there are so many ruins all over the country. Many people were killed in that way because their chiefs became angry and invited some chief or inhabitants from other villages to destroy their people."

There are Hopi recollections of a drouth and a great prairie fire during the Spanish era. The fire is said to have originated along the Little Colorado River and swept northward, eventually consuming the corn of many Hopi villages. According to tradition, only the cornfields of Awatovi were spared. The conflagration featured in the Pivanhonkapi story, and its alleged start at the San Francisco Mountains, could be a particularized remembrance of a real event.

The Yayaponcha (also called Yaponcha, Yaya, Yayaponchatu and

Yayatu) people are generally known among the Hopis as a group or secret society with special powers, some of which are indicated in the present story. There are conflicting accounts of their origins. One explanation says that they had their own village, had their own distinctive dress and hair styles, and were not really Hopi. Another explanation says that they were Hopis and lived in the First Mesa villages, where they frequently put on exhibitions of their magical prowess. The Yayaponchas have not been active for some years, and their ritual paraphernalia is said to be sealed up in a cave on First Mesa.

The precipitating event in this drama—the rape of the chief's daughter-in-law—appears in some versions of the Awatovi and Palatkwapi stories with minor differences of detail.

This section appeared previously, in slightly different form, in Courlander, *People of the Short Blue Corn*, and is used with permission of Harcourt Brace Jovanovich.

Sources: Informants 1, 3, 5, 6, 7.

XIII. The Antelope Boy of Shongopovi

THE THEME OF CHILDREN turning into animals of various kinds is widespread in the Hopi tales and legends. In many such tales the metamorphosis comes because the children have been treated unkindly by their parents or their villages. The theme is frequently encountered, also, in the stories of the Eastern Pueblos.

Here, once again, we have an example of the Hopi view that all living things are closely related, and that only an outer skin makes one species distinguishable from another.

The young woman's anxiety about her pregnancy is not easily explained in the context of contemporary Hopi life. Hopis—despite strongly stated standards of proper behavior—are uncommonly generous in their attitudes toward so-called "illegitimate" mothers and children. But, as in this story, the parents of the "illegitimate" child are expected to assume their full parental responsibilities.

Source: Informant 3.

XIV. The Races Between Payupki and Tikuvi

THE VILLAGES OF TIKUVI and Payupki were situated on the eastern edge of Second Mesa a little north of Shipaulovi, and their ruins are still visible. The Tikuvis were Hopis and the Payupkis, as their name indicates, were settlers from the Rio Grande Valley, from which region they are believed to have emigrated in the middle years of the seventeenth century.

According to Hopi tradition the Payupki people returned eventually to their homeland, settling at San Felipe Pueblo. Some older informants indicate that the Payupkis and neighboring Hopis on Second Mesa did not get along together very well. It was during this period that numerous Eastern Pueblo groups were seeking sanctuary from Spanish rule, and it is probable that the continual arrival of outsiders was disturbing to the Hopi villages, primarily because of the limited resources of the mesas.

As stated by one authoritative work: ". . . As the 18th century rolled on, most of the easterners, little by little, group by group, returned to their homelands. Home ties, aided in all probability by the economic limitations of the Hopi country which must indeed have been strained by the increased population of the early decades of the 18th century, combined to force the eventual capitulation of the refugees to God and King." (Montgomery, Smith and Brew, *Franciscan Awatovi*, 1949, p. 24.)

This description of the circumstances surrounding the vacating of Payupki contains many of the motifs found elsewhere in the Hopi literature—Spider Grandmother's intervention in a time of crisis, footracing and gambling, for example. Even the Castilla is infected with the gambling urge. Somewhat unusual is the theme of a girl racing champion, but this is so only because footracing is primarily a young man's sport. Girls are also represented in traditional literature as playing nahoydadatsia (field hockey). But it is not only in footracing that women triumph in this story. In the original narration the almost total inability of the men of Tikuvi to perform ordinary female tasks is made much of:

"The men of Tikuvi, they were not feeling very bad about losing their wives, because they said they could work just as well as the women. They had seen their wives grind corn and it looked easy. They could do that, and they could shell corn and make piki. They had also seen their wives make piki. And so they didn't feel too bad. The women had left a supply of piki. A Hopi woman usually has a supply of piki on hand all the time, and so the men had this to eat. And some of them who didn't want to cook anything would go to another man's house and they would fix something together and eat there. As time went on they used up all their piki, and soon they used up all the corn flour that the women had on hand. And so they said they would grind corn and make piki. So they would get busy shelling corn, and some who were not very good at this made the corn scatter all over the floor instead of the place where they had put the cloth down. And so they would have a time picking up all the corn that scattered all over the place. When they got through they would start grinding. They had these mata stones the women grind on. They sat down behind this grinding stone, and they took the matati (it's a long piece of stone just wide enough to hold with two hands) and they would put the corn between the mata and the matati and start grinding. And the men had a time doing that because the corn is slippery and would slide right under the matati and whole kernels would come out underneath and they are supposed to be cracked when they come out from underneath. Well, they tried and tried, and they worked hard enough so they ground some. They didn't know it was so hard. They didn't know it was so much work. It took a lot of time to grind enough corn so that it would last them for a while. And then some of the men decided that they would make piki the way their wives did. And so they went to the piki house and made a fire under the big black flat stone. And when the fire was good and hot (of course they had mixed the batter already, the flour and water and juice from a certain kind of bush ashes) and so with their hands they would spread this batter across the stone. They discovered it was not so easy. The stone burnt their hands, and they would shake their hands around till they cooled. And before they were through putting the batter onto the stone, the first part of the piki was already rolling up. And they made the piki so heavy that when they were through they had to put it out to dry, and it dried in hard sheets that had to be soaked in water for them to eat. This went on for a long time until they decided they could not go on living this way."

The account of the Payupki dispersal given here originally appeared in Courlander, *People of the Short Blue Corn,* and is used with permission of Harcourt Brace Jovanovich.

Source: Informant 3.

XV. The Castillas at Oraibi

THIS IS A STANDARD VERSION of the events leading up to the Hopi attacks against the Catholic missions, though some of the accounts from Oraibi suggest that it was the Bear Clan chief of that village—rather than Popay—who initiated the rebellion against the Spanish. One narrator stated it this way: "The Catholics put their church over in Old Oraibi. And then the people started, you know, the same kind of life the people around here have now, getting wild and all that sort of thing. And pretty soon it got to be that the chief's wife got to going to these parties and things. [Note the Palatkwapi corruption theme.] The chief didn't like it and so he went to Zuni. All the chiefs of the villages out toward Santa Fe were there. I guess they sent out a message telling the chiefs to gather at Zuni. The Catholics [the missionaries] were scattered all over those villages. They were doing the same thing, the same thing as at Oraibi. And the chief of Oraibi wanted them killed. And so they agreed, and they gave them all the strings with the knots. . . ." (Informant 2)

From time to time remnants of the destroyed church in Oraibi are uncovered: "Just lately they were digging over there and found some of the stone pillars." (Informant 2) Some of the beams from the church are still in place as supports for various kiva roofs.

While some of the paraphernalia from the churches were buried or lost track of, various items were preserved by the fraternal societies. According to the version given here, the lances of the Spanish soldiers were taken and saved by the One Horn Society. A narrator on First Mesa declared: "We One Horn Society got all those small brass bells like sleigh bells from the church in Koechaptevela. Whenever the One Horn people have a chant they ring those bells." (Informant 1)

Sources: Informants 1, 2, 9, 10. Some additional details were taken from Voth, *Traditions of the Hopi*, pp. 268–71. Voth's informant was Wikvaya of Oraibi.

XVI. The Arrival of the Tewas

HANO, OR TEWA VILLAGE, is the only Eastern Pueblo settlement surviving among the Hopis. It is one of three villages tightly clustered at the southern tip of First Mesa. Somewhat later than the founding of Hano, a middle village, Sichomovi, came into being as an offshoot of Walpi. There is little to distinguish the Tewa settlement from the other two. A casual visitor can walk from Hano into Sichomovi without being aware he has crossed a boundary line. Most First Mesa dwellers, in fact, tend to think of the three settlements as a unit, although there are some subtle distinctions. The Tewas still speak Tewa among themselves, and their religious ceremonies are different in many respects from those held in Walpi. But Tewas and Walpis are members of the same secret religious fraternities and they share responsibilities in the kachina dances. There has been considerable intermarriage between the villages and there are strong clan ties. Nevertheless, in recent years there has been some contention over the lands that were originally designated by Walpi for Tewa use. Some Walpi people are insisting that the lands were only loaned, and that the Tewas have no permanent claim to them. Tewas reject this contention and insist that they were given absolute title to the lands as part of the original compact.

There are some minor differences between the Tewa story of the compact and the Hopi version. As some Hopi accounts go, the Tewas were refugees from the Spanish and asked for permission to come to First Mesa. The Tewa version is the one given here. However, a number of Hopis on First and Second Mesas support the Tewa assertion that Walpi specifically sent to Tewageh to ask for help from the Utes.

Following herewith are textual excerpts from comments made by the Tewa informant who narrated this story.

On Tewa Village: "It's Tewa Village, not Hano. The 'Hano' comes from the Hopis. The word is really T'hano, but the Hopis can't say T'hano. They say Hano. . . . The Tewas still consider themselves separate from the Hopis. They still speak their language. They have their own ceremonies. The ceremonies are different, but the kachina dances are more or less a common thing between the Hopis and the Tewas. Most of the kachina dances they have in Tewa Village originated with the Hopis. But the ceremonies are different. And you'll hear the [Tewa] people converse in Tewa. You can't find a Hopi that talks Tewa. But the Navajos, they can learn it. We have some Navajos that are adopted. You talk to them in Tewa and they can talk it fluently. Your Hopi, he may understand but he can't talk to you in Tewa. . . . We Tewas now have more or less intermarried into the Hopis, even into other villages. You have a big bunch of half-Tewas in Shongopovi. They play a very important part in that village. They still call them Tewas."

On Sichomovi, the middle village: "Sichomovi is a branch from Walpi. The Water Clan started that village. And today [1970] a woman named Matilda Siwonka, she is you might say the mother of that village. She belongs to the Water Clan. The Water Clan was increasing and because Walpi was so small they asked, 'Why couldn't we branch out to the middle village?' 'You can, but if you form that village you will have to be the one at the head of it, and anything that takes place you Water Clan people will be responsible. [You have to be responsible] for the ceremonies that take place in Sichomovi.' The Water Clan accepted and started to branch out to Sichomovi. Then others came in, like your Badger Clan from Oraibi. Then your Coyote Clan because of the Sikyatki affair, some of them returned from Oraibi to First Mesa and settled in Sichomovi. They're living on the east side of the village now, the Coyote Clan. Badger Clan is in the corner. Then later on the Mustard Clan came from around Poyay during the uprising of the Pueblos. They're the ones really should be called Hano or T'hano. Tewas aren't T'hanos."

On paraphernalia and ceremonies brought from Tewageh: "It used to be that every ten years they would perform a ceremony where all the four you might say 'dignitaries' [heirloom masks] showed themselves. This black mask (they call them sempengyi) takes the lead. The mask has diamond-shaped eyes, mouth with lots of teeth, long hair, great big eagle feathers, horns, and he's dressed up in a bearskin. Underneath he has a kilt and shells all around. He leads [a procession] around in the village four times. He's taken to a place where he has to sit up on his haunches all day with no water until it's all over. They have these different kachinas. Each kiva has organized clowns. They perform all day. The Tewa kivas take part first. This goes on clear down to the last kiva in Walpi. They whip these clowns with willow or yucca. This is part of the ceremony of purifying the whole community, that's the meaning of the whipping."

On the all-night chant containing the history of the Tewas: "How we separated. . . . When we got over from Sibopay we went to Oga'akeneh, a body of water. We came from there and hit Slippery Point, Shokugeh. All those things are in our chant. When they have the midwinter ceremony at Tewa Village they sing that chant. It's a long one. We repeat in the song where we come from, Sibopay. . . .

> *Hay-ay ay-ya-ah ah-ah-ha oh-o way ma*
> *Hay-ay-ya ay-ya ma-hay ya-hay ya-hay minu.* . . .
>
> *Somewhere, somewhere.* . . .
>
> *Hay-ay-ya hay-ya ma hay ya-hay-ya ay-ma-ha.* . . .
> *Ka ya.* . . .
>
> *That means far away.* . . .
>
> *Ka-ya-a-oh ay-ma-a*
> *Si-bo-pay dimaan o nohn-ka dimaa-haan-a ohm-oh.* . . .
>
> *What are you at Sibopay when you were born, that's what it means.* . . .
>
> *Hay-ay emba-go na-ka dimaan-oh nohn-ka-la aw-tawn.* . . .
>
> *That's what I am asking, what am I going to be, myself.*
> *Then when they get through with Sibopay, then they go to.* . . .
>
> *Oh-oh-oh-a-keneh way-ma.* . . . *(etc.)*

It's a long one. It repeats how life starts, how you're born, in your childhood, up to manhood after you get to be mature, how you're going to conduct yourself until the Great Spirit calls you. It's kind of tiring. It's a long ceremony. They watch the stars. And when the stars are at a certain point—the great big Hunter, those three stars, they call them Kwidi, it means Strung Together—they watch that through the kiva hole. 'Ah, the Kwidi's at the right place. Okay.' Everybody goes down below. Nobody stays up. They all get in a circle. First they purify themselves. They have a purifying song. 'Anybody that's got a guilty conscience, wipe it out of your mind, out of your heart, because we're going to start in repeating our chant from Sibopay.'

"After they get through with Sibopay, then when they came here to Hopi country, that's a different song from there. They sing how we participate in this ceremony, we have the great power to make it rain, give plentiful crops and all that. That is the chant. It talks about the different waters and the four directions, the different colored clouds, all those things mean something. It takes all night. And then about daybreak they keep watching [through the kiva entrance]. 'I think one more would be about enough.' 'No, let's finish it.' They kind of start to sing faster, up till the last one. Then they purify themselves again. The fellow with the purifying feather—buzzard feather, buzzard is a great purifier because he cleans up all the dirt—puts ashes on the feather. They start a purifying song. He puts ashes on the feather and when the song comes to an end everybody blows the ashes away."

This story appeared in a less extensive version in Courlander, *People of the Short Blue Corn,* and is included here by permission of Harcourt Brace Jovanovich.

Source: Informant 1.

XVII. The Destruction of Awatovi

IN ITS GENERAL OUTLINE, this traditional story of Awatovi's destruction is consistent with contemporary Spanish chronicles. Those chronicles were far from complete, and they were strongly colored by a sense of righteousness about the propriety and morality—as it was frequently phrased—of "reducing" the Hopi villages. But they do provide us with some details about the Awatovi affair and events that preceded it that are missing from Hopi oral accounts. At the same time they give support to Hopi recollections of what occurred. Spanish accounts agree with the Hopi tradition that in the year 1700, twenty years after expulsion of the church from the villages, a Franciscan missionary, Father Garaycoechea, appeared in Awatovi with the intention of rebuilding the church establishment in that village, in Walpi and in other more westerly settlements.

Although there appears to have been a large body of converts in Awatovi (over-enthusiastic chronicles assert that virtually all the Awatovis had been baptized), the prospect of renewed Spanish and religious meddling in Hopi affairs was infuriating to other Hopis. Hopi tradition says that Awatovi was split about half and half, accounting for the frictions that existed within the village before the final tragic event. The fact that the church buildings were destroyed by Awatovis and the resident priest killed in 1680 is explicit evidence that the anti-Catholic element in the village was strong. An informant stated: "When half of the people became Catholics they moved away from their old places and built new houses on the north side, closer to the church." (Informant 1) Thus the intra-village split was externalized.

The destruction clearly was a traumatic experience for the entire Hopi community, and guilt feelings and embarrassment about the massacre have not yet disappeared. Among older people there is a desire to let the episode be forgotten. Several reliable informants declared that few persons know the details of the destruction, and that fewer still are willing to recount those details. Some of the Hopi narrations avoid direct reference to the missionary issue, substituting traditional elements from old legends to explain the motivations behind the Walpi-Oraibi attack. But the evidence is clear that the villages of Walpi and Oraibi (some variants include Mishongnovi) acted out of frustration and anger over the return of the missionaries to Awatovi, which, in their view, was in collusion.

One long and detailed version of the story made no mention of the missionaries, but on being questioned about this the informant declared: "Yes. Of course it was the missionaries. They were the cause of all the trouble. They took the people away from the Hopi religion. The ones who were converted acted crazy. They didn't have to obey the Hopi religion any more. The young ones wouldn't listen to anybody. They went wild. The village was full of powakas [sorcerers]. The Castilla missionaries were responsible. That is why they were killed in the [1680] revolt and why all the churches were torn down. After that things settled down. Then the Castillas sent the missionaries to Awatovi again, and the trouble started all over. That's why the kikmongwi of Awatovi decided his village had to be wiped out. That's why the Walpis and Oraibis did it for him." (Informant 6)

Another First Mesa informant stated that many of the Awatovi accounts are distorted because of a general desire to mute the event. "They don't like to talk about it. There was a Catholic father that came one time. He wanted to turn Awatovi into a national monument. His party came to Keams Canyon. I had been acting as interpreter all those years since 1914, and I was sent out with the father to approach a man named Na'i, the head of the Reed Clan. They are the ones that control that village [Awatovi] now, the water and everything. (The Oraibis don't help with that because the Reed Clan of Walpi took the responsibility.) When we got to Na'i I talked to him in Hopi, told him the priest wanted to talk to him. 'What about?' 'The Catholic Church would like to have Awatovi as a national monument, to be set aside by the government. They'll kind of reconstruct the walls, things like that.' He said, 'No. Nobody's to do anything there after all those things that happened.' The priest said, 'Well, that thing happened a long time ago.' Na'i told him, 'Yes, we know it happened a long time ago. But I don't care for my people to know anything about it.' " (Informant 1)

Had Awatovi survived to the present day it would be reckoned the oldest of the Hopi villages, for it is widely agreed that it was already established on Antelope Mesa when the Bear Clan first arrived and settled at Shongopovi. The Spanish considered it to be the most important Hopi settlement. And it was the source of a number of cultural elements taken over by the other villages. While it was considered an essentially Hopi community, it is known to have sheltered a considerable number of non-Hopis from the Eastern Pueblos, and to have had close ties with neighboring Moesiptanga and Kawaika, built by peoples from the Rio Grande Valley. Said one informant: "Moesiptanga and

Kawaika, those were Laguna people. Now, all the Two Horn and Wu-wuchim songs we have on First Mesa, they are in the Laguna language. How did we learn that? We don't have any Lagunas living here. We got those things from Awatovi, and Awatovi got them from the Lagunas living there and in the other two villages, Moesiptanga and Kawaika. The Lagunas and Acomas were there in Awatovi. The important initiation songs we have in Walpi all came from over there." (Informant 1)

Sources: Informants 1, 2, 5, 6, 7, 8.

Initiation Song in Laguna

XVIII. The Navajo Attack on Oraibi

SOME OF THE ELEMENTS of this narrative suggest that it refers to the same Navajo attack described in a text taken by Voth (*Traditions of the Hopi*, pp. 258–66), though the details are different in many respects. In the Voth story the Oraibis discover renegade Walpi warriors among the Navajo attackers. In the present version a Hopi appears among the Navajos, but his loyalties are divided. There is also here a perhaps unconscious effort to place relatively recent events in the context of legend, as indicated by the crucial intercession of Spider Grandmother and the young warrior gods.

Source: Informant 11.

XIX. The Founding of Moencopi

SETTLED BY FAMILIES FROM ORAIBI, Moencopi reflects to this day the frictions within the mother village that caused the split in 1906. (See the story, "The Breakup of Oraibi.") There are still two factions, the Traditionals and the Progressives, separated by contention over the extent to which the community should move toward the mainstream of American life. The factionalism was polarized by application of the Indian Reorganization Act of 1934, which provided that Indians should assume a greater role in governing themselves under constitutions written to assure majority rule. In a referendum held in Moencopi, a large majority did not vote at all, on the grounds that the Hopis already had their own system of government and did not need another one superimposed on it. Those who did vote in the referendum were largely persons of the Progressive faction, and they overwhelmingly endorsed the provisions of the political reform. It was the Progressive element, therefore, with whom the Federal Government thenceforth dealt, ignoring the fact that perhaps 85 percent of the Hopis had not approved of the new arrangement. The concentration of local political power in the hands of the Progressives heightened feelings between the factions and kept alive old dissensions dating from the turn of the century.

Following herewith are textual excerpts from comments by an elder of the Moencopi community on circumstances of the founding of that village.

On early-day farming practices: "The people lived at Oraibi a long time, and they found there was a lot of water down here in Moencopi. In Oraibi, they don't have much water there. So some of those Hopis came back down here to plant some vegetables and irrigate the fields, just little pieces of ground here and there. Of course, in those days there were no Navajos, no white men around here, only Hopis. The Oraibi farmers, they would start coming here at daylight, running all the way. They'd work on the fields and then toward sundown they'd start running home. It's a pretty good run, about forty-five miles. At that time the Hopis were good runners, been practicing since they were kids. That's the way they trained us old-timers. They had to run all the way here and all the way back, and maybe the next morning they'd come to Moencopi again. That's the way they did in those times. After the harvest they didn't come back till spring, just stayed in Oraibi doing winter ceremonials." (Informant 9)

On Tuvi, the first permanent settler: "He stayed down here by himself with his wife in the winter for some years. The rest of the Oraibi people stayed home in the winter. By the time Tuvi was here a few Paiutes were around. They're enemies. So this man wanted somebody to protect him down here. Before that, some Mormons came around at Oraibi and made friends with the Hopis. I don't know how long after that, but Tuvi went to Utah with them, the Mormons, to Salt Lake City. Stayed there a year and then came back again. He was an old man and he wanted the Mormons to protect him so he'll be safe from the Paiutes. Some years after that the Mormons came. This old man found a place for them up on top where the day school is now. He asked them if they could stay there. They said, 'Okay, you're the boss.' " (Informant 9)

On the school problem: "In 1884 that government school was established at Keams Canyon. The people used to send their children to Keams Canyon from here [Moencopi]. It's a long way to ride on those burros. We had nothing but burros then. The Hopis down here wanted a school closer to the village. The government picked out a place up here at Blue Canyon, about twelve miles from here in the wash. There used to be a trading post there and the man left it. There was a building there and the government built it up again for a school. That was around 1900. I was here then, and I saw it for myself. But it was still too far and after two years the Hopis wanted a school over here. So the government bought this place from the Mormons. Paid four hundred and fifty dollars for the property and the trees, the orchards. There were a lot of orchards. When I was a kid I used to work here picking apples, peaches and apricots. In 1904 they started to build this school over here. Then the Mormons had to go away. They didn't want to take the money, said it wasn't enough. The government told them that if they didn't want the money they could go away empty. And they had to go, in 1904, in July. They went away in all directions. Some went to Salt Lake and some went east to Winslow." (Informant 9)

On Navajos: "I don't see how the Navajos can claim this country around here. The Hopis were here all the time. The Navajos came in late. They came to Oraibi and fought with the Hopis for food or stock. Sometimes they killed the Hopis with bows and arrows. If they saw a sheep herder they'd kill him and take the sheep." (Informant 9)

Sources: Informants 1, 2, 9.

XX. The Breakup of Oraibi

FOLLOWING HEREWITH are textual excerpts from comments made by various informants on the Oraibi split.

On the push-of-war: "I was in that business. I was a boy about ten or eleven years old when that thing happened, about the right size to be in school. They [the Hostiles] were hostile to the government, to the whites. They don't want to get help from the government. They like to be left alone. The Hostiles were mixed clans. It was kind of sad, things turned upside down. Now at the beginning of the Niman ceremonies the Hostiles had their own ceremonies at the same time. When we friendly people had our ceremonies, they had theirs by themselves. And we were not living peaceably until nineteen hundred six. That was the time that we planned to do something to them so we could live peaceably. It was on September the 8th, 1906, that it happened. We drove those hostile people from the village out that way, and all the hostile people were gathered there. And in the afternoon it was getting pretty bad and the Hotevilla chief [i.e., the chief of the Fire Clan] wanted to stay there [Oraibi], wanted us Friendlies to leave that place. So about three o'clock they make a line on the ground, four lines [outside the village]. Then he [Yukioma] said, 'Well, it have to be this way now, that when you pass me over this line it will be done. We're going to have a tug-of-war. If they push us out of our village, we are the ones that are going to leave.'

"So our chief called on all our strong men to do the work. 'We'll get together and then we'll push each other, we'll push them back that way. If we pass those four lines it will be done.' We had a hard struggle. Our chief was in the center. He had a hard time to get his breath. And then we shoved them over the four lines. Then 'it was done,' that's what he said. Then before the setting of the sun he departed. Our chief said, 'You people of those clans are supposed to go out where you come from, Kalewistima.' And that [Fire Clan] chief was planning to go out toward Kayenta. So after they left they make a footprint on the rock making a step toward the west. They made about three footprints on the rock. Then a fellow named Robert Silena and Charles Addington, they put the words that the chief had said [in the rock]. So they went. They must be out by sundown. They cut down trees and made hogans for themselves. Then after that we were going to the government school where we could learn and know how white people live. And it sounded good to get our education so some of the younger people will know something about what they learn in school to help the older people to live in the right way of life." (Informant 8)

On the Fire Clan tablet: "The Fire Clan of Oraibi which moved to Hotevilla have a broken piece, and half of it is what they're expecting the eastern people [Bahanas] to bring and fit that tablet. The old man that's dead and gone, Yukioma, he was head of the Fire Clan while they were all living in Oraibi, and when the Oraibis drove them out he took the stone tablet with him. We have had them [the Fire Clan men who went to Hotevilla] at Keams Canyon as prisoners on account of their not sending their children to school. The superintendent [of the Indian Agency] at that time wanted to take the old man to Washington, to really make out what he means by having a stone tablet in his possession and waiting for people to come from the east to bring the other half. That's when they claim there'll be peace, or approach to peaceful times. The old chief Yukioma thinks that it's going to come to pass. . . .

"Now it [the tablet] is in the hands of a man named James George in Hotevilla. He comes down to Parker, he works there in the fields. He told me one time he was visiting me, he said, 'You remember when my old uncle went to Washington?' I said, 'Yes.' 'You were interpreter then.' 'I was, with my half brother. When they made this trip my half brother went along as interpreter for your uncle. I saw the tablet, half of it, when he brought it to Keams Canyon. It had a design there with a body, the lower part, but the head was off. And then there was a line along the edge. I don't know what it signified, but this other half, the head part, was gone.' He said, 'Did you see that?' I said, 'Yes.' 'There's another stone tablet at Shongopovi,' he said. 'What does it look like?' He said, 'I don't know, but we understand that the Shongopovi people have another tablet.' It was the first time I'd heard of it. He said, 'Yes, they have it.' " (Informant 1)

On the decay of ritual in Oraibi: "The people started to come down to New Oraibi after the split. Before the split there were only three families that moved down. They had stone houses. But after the split the people came down leaving, you might say, anything that was connected with their tradition. So I say today, and I tell those people, 'You Oraibis got nothing, you threw it up. You threw it all away.'

"They've done away with it, because those who are supposed to carry on as priests and so on, they don't want to carry on. When they split up they didn't carry anything on. The following generation wanted to bring it back, even to have initiations. Somebody told them, 'How could you? Your paraphernalia is no more.' The paraphernalia was all gone. Some of the people burned it. Just like J—— over there in Oraibi. When he became a Christian, he took all the paraphernalia from his kiva and threw it all out and burned it. . . .

"Now with all the paraphernalia gone, how could the four societies be true? All the altar things were gone, and the priests weren't carrying the traditions on, and they didn't know how to do it any more anyway. In Oraibi it is finished. But the four societies are almost gone now on First Mesa too. Very few get to go through the initiations. It isn't like it used to be." (Informant 1)

On the missionary Voth: "They must have sent a German here because they wanted a stern man. That's what Voth was. He did not stay in the back. He always pushed to the front, anywhere he wanted to be, even in the kivas. Nobody could stop him. One time a Two Horn priest tried to stop him from going into a kiva. He kicked the Two Horn priest out of the way and went in. . . . Most of the stories they told Voth is because they didn't want to tell him the true story." (Informant 7)

"I don't think it was right, what he did. He came here to teach the Bible, to convert the people. Instead of doing what he was supposed to, being a church man, he got into all the secrets, stole them and some of the altar things too, and revealed all the sacred things in his books." (Informant 8)

Sources: Informants 1, 2, 7, 8.

Glossary and Pronunciation Guide

PRONUNCIATION OF HOPI WORDS varies from village to village, and particularly from mesa to mesa, reflecting the relative isolation of village groupings from one another in earlier times, and also the different speech patterns brought in by immigrating clans. The pronunciations given below do not conform to any one of the mesa dialects, but are reproduced as heard from informants. Pronunciation is shown in parentheses following each word, capital letters indicating accented syllables, with these vowel sounds:

ah—*a* as in *mama*
ee—as in *need*
eh—short *e* as in *pet*
eu—French *eu* as in *peu*
i—short, as in *it*
o—as in *blow*
ö—German *ö*
oo—as in *book*
u—long, as in *jute*
uh—*u* as in *luck*

AAL, sometimes ALA (AHL, AH-lah)—Horn. The Aal or Two Horn Society (also called Aaltu, a plural form) is one of the four major religious fraternities among the Hopis.
ACOMA (AH-ko-mah)—An Eastern Pueblo people, some of whom settled for a time in Hopi country.

AGAYOPING, AGAYOTSAY (ah-GUY-o-ping, ah-GUY-o-tsay)—A Tewa personal name. The leader of the Tewa relief expedition to Walpi.

AKOKAVI (AH-ko-kah-vee)—An Acoma settlement on Antelope Mesa, now extinct.

ANANGTANA (ah-NAHNG-tah-nah)—Place of Hearts. The site where the Tewas buried the hearts of their slain Ute enemies.

ANASAZI (AH-nah-SAH-zee)—Navajo for Ancient People. The ancestral people of the Southwest, particularly of northern Arizona.

ATU'I (ah-TU-ee)—A form of bridal shawl.

AWATOVI (ah-WAHT-o-vee)—Bow Height. The Bow Clan Village on Antelope Mesa that was destroyed by an expedition from Walpi and Oraibi.

AWPIMPAW (aw-PIM-paw)—Tewa for Duck Spring. A site near the present town of Grants, New Mexico. The Tewas camped here on their relief mission to Walpi.

BAHANA (bah-HAH-nah)—White man, white person.

BAKAVI (BAH-kah-vee, sometimes BAH-ko-bee)—A Third Mesa Hopi village.

BALOLOKONG, PALOLOKONG (BAH-lö-lö-kong, PAH-lö-lö-kong)—The Great Water Serpent, generally but not exclusively referring to the snake deity of Palatkwapi.

BETATAKIN (beh-TAH-tah-kin)—A cliff village ruin near Kayenta, Arizona, claimed by the Hopis as one of their ancestral settlements.

BOPAW (BO-paw)—Tewa for Reed Spring. A site near Ganado, Arizona, where the Tewa relief expedition to Walpi stopped to rest.

CASTILLA (KAH-steel-ah)—Spaniard.

CHAKMONGWI (CHAHK-mong-wee)—Crier chief, responsible for making announcements in the village.

CHAKPAHU (CHAHK-pah-hu)—A village on Antelope Mesa, now extinct.

CHIMOENVASI (chi-MÖN-vah-see)—A village, now extinct, about six miles northwest of Oraibi, settled by Eastern Pueblos.

CHOONG'O (CHOONG-o)—A personal name meaning Smoke Pipe.

COOYOKO, COYOKO (KO-o-yo-ko, KO-yo-ko)—A monster, represented as a kachina.

EOTOTO (EE-o-toh-toh)—A variety of kachina.

GOGYENG SOWUHTI (GO-gyeng so-WÖ-tee, sometimes KO-kyeng so-WÖ-tee)—Spider Grandmother. Literally, Spider Old Woman. One of the creator deities of Hopi mythology.

GOGYENGVA (GO-gyeng-vah, KO-kyeng-vah)—Spider Spring, situated at the foot of First Mesa.

HANO (HAH-no)—The Hopi name for Tewa Village on First Mesa.

HEMIS (HAY-mis)—An Eastern Pueblo people, now situated at a Rio Grande village by the same name. Sometimes improperly written as Jemez.

HIMSUNG (HIM-soong)—The Hair-Cutter kachina.

HOHOKYAM (HO-hok-yahm)—One of the villages settled by the Palatkwapi clans during their migration northward.

HOMIKOPU (ho-MEE-ko-pu)—A temporary settlement of the Spider Clan during the migrations.

HOMOLOVI (ho-MO-lo-vee)—Small Mound. A village site near Winslow, Arizona, where the Palatkwapi clans settled for a time during their migrations northward.

HOPI (HO-pee)—The western Pueblos of Arizona. Hopis do not, however, regard themselves as Pueblos.

HOTEVILLA, HOTEVALA (HOHT-vi-lah, HOHT-vah-lah)—A village on Third Mesa, settled by the Fire, Coyote and other clans after the breakup of Oraibi.

HUCKOVI (HU-ko-vee, HÖ-ko-vee)—An extinct Third Mesa village which was located a little north of Oraibi.

HUCKYATWI (huk-YAHT-wee, hök-YAHT-wee)—A now extinct village site at Five Houses Butte, about four miles south of Walpi.

HURUING WUHTI (hu-RU-ing WÖ-tee, sometimes heu-REU-ing, French eu)—Hard-Substances Old Woman or Sea Lady. In some myths one of the principal creators. Said to be the "owner" of hard substances such as coral, shells and turquoise.

ISLETA (iss-LEH-tah, iss-LAY-tah)—An Eastern Pueblo village belonging to the Tiwa Language group.

KACHINMANA (kah-CHEEN-mah-nah)—Kachina girl, in this case a personal name.

KACHINVA (kah-CHEEN-vah)—Kachina Spring. The name of a village, now extinct, five or six miles northeast of Walpi.

KAIOTAKWI (kye-O-tah-kwee)—The old village, now extinct, at Corn Rocks, below the rim of Second Mesa near Mishongnovi.

KALATAKA (kah-LAH-tahk-ah)—Warrior.

KALATAKMONGWI (kah-LAH-tahk-mong-wee)—War chief.

KALEWISTIMA, KAWESTIMA (kah-leh-WIST-i-mah, kah-WEHST-ih-mah)—The Hopi ancestral villages in the Tsegi Canyon complex about fifteen miles west of Kayenta, Arizona. They include the cliff villages now identified as Betatakin, Keet Seel and Inscription House.

KANELVA (kah-NEHL-vah)—A spring at the western edge of First Mesa a few miles north of Walpi.

KATESHUM (KAH-teh-shoom)—An extinct village east of First Mesa.

KAWAIKA (kah-WYE-kah, kah-WYE-ah-kah)—An Eastern Pueblo people now usually called by the Spanish name Laguna. They call themselves Kawaiks or Kawaikas. During the time of the Spanish occupation Kawaika people migrated to Hopi country and established a village on Antelope Mesa, near Awatovi, and this settlement was known as Kawaika. According to some traditional accounts, the Antelope Mesa Kawaika was destroyed by the Spanish.

KIAVAKOVI (ki-AH-va-ko-vee)—"Someone is coming."

KIKMONGWI (KIK-mong-wee)—Village chief.

KIKOECHMOVI (kee-KEUCH-mo-vee, kee-KÖCH-mo-vee)—The village of New Oraibi.

KISAKOVI (kee-SAHK-o-vee)—An old village site on a lower ledge of First Mesa near Walpi.

KISIWU (KI-si-wu)—A former village site about sixty miles northeast of Oraibi.

KIVA (KEE-vah)—The underground ceremonial chamber of the Hopi and other Pueblo peoples. Used for ritual, ceremonial and sometimes social activities.

KIWAN (KEE-wahn)—A kind of kachina.

KOECHAKTEWA (kö-CHAHK-teh-wah)—White Sand, the Hopi name for Tuba City.

KOECHAPTEVELA (KÖ-chahp-teh-veh-lah, KEU-chahp-teh-veh-lah), sometimes called KOECHAPTEKA (KÖ-chahp-teh-kah)—Ash Hill or Ash Mound. The original First Mesa settlement of the Bear and Snake clans. When the people of Koechaptevela moved to the crest of the mesa they called their new village Walpi. Reed Clan tradition says that the Reed people were the founders of Koechaptevela.

KOEKUCHOMO (kö-KUCH-o-mo, kö-KÖCH-o-mo)—A mesa-top branch or suburb of Sikyatki, said to have been a guardpost village. The site is on the top of First Mesa a few miles north of Walpi.

KOKOTUKWI (ko-KO-tuh-kwee)—A hidden ball or stone game played with small tubes or cups.

KOYAMSI (ko-YAHM-see, ku-YAHM-see)—A clown kachina, usually called Mud Head in English.

KUNCHALPI (KUN-chahl-pee)—A southern site where the Palatkwapi clans settled temporarily on their northward migration.

KWAKTAPAVI (KWAK-tah-pah-vee)—A place where the combined Horn-Flute Clan camped on its journey to Koechaptevela.

KWAKWI (KWAH-kwee)—A kind of wild grain.

KWALAIPKA (kwah-LAH-ip-kah)—Eagle Mesa Point.

KWALALATA (kwah-LAH-lah-tah)—Place of Bubbling Water. A site somewhat northeast of Walpi. The Tewas rested here during their relief expedition to Walpi.

KWAN (KWAHN), KWAKWAN (KWAHK-wahn)—Lance. The One Horn Society, one of the four major religious fraternities.

KWATSKIAVU (KWATS-kyah-veu, KWATS-kyah-voo)—One of the so-called bridal robes or shawls, the under shawl used in combination with the OVA, or covering shawl.

KWIDI (KWI-dee)—The stellar constellation Orion.

KWITAMUH (KWEE-tah-muh)—Hooligans, roughnecks.

KWOKWADEH (kwo-KWAH-deh)—Stone Wall. Name of a site featured in the Tewa battle against the Utes.

LAGUNA (lah-GOON-ah)—Name of an Eastern Pueblo people. See Kawaika.

LALAKON (LAH-lah-kon)—Basket Dance, ceremony performed by the Lakone religious fraternity. The Basket Dance traditionally has as participants women belonging to the Water Clan and its affiliates.

LAMEHVA (lah-MEH-vah)—A spring at the foot of Second Mesa near the village of Mishongnovi. An old village which stood at this site, also called Lamehva, is said by Reed Clan people to be the place of their creation.

LENYANOVI (LEHN-yah-no-vee)—Place of the Flute. The ancient Flute Clan village from which the combined Horn-Flute Clan migrated to Koechaptevela.

LOLOMA (LO-lo-mah)—An Oraibi village chief, a leader of the faction friendly to the whites somewhat before the Oraibi split.

MASAUWU (MAH-sah-wu)—Spirit of Death, the deity who owned the Upper World at the time of the emergence of the people through the sipapuni.

MASHILAYWI (mah-SHEE-lye-wee)—A woman's name. The first kikmongwi of Moencopi.

MASIPA (mah-SEE-pah)—The name of the first site of Shongopovi.

MASITO, Sometimes MACHITO (mah-SEE-toh, mah-CHEE-toh)—The founder and first chief of Oraibi.

MASJUMO (MAHS-ju-mo)—Dead Persons Hill. A site associated with the Awatovi massacre.

MASKI (MAHS-kee)—Land or dwelling place of the dead.

MASKOTEU (MAHS-ko-teu)—Skull Mound. A site associated with the Awatovi massacre.

MASTOEKI (MAHS-tö-kee)—Place of Dead Persons. A site associated with the Awatovi massacre.

MATA (MAH-tah)—The lower grinding stone against which the matati is worked.

MATATI (MAH-tah-tee)—The upper grinding stone, the one held with the hands.

MATOVI, also heard as MACHOVI, MAKOVI (MAH-toh-vee, MAH-cho-vee, MAH-ko-vee)—A spring, formerly a village, about fifteen miles south of Shongopovi.

MISHONGNOVI (mi-SHONG-no-vee)—The most easterly of the Second Mesa villages.

MOENAVI (MOON-ah-vee, MÖN-ah-vee)—Flowing Water. A spring not far from Moencopi.

MOENCOPI (MOON-kah-pee, MÖN-kah-pee)—Running Water. The most westerly of the Hopi villages, adjacent to Tuba City.

MOESIPTANGA (mö-SIP-tahng-ah)—Place of Gourds. An Antelope Mesa site formerly settled by Lagunas and other Eastern Pueblo peoples.

MOMO'A (MO-mo-ah)—A personal name.

MUYINGWA (MUY-ing-wah)—A germination deity.

MUYOVI (MUY-o-vee)—Hopi name for the Rio Grande and the Rio Grande Valley.

NAHOYDADATSIA (nah-HOY-dah-dahts-yah)—A Hopi stickball game similar to field hockey.

NA'I (NAH-ee)—A personal name.

NEUVAKWIOTAKA (neu-VAH-kwee-o-tah-kah)—A site near Chaves Pass, Arizona, where the Palatkwapi clans settled for a while during their migration northward.

NEUVATIKYAO (neu-VAH-tik-yah-o)—Hopi name for the San Francisco Peaks.

NIMAN (NEE-mahn)—The annual festival celebrating the departure of the kachinas. During the dance, which is an aspect of the festival, the kachinas give out bread, piki, fruit and other gifts to the spectators. Small boys receive bows and arrows; and small girls receive kachina dolls.

NUVA (NU-vah, NEU-vah)—Snow.

NUVAKWAHU (NU-vah-kwah-hu, NU-vah-gwah-hu)—Snow Eagle. A personal name.

OGA'AKENEH (o-GAH-ah kehn-eh)—(Tewa) A great body of water. The ocean.

OJAIVI (o-JYE-vee, soft j)—Round Rock. The original name of Oraibi.

ORAIBI (o-RYE-bee)—An old Hopi village on Third Mesa.

OVA (O-vah)—Bridal shawl. This shawl is frequently used for magico-religious purposes.

OWHALANI (OW-hah-lah-nee)—A kachina. Fewkes calls him "the returning one," meaning the sun god, Tawa.

PAHO (PAH-ho, BAH-ho)—Prayer feathers, prayer sticks.

PAKABVA (PAH-kahb-vah)—Reed Spring. Name of an extinct village.

PAKATKOMO (pah-KAHT-ko-mo)—An extinct village site of the Water and Sand clans not far from Walpi.

PAKUSHKASHA (pah-KOOSH-kah-shah)—A personal name.

PALATKWAPI, sometimes PALATKWA (pah-LAHT-kwah-pee, pah-LAHT-kwa)—An ancestral village far to the south of Hopi country, said to be the place where the Water, Sand, Tobacco and other clans started their northward migrations.

PALATKWAVEHE (pah-LAHT-kwah-veh-heh)—"At the place of Palatkwa."

PATKI (PAHT-kee, BAHT-kee)—A dwelling on water, houseboat. The Patki Clan is literally the Dwelling-on-Water Clan, though in translation it is usually called the Water Clan or the Rain-Cloud Clan.

PATOWAKACHEH (PAH-toh-wah-kah-cheh)—The great water, ocean.

PAYUPKI (pye-UP-kee)—An extinct village site in Hopi country, once a settlement of the Rio Grande Payupkis.

PIKI (PEE-kee)—A paper-thin bread, shaped into rolls while it is still warm.

PIKOYSA (pee-KOY-sah, pi-KOY-sah)—A forehead strap for carrying heavy loads.

PINTOY (PIN-toy)—Tewa for Place of Hearts, the spot where the Tewas buried the hearts of their slain Ute enemies.

PIVANHONKAPI (pee-VAHN-hon-kah-pee), also heard as PIVANOVEH (pee-VAHN-o-veh)—A now extinct village, once located on Third Mesa a few miles from Oraibi.

POJOAQUE (po-HWAH-kee or po-HWAH-kay)—A Tewa village in the Rio Grande Valley.

POKANGHOYA (po-KAHNG-hoy-ah)—The elder of the young warrior gods.

POLONGAHOYA (po-LONG-ah-hoy-ah)—The younger of the two warrior gods.

POPAY (PO-pay, BO-pay)—Mosquito Larva, the name of the Tewa generally acknowledged to have organized the Pueblo uprising against the Spanish in 1680. He is said to have been given this name because he was so hard for the Spanish to catch. In Hopi he was called PA'ATEU (PAH-ah-teu), meaning Water Flea.

POVOSLOWA (PO-vo-slo-wah)—Diviner.

POWAKA (po-WAH-kah)—Sorcerer, witch.

POYAY (po-YAY)—A Rio Grande village site.

SAKIEVA (SAHK-ee-eh-vah)—A personal name.

SAN FELIPE (sahn-fay-LEE-pay)—A Rio Grande Pueblo village.

SAN JUAN (sahn-HWAN)—A Rio Grande Pueblo village.

SANTA CLARA (SAHN-ta KLAHR-ah)—A Rio Grande Pueblo village.

SHIPAULOVI (shi-PAWL-o-vee)—A Hopi village on Second Mesa.

SHOKUGEH (shō-KU-geh)—Slippery Point. In Tewa tradition, the spot where the Tewa people rested after their crossing of Oga'akeneh, a great body of water.

SHONGOPOVI (shong-O-po-vee, frequently heard as shi-MO-po-vee or sam-O-po-vee)—One of the old Hopi villages on Second Mesa. It is not now on its original site. According to tradition, the original Shongopovi was the first Hopi settlement except for Awatovi.

SHONOTEKA (sho-NO-tehk-ah)—A place on Third Mesa not far from Oraibi.

SIBOPAY (see-BO-pay, see-PO-pay)—The Tewa place of origin, said to signify the First Mother. In some accounts, the equivalent of the Hopi sipapuni.

SICHOMOVI (see-CHO-mo-vee)—The middle village on First Mesa, lying between Walpi and Hano (Tewa Village).

SICHTILKWI (SICH-til-kwee, German ch)—Flower Mound. The site of Walpi. According to recollections of the Hopis, this site was once covered with flowers.

SIKAKOKUH (si-KAH-ko-kuh)—A personal name.

SIKYATITI (sik-YAHT-tee-tee)—Yellow Bird. A personal name.

SIKYATKI (sik-YAHT-kee)—A village, now extinct, settled by the Coyote Clan below the mesa rim just a little northeast of Walpi.

SIPAPUNI, SIPAPU (SEE-pah-pu-nee, SEE-pah-pu)—The hole in the sky above the Lower (Third) World, through which the people emerged into the Upper (Fourth) World.

SOMIVIKI (so-MI-vi-ki)—A kind of bread made of finely ground blue corn. The meal is wrapped in corn husks and boiled.

SOWITUIKA (so-WEET-wee-kah)—A now extinct village south and west of Oraibi.

SOWUHTI (so-WÖ-tee)—Old woman, grandmother.

SOYAL (SOY-ahl)—An important winter solstice ceremony. Also the name of a kachina representing the sun spirit.

SOYOHIM (so-YO-him)—Mixed kachinas, Mixed Kachina Dance.

SOYOKO (SO-yo-ko)—A monster, represented by a kachina.

SUCHAPTAKWI (su-CHAHP-tah-kwee)—A legendary village in the east, probably at the Rio Grande. In the tradition of the Reed Clan, the home of the Dog People.

TALAVAI (tah-LAH-vye)—The Dawn Kachina.

TAOS—(TAH-os, TOWSS)—The northernmost of the Eastern Pueblo communities.

TAOTOYKYA (TAH-o-toy-kyah)—An ancestral village, said to have been in what is now California, from which people (later to become the Snake and Horn clans) migrated to Tokonave.

TAWA (TAH-wah)—Sun, sun spirit or deity.

TAWAKWAPTEWA (ta-WAH-kwahp-teh-wah)—Village chief of Oraibi at the time of the Oraibi split.

TEHTUVANI (TEH-tu-vah-nee)—A large flat rock on the old salt trail to Grand Canyon. In former times members of the salt expeditions passing that way left their clan marks on the rock.

TERKINOVI (ter-KEE-no-vee)—A village, now extinct, on First Mesa above Sikyatki.

TESUQUE (teh-SOO-key or teh-SOO-kay)—A Tewa village on the eastern side of the Rio Grande.

TEWA (TAY-wah)—One of the Rio Grande Pueblo peoples. A group of Tewas settled on First Mesa close to the Hopi village of Walpi.

TEWAGEH, TSEWAGEH (teh-WAH-geh, tseh-WAH-geh), sometimes CHEKWADEH (chek-WAH-deh)—The Rio Grande village from which the Tewas came on the relief expedition to Walpi.

TIKUVI (ti-KU-vee, sometimes heard as tsi-KU-vee, ti-KU-veh, or chi-KU-vi)—A village, now in ruins, a short distance north of Shipaulovi.

TINTOPAKOKOSHI (TIN-toh-PAHK-o-kuh-jee, soft j)—"Spotted in Back" or "Spotted Behind." Name given to a dog in the Lamehva story.

TOKONAVE (toh-KO-nah-veh, sometimes toh-KO-ah-nah-veh)—"Black Mountain," the Hopi name for Navajo Mountain.

TOKPELLA (TOHK-peh-lah, sometimes heard as DOHK-peh-lah)—Endless space, outer space, space without form or order.

TOTOLOSPI (toh-TOH-lohs-pee)—A gambling game played by throwing or dropping flat marked sticks. The sticks are marked on one side, plain on the other. Two points are earned if the thrown sticks show three unmarked sides, one point if all sticks show three marked sides.

TSAVEYO (TSAH-veh-yo, TSAH-vay-o)—A monster, depicted as a kachina.

TUKCHU (TOOK-chu)—Meat Point. A spot figuring in the battle between the Tewas and the Utes.

TUSHI (TU-shee)—A food prepared from cornmeal.

TUVI (TÖ-vee, TÖ-bee)—The original permanent Hopi settler at Moencopi, after whom Tuba City is named.

TUWAKOMOVIKI (tu-WAHK-o-mo-vi-kee)—A supernatural being.

WAKI (WAH-kee)—Place of Shelter. In some accounts, the first name of Shipaulovi.

WALPI (WAHL-pee)—The Gap. The First Mesa village established when the people of Koechaptevela moved to the mesa top.

WEPO (WEE-po)—A spring on the west side of First Mesa not far from Walpi. Also the name of the wash on the west side of First Mesa.

WIKOSHUWOMA (wi-KO-shu-wo-mah)—Grease Cavity Clan.

WUHKOKIEKEU (WUH-ko-kee-eh-keu)—The village at Tokonave (Navajo Mountain) from which the Snake and Horn people began their southward migration.

WUPATKI (wuh-PAHT-kee)—A village (or villages), now in ruins, about thirty-five miles northeast of the present city of Flagstaff, Arizona. Some of the clans or parts of clans went to Wupatki from Homolovi at the time of the northward migration from Palatkwapi.

WUWUCHIM (WU-wu-chim, sometimes heard as WU-chim or WU-wu-chim-tee)—The New Fire Ceremony, performed in November. Wuwuchim is also the name of one of the major religious fraternities.

YAWPA (YAW-pah, YAWL-pah)—Mockingbird.

YACHAKPA (yah-CHAHK-pah)—A personal name.

YAYAPONCHA (YAH-yah-pahn-chah, sometimes abbreviated to YAH-yah)—A secret society, now generally considered to be extinct.

YUKIOMA (yu-KEE-o-mah, yu-KYU-mah)—The Fire Clan chief who took the Hostiles out of Oraibi at the time of the split.

YUTEU (YU-teu)—A personal name.